THE KEY TO UNLOCKING
THE DOOR TO THE TRUTH

THE KEY TO UNLOCKING THE DOOR TO THE TRUTH

*Father Ignacio Gordon, SJ, and His Contribution
to the Discipline of Canonical Procedural Law*

William L. Daniel

The Catholic University of America Press
Washington, D.C.

The paper used in this publication meets the minimum requirements of
American National Standards for Information Science—Permanence of Paper for
Printed Library materials, ANSI Z39.48-1992.
ISBN 978-0-8132-3641-4 (cloth) | ISBN 978-0-8132-3642-1 (ebook)

∞

Cataloging-in-Publication Data available from the Library of Congress

In Rev.mi Patris Ignatii Gordon, S.I. memoriam ~
ut, deprecans eundem sacerdotem filiumque Ecclesiae
fidelem pace sempiterna frui et in lumen vultus piissimi
Iudicis divini admitti, multi eius studium servitio Ecclesiae et
curam in sacra disciplina investiganda aemulentur.

"Etenim nisi clavis processualis (sit venia comparationi) tot habeat dentes, quot serratura naturae humanae habet sinuositates, porta iustitiae nunquam aperietur!"[1]

+

"I recall the image used by the professor of canonical processes at the Pontifical Gregorian University, Father Ignacio Gordon, SJ, during the years of my study. He observed that the canonical process with its various elements is like a key whose teeth must match the winding contours of the lock of human nature, and only when all the teeth are cut correctly can the key open the door to truth and justice."[2]

---

1. Ignacio Gordon, *De iudiciis in genere. I. Introductio generalis. Pars statica*, 2nd ed. (Rome: Pontificia Universitas Gregoriana, 1979), 22, no. 1/26. "For only if the procedural key (pardon the comparison) has as many teeth as the complexity of human nature has winding curves, the gate of justice will never be opened!" All translations in this book are the author's.

2. Raymond Leo Burke, "The Canonical Nullity of the Marriage Process as the Search for the Truth," in *Remaining in the Truth of Christ. Marriage and Communion in the Catholic Church*, ed. Robert Dodaro (San Francisco: Ignatius Press, 2014), 214. Elsewhere the same author, relating the same imagery, refers to Fr. Gordon as "my revered professor" (*mio venerato professore*): idem, "Introduzione ai lavori," in *La ricerca della verità sul matrimonio e il diritto a un processo giusto e celere. Temi di diritto matrimoniale e processuale canonico*, Subsidia canonica 6, ed. Héctor Franceschi and Miguel A. Ortiz (Rome: EDUSC, 2012), 17–18.

Table of Contents

Abbreviations

A) General Sources

AAS	*Acta Apostolicae Sedis.*
APN	("American Procedural Norms") Council for the Public Affairs of the Church. Rescript *Attentis precibus*. Prot. n. 3320/70. April 28, 1970. In *DR* 1:243–252.
CIC	*Codex iuris canonici* (preceded by 1917 or 1983, if not evident from the context).
CM	Paul VI. Motu proprio *Causas matrimoniales*. March 28, 1971. *AAS* 63 (1971) 441–446.
DC	Pontifical Council for Legislative Texts. Instruction *Dignitas connubii*. January 25, 2005. Vatican City: Libreria Editrice Vaticana, 2005.
FICPUG Archives	Archives of the Faculty of Canon Law of the Pontifical Gregorian University (Rome, Piazza della Pilotta, 4, 3rd floor, room XII: *Seminarium Iurisprudentiae*).
LP	Benedict XVI. Motu proprio *Antiqua ordinatione*. June 21, 2008. *AAS* 100 (2008) 513–538. English translation in *Ministerium Iustitiae vol. II. The "Lex propria" and More Recent Contentious-Administrative Jurisprudence of the Supreme Tribunal of the Apostolic Signatura*. Translated by William L. Daniel, 11–56. Gratianus Series. Montréal: Librairie Wilson & Lafleur Inc., 2021.
MI	Francis. Motu proprio *Mitis Iudex Dominus Iesus*. August 15, 2015. *AAS* 107 (2015) 958–970.
NS	Supreme Tribunal of the Apostolic Signatura. *Normae speciales in Supremo Tribunali Signaturae Apostolicae ad experimentum servandae*. March 23, 1968. In *DR* 1:372–397.
PB	John Paul II. Apostolic constitution *Pastor bonus*. June 28, 1988. *AAS* 80 (1988) 841–934.
PCCICR/PCCICAI/ PCTLI Archives	Archives of the Pontifical Commission for the Revision of the Code of Canon Law, the Pontifical Commission for Authentically Interpreting the Code of Canon Law, or the

Pontifical Council for the Interpretation of Legislative Texts (Vatican City, Piazza Pio XII, 10, 4th floor).

PCLT Archives   Archives of the Pontifical Council for Legislative Texts ("Archivio protocollo").

PME   Sacred Congregation for the Discipline of the Sacraments. Instruction *Provida Mater Ecclesia*. August 15, 1936. *AAS* 28 (1936) 313–361.

REU   Paul VI. Apostolic constitution *Regimini Ecclesiae universae*. August 15, 1967. *AAS* 59 (1967) 885–928.

SSAT Archives   Archives of the Supreme Tribunal of the Apostolic Signatura.

B) Cited Published Works of Fr. Ignacio Gordon, SJ

For the sake of simplicity, the full citation of the major published works of Father Gordon is given only here and in Chapter X. All references in this book are from works of Father Gordon, unless otherwise indicated. His works are cited according to the abbreviated version indicated here:

Adnotationes in m.p. "Causas matrimoniales"
> *Adnotationes in m.p. "Causas matrimoniales" (Excerptum ex "Adnotationibus Professorum", 3ª edit., pp. 241–287 addito brevi commentario 20 paginarum circa appellationem)*. Cursus renovationis canonicae pro iudicibus. Rome: Pontificia Universitas Gregoriana, 1979.[1]

"Codificationes legum"
> "Codificationes legum Signaturae Iustitiae a Pio VII et Leone XII elaboratae." In *Miscellanea in onore del Professore P. Esteban Gomez O.P.* Edited by Pontificia Università S. Tommaso d'Aquino – Roma, 79–100. Milan: Massimo, 1984.

"De appellationibus"
> "De appellationibus iuxta m.p. '*Causas matrimoniales*.'" *Periodica* 63 (1974) 285–316.

"Decisio Signaturae Iustitiae"
> "Decisio Signaturae Iustitiae diei 19 iunii 1834 qua nova forma contentiosi-administrativi in Statu Pontificio introducta est." In *Investigationes theologico-canonicae*, 185–210. Rome: Università Gregoriana Editrice, 1978.

---

1. This text is included also in a *dispensa* in which were collected three works written by Fr. Gordon: *Tribunalia et processus (excerpta quaedam)* (Rome: Pontificia Universitas Gregoriana, 1974) 241–287.

"De Curia Romana renovata"

"De Curia Romana renovata. Renovatio 'desiderata' et renovatio 'facta' conferuntur." *Periodica* 58 (1969) 59–116.

"De diverso regimine appellationum"

"De diverso regimine appellationum inducto in m.p. '*Causas matrimoniales.*'" In *Studi di diritto canonico in onore di Marcello Magliocchetti*, 2:713–724. Rome: Catholic Book Agency, 1975.

"De iustitia administrativa ecclesiastica"

"De iustitia administrativa ecclesiastica tum transacto tempore tum hodierno." *Periodica* 61 (1972) 251–378.[2]

"De nimia processuum matrimonialium duratione"

"De nimia processuum matrimonialium duratione. Factum – Causae – Remedia." *Periodica* 58 (1969) 491–594 and 641–735.

"De obiecto primario competentiae"

"De obiecto primario competentiae 'Sectionis Alterius' Supremi Tribunalis Signaturae Apostolicae." *Periodica* 68 (1979) 505–542.

"De procedura sequenda"

"De procedura sequenda coram Signatura Iustitiae inde a saeculo XVI ad saeculum XVIII." *Periodica* 74 (1985) 575–604.

"De referendariorum ac votantium dignitate"

"De referendariorum ac votantium dignitate, privilegiis, labore, in aetate aurea Signaturae iustitiae." In *Dilexit iustitiam. Studia in honorem Aurelii Card. Sabattani.* Edited by Zenon Grocholewski and Vicente Cárcel Ortí, 197–210. Vatican City: Libreria Editrice Vaticana, 1984.

"De Signaturae Iustitiae competentia"

"De Signaturae Iustitiae competentia inde a saec. XVI ad saec. XVII." *Periodica* 69 (1980) 351–386.

"De Tribunalibus administrativis"

"De Tribunalibus administrativis propositis a Commissione Codici I. C. recognoscendo et suffragatis ab Episcoporum Synodo." *Periodica* 57 (1968) 602–652.

---

2. Cf. *Tribunalia et processus (excerpta quaedam)*, 207–238, which is drawn both from this article and from "La renovación de la Signatura Apostolica" (*vide infra*). He cites this section in *Pars statica*, 19 (note 36g), 51 (note 15d), 52 (note 15f), 282 (note 3), *et passim*.

"De Tribunalibus Regionalibus"
> "De Tribunalibus Regionalibus cum respectu ad iudicum delectum et ad processus breviationem." *Periodica* 56 (1967) 579–596.[3]

"Dichiarazione di nullità"
> "Dichiarazione di nullità e dispensa del matrimonio." In *Amore e stabilità nel matrimonio*, 133–150. Rome: Università Gregoriana Editrice, 1976.

"Discorso generale"
> "Discorso generale sui libri IV e V del *Codex*." *Apollinaris* 52 (1979) 62–79.

"*DR 1*"
> Gordon, Ignacio, and Zenon Grocholewski, eds. *Documenta recentiora circa rem matrimonialem et processualem cum notis bibliographicis et indicibus*, vol. 1. Rome: Pontificia Universitas Gregoriana, 1977.

"*DR 2*"
> Grocholewski, Zenon, ed. *Documenta recentiora circa rem matrimonialem et processualem cum notis bibliographicis et indicibus*, vol. 2. Rome: Pontificia Universitas Gregoriana, 1980.[4]

"El contencioso-administrativo eclesiástico"
> "El contencioso-administrativo eclesiástico. Génesis, historia y competencia actual." In *Curso de derecho matrimonial y procesal canónico para profesionales del foro (IV)*. Bibliotheca Salamanticensis, Estudios 31, 145–171. Salamanca: Universidad Pontificia, 1980.

"Elementi innovativi nei processi"
> "Elementi innovativi nei processi per il rispetto della giustizia e della verità." *L'osservatore romano* 123/89 (Lunedì–Martedì, 18–19 Aprile 1983) 8.

"El M. P. '*Causas matrimoniales*' y las normas americanas"
> "El M. P. '*Causas matrimoniales*' y las normas americanas." In *Curso de derecho matrimonial y procesal canónico para profesionales del foro (IV)*. Bibliotheca Salamanticensis, Estudios 31, 191–216. Salamanca: Universidad Pontificia, 1980.

"El recurso contencioso-administrativo canónico"
> "El recurso contencioso-administrativo canónico." *Sal Terrae* 61 (1973) 641–648.

---

3. Cf. *Tribunalia et processus (excerpta quaedam)*, 174–203. He cites this section in *Pars statica*, 321, no. 469.

4. While this was indeed the work of Grocholewski, it contains a preface written by Fr. Gordon (5–7).

"Interessi legittimi"
  "Interessi legittimi, diritti soggettivi e giustizia amministrativa ecclesiastica." In *Persona e ordinamento nella Chiesa. Atti del II Congresso Internazionale di Diritto Canonico, Milano 10–16 settembre 1973*, 391–401, 455. Milan: Vita e Pensiero, 1975.

"La renovación de la Signatura Apostólica"
  "La renovación de la Signatura Apostólica." *Revista Española de Derecho Canónico* 28 (1972) 571–610.

"La responsibilità"
  "La responsibilità dell'amministrazione pubblica ecclesiastica." *Monitor Ecclesiasticus* 98 (1973) 384–419.

"La soppressione dei tribunali ecclesiastici"
  "La soppressione dei tribunali ecclesiastici negli scritti di Mons. St. J. Kelleher (1966–1969)." In *Atti del Congresso internazionale di diritto canonico: La Chiesa dopo il Concilio. Roma, 14–19 gennaio 1970*, 2.1:737–751. Milan: Giuffrè Editore, 1972.

"L'oggetto primario"
  "L'oggetto primario della competenza della 'Sectio altera.'" In *De iustitia administrativa in Ecclesia—La giustizia amministrativa nella Chiesa*. Edited by Pio Fedele, 167–195. Rome: Officium Libri Catholici, 1984.

"Normae speciales"
  "Normae speciales Supremi Tribunalis Signaturae Apostolicae. Editio aucta introductione, fontibus et notis." *Periodica* 59 (1970) 75–165.

Novus processus nullitatis matrimonii
  Novus processus nullitatis matrimonii. Iter cum adnotationibus. Rome: Pontificia Universitas Gregoriana, 1983.

"Octavus Cursus pro Iudicibus"
  "Octavus Cursus pro Iudicibus (2 nov. – 14 dec. 1979)." *Periodica* 68 (1979) 733–739.

"Origine e sviluppo"
  "Origine e sviluppo della giustizia amministrativa nella Chiesa." In *De iustitia administrativa in Ecclesia—La giustizia amministrativa nella Chiesa*. Edited by Pio Fedele, 1–18. Rome: Officium Libri Catholici, 1984.

Pars dynamica
  De iudiciis in genere. II. Pars dynamica. Rome: Pontificia Universitas Gregoriana, 1972.

Pars statica

> *De iudiciis in genere. I. Introductio Generalis, Pars statica.* Rome: Pontificia Universitas Gregoriana, 1976 (second printing: 1979).

"Paulus PP. VI alloquitur"

> "Paulus PP. VI alloquitur IV Cursum renovationis canonicae pro iudicibus et tribunalium administris." *Periodica* 64 (1975) 5–11.

Processus nullitatis matrimonii

> *Processus nullitatis matrimonii sub luce Schematis Codicis I.C. recogniti cum notis et appendicibus.* Cursus renovationis canonicae pro iudicibus. Rome: Pontificia Universitas Gregoriana, 1981.

"Responsio nonnullis quaestionibus"

> "Nota. Responsio nonnullis quaestionibus de interpretatione quorundam canonum Libri VII C.I.C." *Periodica* 75 (1986) 639–645.

"Septimus Cursus pro Iudicibus"

> "Septimus Cursus pro Iudicibus (3 nov.–14 dec. 1977)." *Periodica* 68 (1979) 159–170.

"Votum de revisione sententiae"

> "Votum de revisione sententiae primo affirmantis nullitatem matrimonii." August 10, 1981. In *Congregatio plenaria diebus 20–29 octobris 1981 habita.* Acta et documenta Pontificiae Commissionis Codicis Iuris Canonici recognoscendo. Edited by Pontifical Council for the Interpretation of Legislative Texts, 111–127. Vatican City: Typis Polyglottis Vaticanis, 1991.

Introduction

1. – The Church, like her divine Founder, while endowed with divine glory, is increasingly held in low esteem in the eyes of the world, which may not even notice her or may only notice her with suspicion or in jest. The canonist is one engaged in reflection, research, and service in regard to that which is just (*ius*) in the social relations of the same Mystical Body of Christ. And so he shares in this secular low estate. His position within the Church, too, is typically one to which the ambitious do not aspire, since, on the one hand, he may often be spurned by those harboring an antijuridical mentality while, on the other hand, become weighed down with grave and even unpleasant matters when the Church's shepherds place their confidence in him. As a result of these factors, the work of the canonist is usually carried out in the peripheral offices of the chancery and rooms of the university. It is a work that is often hidden, and its good fruits frequently bear the name of another, whom the canonist is privileged to serve. When this is done with virtue, it amounts to a service that is quiet yet intense, initiated out of duty and completed with devotion and even love, and often with the bulk of the work accomplished in solitude even while motivated with zeal for those souls who will be affected by it.

2. – One canonist who has long intrigued me for his excellence in these respects is the Spanish professor of procedural canon law (*ius processuale canonicum*) who taught at the Pontifical Gregorian University in Rome from 1960 until 1985, the Very Reverend Father Ignacio Gordon, SJ. His academic service has captured my attention because of my own fascination with procedural law. I have thus been inspired to dedicate a period of research to the study of his contribution to procedural law. Scholars of procedural law soon encounter his name as one of those outstanding in the field, at work during a period of great transition—the celebration of the Second Vatican Ecumenical Council and the subsequent revision and promulgation of the Code of Canon Law. I took particular notice of his work, especially his latest writings, on the occasion of my own rudimentary study of the history of the Apostolic Signatura.[1] I also began to detect in diverse ways

---

1. See my "The Strictly Judicial Function of the Supreme Tribunal of the Apostolic Signatura," *Studies in Church Law* 5 (2009) 119–172 and *CLSGBI Newsletter* 175 (September 2013) 42–75; "The Historical Development of the Power of Governance of the Supreme Tribunal of the Apostolic Signatura," *Studia canonica* 43 (2009) 47–80; "The Power of Governance of the Supreme Tribunal

his formative influence on canonists whose ecclesial service and work I greatly admire, not least of whom are Their Eminences Raymond Leo Cardinal Burke and Zenon Cardinal Grocholewski (*r.i.p.*), His Excellency Archbishop Frans Daneels, OPraem, and others.

3. – This research on Father Gordon's contribution naturally required that I study all of his published writings in the area of procedural law. These are more or less listed in the Abbreviations section and in Chapter X. The method used consisted of a careful reading of each of his writings according to theme and, secondarily, according to date of publication. They were read in this general thematic sequence: the marriage nullity process, the judicial process in general, contentious-administrative recourse or administrative justice, and the history of the Apostolic Signatura. The chapters concentrating on these themes naturally focus on the writings pertaining primarily to them, but the reader will note a great many instances of interrelationship among all of his writings.

4. – However, Father Gordon's contribution clearly cannot be adequately identified and assessed merely by reading his published writings. In the first place, his work's value in the formation of students in the Church's judicial discipline is inestimable, since that work is not confined to print but has lived and lives in the men and women who learned from him and who, in turn, have formed others in what they learned.

Furthermore, as his colleague, Father Jean Beyer, SJ, remarked, Father Gordon's publications do not fully represent even his written, technical contribution, "since much remains modestly hidden away in silence."[2] Far from compromising his modesty, this work strives to break the silence, or better to bring into the light the great work that has been hidden away. Given his service both to his university and to the Roman Curia, this was only possible by consulting the archives of the Pontifical Gregorian University, of the Supreme Tribunal of the Apostolic Signatura, and of the Pontifical Council for Legislative Texts, which I was able to do in May 2018. What a privilege it was for me to study all of these archives in the very buildings and rooms that Father Gordon frequented while

---

of the Apostolic Signatura with Historical Antecedents," *Ius Ecclesiae* 21 (2009) 631–652; "Brief Note on the Judicial Figure of the Secretary of the Supreme Tribunal of the Apostolic Signatura," *The Jurist* 73 (2013) 256–269.

2. See Jean Beyer, "Magisterii in iure canonico R.P. Ignatii Gordon, S.J. felix faustaque recordatio," *Periodica* 75 (1986) 18.

he lived and worked, and to handle and study some of the very pages that he touched and worked with.

5. – A few explanations about the content of this work are in order. Father Gordon carried out most of his academic service prior to the promulgation of the 1983 Code of Canon Law. He thus cites the 1917 code in most of his works, as well as other norms that have been abrogated (e.g., *PME, NS*). Nevertheless, both the originally cited norms and those that entered into effect after his time of writing will be cited appropriately. This should be taken not as an anachronism but as a proof of the lasting relevance of his investigations and, to some extent, the lasting influence he had on the Church's procedural order, since his own work had some impact on the development of the law that is currently in force.

Some choices have been made along the way to refrain from dwelling on doctrinal questions that are now resolved or obsolete due to normative development (e.g., the local transfer of competence of a tribunal, active legitimation to introduce a cause of nullity of marriage). Also, at times he is merely commenting on the text of the law, especially in his course *dispense,* which are meant to impart a complete teaching of the subject matter and not primarily to advance his own doctrine. Such commentary is omitted when his comments are simply explanatory or demonstrative of the teaching of others. While he consistently draws generously from other authors, he tends to show a greater independence from them when treating a topic about which he seems to have thought more deeply and that is more central to his doctrinal contribution. This book omits some of his teachings written for the purpose of offering a complete treatment of procedural law to his students, since he sometimes relied heavily on or even drew completely from particular authors in certain sections.

6. – Some indications about the stylistic presentation of the material may also be helpful. The common and seemingly preferred style of Father Gordon in his various monographs was the conceptual division of the body of his writing into numbered paragraphs or sections, such as one sees in this Introduction. This allowed him to make facile and useful cross-references within the same work or in other works. Following his example and in order to reflect Father Gordon's work, which is the inspiration for this one, this book emulates this technique. And the indices take this numeration as their point of reference.

The vast majority of footnotes cite works written by Father Gordon, whether published writings (according to the abbreviations indicated above), unpublished *vota*, or reports of his interventions in the *Coetus "de processibus."* The stylistic approach taken follows these rules:

a) when his very words are quoted in the original language, the work is cited without qualification;

b) when his words are presented in English—a language in which he published almost nothing—the reference is preceded with the word "See," since one would need to look to the cited passage in order to see his very words, which typically are not provided; and

c) when his teachings are summarized or their meaning is implied in the text, the abbreviation "Cf." (*confer*, "compare") is used, since one would need to compare my synthesis of his teaching with the original.

7. – I would like to express my heartfelt gratitude to His Eminence, Dominique Cardinal Mamberti, the Prefect of the Apostolic Signatura, who permitted me to consult the archives of the Supreme Tribunal.[3] I am so grateful also to the officials diligently working there, who gave me practical access to the archives and explained the manner in which Father Gordon's *vota* were able to be located. I likewise thank deeply the abovementioned Pontifical Council for admitting me to its archives. I am particularly honored that it has granted me permission to cite unpublished documentation and unpublished indications about Father Gordon's precise interventions in the *Coetus "de processibus."*

And I am heartily grateful to the Faculty of Canon Law of the Pontifical Gregorian University, especially to the Very Reverend Father Janusz Kowal, SJ, Ordinary Professor, who generously discovered those archives related to Father Gordon that exist, helped me prepare the scope of my research at that University, and most hospitably made the archives conveniently available to me. Particular thanks are likewise offered to Reverend Monsignor Gianpaolo Montini who, as editor of *Periodica de re canonica*, graciously published my article presenting some of this research in that faculty's journal wherein many of Father Gordon's works were published.[4]

---

3. Supreme Tribunal of the Apostolic Signatura, rescript of the Prefect, *Romana, Consultationis archivi ad opus Rev.di P. Gordon extollendum*, prot. n. 53310/17 VAR, December 6, 2017; decrees of the Secretary, [*eodem de casu*], May 17, 2018 and April 16, 2019.

4. It appears in an issue of that journal containing three articles published in Fr. Gordon's honor on the occasion of the 20th anniversary of his death: William L. Daniel, "Commemorative Notes on Father Ignacio Gordon, S.J.'s Contribution to Canonical Procedural Law," *Periodica* 111 (2022) 3–31; Gianpaolo Montini, "La competenza di merito della Segnatura Apostolica nel pensiero di p. Ignacio Gordon, S.J.," ibid., 33–64; Emanuele Spedicato, "'Ab imo ad summum': il contributo alle cause dei santi di Padro Ignacio Gordon, S.J.," ibid., 66–88."

A number of Father Gordon's former students have served the Church with distinction as experts in her sacred discipline. I am deeply grateful to each of those who sent me their recollections of Father Gordon and authorized me to quote them in print, which I do below, especially in Chapter I.

8. – Finally, I am deeply grateful to the Senior Vice Provost for Academic Administration and Dean of Graduate Studies of The Catholic University of America, Dr. J. Steven Brown, and to the University Institutional Grants Committee, which supported this research as a Grant-in-Aid project. Special thanks, too, to Trevor Lipscombe, Ph.D., Director of The Catholic University of America Press, for his gracious service in bringing this publication to fruition.

With gratitude I also recognize my supportive colleagues in the School of Canon Law, especially the Dean, the Reverend Monsignor Ronny Jenkins, and my colleague Professor Kurt Martens, who both encouraged me to pursue this project. It is worth noting that during the course of this project, our School was deeply saddened by the death of the Reverend Monsignor Thomas J. Green, a beloved colleague and a former student of Father Gordon's, and of the Reverend Father Robert Kaslyn, SJ, who was so kind in orienting me to canonical resources in the Society of Jesus. *Requiescant in pace.*

I offer endless thanks to my beloved wife, Meredith Ann, and our children. She bore extra responsibility while I traveled to Rome, and they all have so graciously endured my stories about Father Gordon and his canonical work. How blessed I am to have them and to materially support them as a canonist.

I wish, too, if I may, to thank Father Gordon himself for his love of the Church, his service to souls, his earnest and meticulous research carried out with such diligence and humility, and his devotion to the Successor of St. Peter and to his students, whom he loved so much. Please pray for me, that I may also in some measure exhibit these gifts in the years the Lord gives me as a canonist.

Ad maiorem Dei gloriam!

Prof. William L. Daniel
The Catholic University of America
Washington, DC
June 29, 2022 + Solemnity of Sts. Peter and Paul

CHAPTER I

Father Ignacio Gordon, SJ— Professor, Jurist, Priest

SUMMARY — Introductory remarks (no. 1). ▪ A. Professor (nn. 2–5). ▪B. Jurist (nn. 6–12). ▪ C. Priest (nn. 13–20). ▪ D. Further Illustrations (nn. 21–23).

1. – Before entering into the matter of the doctrinal contribution of Father Gordon, some biographical notes are necessary. For these reveal what motivated his work, academically, juridically, and spiritually.

Ignacio Gordon Cuvillo was born July 3, 1915 in Seville, Spain, and died in Rome on December 5, 2002 at five thirty in the morning. The funeral was celebrated on December 7 at 10:00 a.m. at the Church of the Generalate of the Society of Jesus. He had suffered from "a long and painful illness,"[1] which at the end of his life included some form of dementia, when he was "like a child."[2] What occurred between July 3, 1915 and December 5, 2002 is the story of a man who was an accomplished professor, a serious jurist, and a devoted priest.

A. Professor

2. – Father Gordon defended his doctoral dissertation before the Faculty of Canon Law of the Pontifical Gregorian University on January 25, 1952. It was written on a theme pertaining to religious and patrimonial law—namely, the dominion that Jesuit colleges have over temporal goods.[3]

After about eight years teaching canon law in Granada,[4] he began teaching at the Pontifical Gregorian University in the academic year of 1960–

---

1. See Pontificia Università Gregoriana, *Liber Annualis, Roma 2003 – Univ. 450°* (Rome: Pontificia Università Gregoriana, 2003) 379.

2. Gianfranco Ghirlanda, conversation with William L. Daniel, May 19, 2018, at the Pontifical Gregorian University, Rome.

3. Ignacio Gordon, *En torno al sujeto de Dominio de los Colegios de la Compañía de Jesús*, Excerpta ex dissertatione ad Lauream in Facultate Iuris Canonici Pontificiae Universitatis Gregorianae (Granada: [no publisher], 1952).

4. Among the subjects he taught was public ecclesiastical law, which no doubt contributed to his rich discussion about the jurisdiction of the Church, including the notions of *res mixtae, privilegium fori, mixtum forum,* and the Pauline principles stated in 1 Cor. 6:1–7 (*Pars statica,* 85–103, nn. 122–147).

1961.[5] In 1961–1962, he taught a special course on the Sacred Congregations and repeated it in 1964–1965.[6] In 1962–1963, he taught the course *De rebus*, including the sections on sacred places and times and aspects of divine worship, and repeated it in 1964–1965.[7] He also taught an optional course on the reform of the Roman Curia by Paul VI.[8]

He was Dean of the faculty of canon law in the 1963–1964, 1964–1965 and 1965–1966 academic years.[9] He would later be a consultor to the Dean.[10]

3. – He was certainly already teaching procedural law in the academic year 1961–1962, using the manual by Wernz-Vidal as his textbook.[11] His course in procedural law taught in 1970 was entitled "De processibus (C. I. C., L. IV, cc. 1552–2194)." The course description was as follows:

An explanation will be imparted especially concerning Part I *De iudiciis* with particular attention: 1. to matrimonial processes, both concerning nullity

---

5. Cf. Pontificia Universitas Gregoriana, *Liber annualis* (Rome: Universitas Gregoriana, 1961) 24. He was hired under Huizing, as the Dean, his colleagues being Bertrams and Robleda (consultors), Bidagor, Bortolotti, Buijs, Cappello, Lo Grasso, Navarrete, Örsy, Risk, Wuyts, and Cereceda (ibid., 55).

6. Cf. Pontificia Universitas Gregoriana, *Liber annualis 1962* (Rome: Universitas Gregoriana, 1962) 31, 328; Pontificia Universitas Gregoriana, *Liber annualis 1965* (Rome: Universitas Gregoriana, 1965) 349.

7. Cf. Pontificia Universitas Gregoriana, *Liber annualis 1963* (Rome: Universitas Gregoriana, 1963) 343, 346; *Liber annualis 1965*, 339, 343.

8. *Programma studiorum 1971–1972*, in FICPUG Archives, *Archivio del primo corso per giudici (1971–1972)*, I.3 at 12 (J13), 14 (J17), 17, 23–24.

9. Pontificia Universitas Gregoriana, *Liber annualis 1964* (Rome: Universitas Gregoriana, 1964) 49–50, 59; *Liber annualis 1965*, 21–22, 33; Pontificia Universitas Gregoriana, *Liber annualis 1966* (Rome: Universitas Gregoriana, 1966) 21–22, 33. See also, e.g., Ignazio Gordon, "Presentazione," in Emilio Ghidotti, *La nullità della sentenza giudiziale nel diritto canonico* (Milan: Giuffrè Editore, 1965) xi–xii, which includes this inscription below his name: "Decano della Facoltà di diritto canonico nella Pontificia Università Gregoriana."

10. Cf., e.g., Pontificia Universitas Gregoriana, *Liber annualis 1970* (Rome: Universitas Gregoriana, 1970) 52.

11. Cf. *Liber annualis 1962*, 356, 360. The manual mentioned here is Franz Wernz and Peter Vidal, *Ius canonicum. Tomus VI: De processibus*, 2nd ed. (Rome: Universitas Gregoriana, 1949). Some authors cite his course notes from a few years earlier as follows: I. Gordon, *De processibus. Adnotationes in Lib. IV Codicis Iuris Canonici* (Roma 1965–1966) (see, e.g., Carlo Gullo and Alessia Gullo, *Prassi processuale nelle cause canoniche di nullità del matrimonio. Terza edizione aggiornata con l'Instr. "Dignitas connubii" del 25 gennaio 2005*, Studi Giuridici 80 [Vatican City: Libreria Editrice Vaticana, 2009] 71, note 2; Linda Ghisoni, "I ministri di giustizia in specie: uditori e assessori (artt. 50–52)," in *Il giudizio di nullità matrimoniale dopo l'Istruzione "Dignitas connubii." Parte Seconda: La parte statica del processo*, Studi Giuridici 76, ed. Piero Antonio Bonnet and Carlo Gullo [Vatican City: Libreria Editrice Vaticana, 2007] 158, note 5).

and concerning ratified and non-consummated [marriage]. 2. to regional tribunals recently established for these causes in Italy (1938), the Philippine Islands (1940, 1956), Canada (1946, 1952), Brazil (1960), France, Algeria, and Tunisia (1965) and Colombia and Chile (1967). *Five hours per week. 1ˢᵗ semester.*[12]

This was a developed form of the course in comparison with what he originally taught the previous decade, taking into account contemporary reforms and his own doctrine in the matter. Its development may have been among the "burdens of a diverse kind which have ever occupied us throughout the academic year 1969–1970."[13]

The content of his course, which is treated throughout this book, is encapsulated in his two volumes of *dispense*, or distributed course notes. They were first issued in 1972, and the first—the general introduction and the *pars statica*—was published in a second edition in 1976, a second printing of which was released in 1979.[14] It had been his hope also to complete a third edition after the eventual publication of the new code; but this was not accomplished, apart from the synthetic and brief treatise on the marriage nullity process itself.[15]

4. – Father Gordon's zeal for the sound teaching of canon law and for correct comprehension on the part of students prompted him to apply himself directly to the teaching of Latin in the university. This was driven by "the fittingness, in fact the necessity that canonists have of comprehending the Latin language in order to have a good understanding of the Code of Canon Law, the *Acta Apostolicae Sedis*, the sentences of the Sacred Roman Rota, etc."[16] And so, for example, in the academic year 1971–1972, aside from the *De processibus* course, which he taught five hours per week the first semester and two hours per week the second semester (for seven weeks), he offered a course called *Latinitas canonica* for five hours per week the first semester for three weeks.[17] The latter had two parts: 1) a

---

12. See *Liber annualis 1970*, 145–146. He also gave a one hour lecture per semester (*exercitatio*) on the procedural steps in causes of nullity of marriage (ibid., 152).

13. See Ignacio Gordon, *votum alterum circa causas [X] et [Y] et aliarum*, prot. n. 270/70 CG, October 24, 1970: in SSAT Archives, 1, no. 2/5.

14. Cf. Jean Beyer, "Magisterii in iure canonico R.P. Ignatii Gordon, S.J. felix faustaque recordatio," *Periodica* 75 (1986) 21 (no. 29), 22 (no. 44).

15. Cf. *Pars statica*, 1; *Novus processus nullitatis matrimonii*.

16. See Ignacio Gordon, *Latinitas canonica. Morphologia* (Rome: Pontificia Universitas Gregoriana, 1987) i.

17. He likewise taught that course, e.g., in 1990–1991, after he had retired from the teaching of canon law (see Pontificia Universitas Gregoriana, *Liber annualis, Roma 1990 Univ. 437º* [Rome: Universitas Gregoriana, 1990] 131).

theoretical part, which recalled principles of Latin syntax and taught vocabulary and expressions proper to canon law, and 2) a practical part, which involved the translation of the code and other juridical documents into vernacular languages.[18] Also, for some years, he was a professor in the Higher School of Latin Letters (*Schola superior litterarum latinarum*).[19]

As was common at the Gregorianum while he taught there, his lectures were delivered in the Latin language, which he did in a "remarkable" way.[20] One of his students, who likewise enjoys a high mastery of Latin, testifies that "Father Gordon taught in a clear fluent Latin."[21] Another recalls: "His spoken Latin—in public and in private—was excellent and very clear."[22] By his example and instruction, he thus promoted knowledge and love of Latin, even calling upon his students to make their own contributions, such as asking them to collaborate in compiling grammars and dictionaries.[23]

5. – So much of the scientific and practical work of this "illustrious author"[24] was done as a service to students, whether formally matriculated in the university or exposed to his teaching in written form. As he explains in reference to one publication, he was motivated to carry out his work by a desire to "offer some aid to judges, ministers of tribunals, advocates, and professors of universities and of tribunals, so that each according to his function might more easily press on in that priceless work both of the administration of justice and of the preparation of stu-

---

18. Cf. Pontificia Universitas Gregoriana, *Liber annualis 1972* (Rome: Pontificia Universitas Gregoriana, 1972) 226, at J17.

19. See, e.g., Pontificia Universitas Gregoriana, *Liber annualis, Roma 1980 Univ. 427º* (Rome: Universitas Gregoriana, 1980) 77; *Liber annualis, Roma 1990 Univ. 437º*, 85, 177.

20. James Conn to William L. Daniel, private letter, June 4, 2018.

21. Private letter to William L. Daniel, June 25, 2018; the person wished to remain unnamed herein.

22. Aidan McGrath to William L. Daniel, "Fr. Ignacio Gordon S.J. – Some personal memories," private correspondence, August 22, 2018, 2.

23. The above-cited *Latinitas canonica* is one example. Another, *Morphologia,* was prepared in collaboration with a Venezuelan canon law student named Fr. Manuel Díaz, and a Latinist-Church history student named Luis Basile, as well as two students (E. Montero and W. Millea) who translated it into English. Additionally, a Latin-English canonical dictionary was prepared by three canon law students "Ignatio Gordon, S.I., rogante." See *Vocabularium canonicum latino-anglicum a Raimundo Burke vocibus Codicis Piani-Benedictini Iuris Canonici primo digestum, curaque Ronaldi Gainer et Michaelis Gorman recognitum, sermonibus etiam Novi Codicis Iuris Canonici auctum* (Rome: Pontificia Universitas Gregoriana, Facultas Iuris Canonici, 1986).

24. See Bassiano Uggé, *La fase preliminare/abbreviata del processo di nullità del matrimonio in secondo grado di giudizio a norma del can. 1682 §2,* Tesi Gregoriana – Serie Diritto Canonico 60 (Rome: Editrice Pontificia Università Gregoriana, 2003) 318.

dents for it."[25] This is all supported by various sources bearing testimony to Father Gordon's character.

Procedural law tends not to be the area of canon law that most spontaneously excites students, even if they may realize its importance. It can become appealing, though, if the professor is not only expert but also zealous about it. In any event, one of his former students explained that Father Gordon's lectures in procedural law were very clear, so that the students could love the subjects explained by him.[26] He was described by another in these terms: "His didactic ability was remarkable, being aided by a wonderful memory . . . and marked by a careful attention to helping the student with the resources then available."[27]

B. Jurist

6. – Pope St. Paul VI appointed him a referendary of the Supreme Tribunal of the Apostolic Signatura on May 30, 1968. On September 4, 1985, Pope St. John Paul II appointed him as a *votans* of the same Supreme Tribunal, which appointment was renewed for another five-year period on October 26, 1990.[28] His body of scholarship and the meticulous work he completed for the Apostolic Signatura reveal his great dedication to that dicastery. He labored extensively to foster its excellence as the supreme organ of ecclesiastical justice, one manifestation of which was his promotion of a most worthy candidate for its service, then-Father Zenon Grocholewski, who was his student and whom he recommended to the Prefect.[29]

---

25. See *DR* 1:9, *in fine*.

26. Gianfranco Ghirlanda, conversation with William L. Daniel, May 19, 2018, at the Pontifical Gregorian University, Rome.

27. Paolo Bianchi to William L. Daniel, "Ricordo di padre Ignacio Gordon," private correspondence, May 6, 2019.

28. Cf., respectively, "Diarium Romanae Curiae. Segreteria di Stato: Nomine," *AAS* 60 (1968) 424 and 425 and "Diarium Romanae Curiae. Segreteria di Stato: Nomine," *AAS* 77 (1985) 1014, 82 (1990) 1650. In the former, we see that he was also appointed a consultor of the Sacred Congregation of Rites for the Causes of Saints on June 1, 1968. In subsequent years, he would also effectively serve as postulator for three causes of canonization: those of St. Angela de la Cruz (canonized after his death), Venerable Antonio Amundarain, and Blessed Marcelo Spínola (cf. Beyer, 15–16; Zenon Grocholewski, "Nota. P. Ignacio Gordon, S.J. e la deontologia dell'insegnamento del diritto canonico," *Periodica* 107 [2018] 365).

29. Cf. Grocholewski, 362, no. 4. We read elsewhere that "in his letter of presentation, Gordon writes the following among other things about Fr. Grocholewski: 'A zealous, prudent priest. He has a gregarious, affable character, a profound and very clear intelligence. He is serious, fast, and tenacious in his work'" (see Paweł Malecha, "Il Cardinale Zenon Grocholewski ed il suo operato nel Supremo Tribunale della Segnatura Apostolica," in *"Quod iustum est et aequum." Scritti in onore del*

7. – As referendary and *votans*, he intervened in many judicial causes and disciplinary matters before the Apostolic Signatura,[30] where—testifies Cardinal Grocholewski, who was his student and a longtime official and superior of the Supreme Tribunal—"the *vota* of Fr. Gordon were highly valued, especially in particularly difficult questions."[31] His interventions would come about, for example, by mandate of the Prefect according to terms such as these: "De mandato Em.mi Cardinalis Praefecti, *votum scribat pro rei veritate R.P. Ignatius Gordon S.J.*, Referendarius Huius Supr. Trib."[32] After writing and submitting his *votum*, he would be called to participate in the *Congresso* in which that cause would be addressed. Thus, sometimes an inscription was handwritten directly on his *vota*, such as: "Die 20 aprilis 1972. – Ad Congressum diei 26 aprilis 1972, h. 10: referet R. P. Gordon S.J. + A. Sabattani, Secr.,"[33] or "22.VII.69. ad proximum Congressum. J.M. Pinna, Sec."[34] At other times, he would simply attend the meeting of the *Congresso* without submitting any *votum*.[35] He was most dedicated to his service of the Supreme Tribunal and carried it out with reverence, even if he was not always in agreement with its judgments.[36]

Cardinale Zenone Grocholewski per il cinquantesimo di sacerdozio, ed. Marek Jędraszewski and Jan Słowiński [Poznań: Archdiocese of Poznań, 2013] 86, citing the file in the archive of the Signatura bearing prot. n. 3166/72 VAR). Fr. Gordon, who was known to encourage and help Grocholewski, is described in the same book as a "leading Spanish canonist" (37) and an "eminent Spanish canonist" (86); see also 53.

30. A search of the archives for this material is difficult, since they are naturally organized according to individual themes (CA – contentious administrative recourse, CG – judicial causes, VT – vigilance over tribunals, etc.). Nevertheless, that search resulted in the discovery of 25 *vota*, and there may even be more.

31. See Grocholewski, 361, no. 1.

32. Supreme Tribunal of the Apostolic Signatura, decree of the Secretary, *Separationis*, prot. n. 4530/73 VT, June 9, 1973: in SSAT Archives, document no. 2. This document is handwritten by then-Archbishop Aurelio Sabattani.

33. Ignacio Gordon, *votum* ("De Tribunalium conflictu"), prot. n. 2695/72 CG, April 30, 1972: in SSAT Archives, document no. 7.

34. Ignacio Gordon, *votum, Nullitatis matrimonii*, prot. n. 336/69 CP, July 18, 1969: in SSAT Archives.

35. He participated in the *Congresso* in the following causes without writing a *votum*: prot. nn. 20012 CA, 19254/87 CG, and 18969/87 VT (see SSAT Archives).

36. Some examples of this are seen below. One that could be mentioned here is his dissent from a principle stated in a response of the Signatura on the territoriality of judicial power (*Periodica* 62 [1973] 593–597). In virtue of this principle, a sentence issued by a judge outside his territory would be irremediably null; but Fr. Gordon thought this to be a title of only relative incompetence, and thus the defect does not cause nullity of the sentence (cf. *Pars statica*, 116, no. 161). He is in fact also self-deprecating in stating this, since he cites no one for support but only three sources that actually suggest otherwise: Roberti, the Signatura, and the Pontifical Commission for Drafting the Code of Eastern Canon Law (*AAS* 45 [1953] 105).

8. – He was still a relatively new scholar of procedural law when the code commission and the study group on processes were being developed, and so he was not named to them initially.[37] Nevertheless, he was already to have some influence on the work of revision through the distribution, requested by the then-secretary of the commission Ramón Bidagor, SJ, to the members of the *Coetus de processibus* of a copy of his thorough and dense article on the excessive length of marriage nullity trials, entitled "De nimia processuum matrimonialium duratione. Factum – Causae – Remedia." Father Gordon in fact prepared that work with the aspiration of aiding "all those to whom the solution of this arduous problem pertains for one reason or another."[38] The secretary perceived its insights pertaining to various elements of the judicial process,[39] and he drew particular attention to it during his interventions in the special commission established on September 2, 1969 by Pope St. Paul VI for examining the proposed particular norms that would become the so-called American Procedural Norms. As the report from the first gathering of that commission explains: "The petitions contained in the USA proposals, and other things besides, were not unknown to the *Coetus de processibus* of the Commission for the Revision of the CIC, also because Father Gordon, S.J., professor at the Gregorian and *Votans* of the Apostolic Signatura made it the object of an open and complete publication—a serious one—in *Periodica de Re Morali, Canonica*, … of that University." And he had the special commission study a particular section.[40]

---

37. Cf. *Communicationes* 1 (1969) 20–21 ("Elenchus Consultorum"), 34 ("Coetus studiorum").

38. See "De nimia processuum matrimonialium duratione," 493, no. 4. On this article of his, *vide infra* Chapter X, no. 3.

39. Cf. Beyer, 17.

40. "Commissione speciale per l'esame delle proposte presentate dalla Conferenza Episcopale USA circa il processo matrimoniale," in PCCICR Archives, *Archivio Card. Felici: Commissione spec. procedura matrim. U.S.A. [II]*, "Verbali riunioni – 6–7.XI.'69 – 26.sett.'69," 2:8–9. At the top of the first volume on that theme in the same *Archivio Card. Felici*, what does one find but two offprints of the first half of the cited article written by Fr. Gordon (i.e., pp. 491–594).

Rightly did Carlo Gullo explain that, "because of the breadth and depth of its arguments, it can be considered a true and proper monograph"; and "in view of the undisputed prestige of the author, it has undeniably constituted the scientific basis for some improvements accomplished by the new code" (see his "Celerità e gratuità dei processi matrimoniali canonici," in *La giustizia nella Chiesa: fondamento divino e cultura processualistica moderna*, Studi Giuridici 45 [Vatican City: Libreria Editrice Vaticana, 1997] 231, note 7). And Thomas J. Green called it "a magisterial study" ("The American Procedural Norms – An Assessment," *Studia canonica* 8 [1974] 318, note 5) and "an extremely detailed and perceptive survey" ("Marriage Nullity Processes in the Schema *De Processibus*," *The Jurist* 38 [1978] 311, note 1) on which he drew frequently in the latter, also with a critical stance. It is cited much in procedural literature, including quite recently by the Prefect of the Apostolic Signatura and the Dean *emeritus* of the Roman Rota: see, respectively, Dominique Mamberti,

9. – In the archives of the faculty in which he taught procedural law for most of his professorship, there is a bound collection of the faculty's observations on the *Schema canonum de processibus* from 1978.[41] No particular author is indicated, but given the fact that Father Gordon was the principal, if not exclusive, professor of procedural law in the faculty at that time, it is likely that it was largely authored by him.

10. – Subsequent to the broad consultation on the *Schema canonum de modo procedendi pro tutela iurium seu de processibus*, a small group was composed for the purpose of examining the observations and suggestions that that consultation yielded. It was in that group that Father Gordon made his entrance into the work of the *Coetus de processibus*. We read: "Father Ignacio Gordon was also added to this Group, even though he was not numbered among the Consultors of our Commission."[42] That seems to have been an informal invitation for Father Gordon's collaboration, since there appears to be no pontifical appointment or even letter of invitation in the archives of the Pontifical Commission for the Revision of the Code of Canon Law.[43] Nevertheless, the essence of his contribution to the work of the *Coetus* was that of a consultor. And it can be said that the commission understood him to be a consultor in fact. For (1) in internal lists of the consultors in the *Coetus*, he was always included among them,[44] and (2) even in *Communicationes* when his name was removed from the discussions (as is done

---

"*'Quam primum, salva iustitia'* (can. 1453). Celerità e giustizia nel processo di nullità matrimoniale rinnovato," in *Studi in onore di Carlo Gullo*, Annales IV (Vatican City: Libreria Editrice Vaticana, 2017) 3:645, note 1; Antoni Stankiewicz, "Alcune considerazioni intorno all'esercizio personale e vicario della potestà giudiziale con riferimento al processo matrimoniale breviore davanti al Vescovo diocesano," in ibid., 765, note 21.

41. Pontificia Universitas Gregoriana, *Animadversiones in "Schema canonum de modo procedendi pro tutela iurium seu de processibus,"* February 11, 1978 (Rome: [P.U.G.,] 1978). It is 92 pages in length, consisting in a preface, the text of several draft canons, and cursive print observations on the text. The material style of the booklet resembles Fr. Gordon's *Processus nullitatis matrimonii*.

42. See *Communicationes* 10 (1978) 209: "Huic Coetui aggregatus est etiam P. Ignatius Gordon, quamvis non adnumeretur inter Consultores nostrae Commissionis."

43. Cf. *Protocollo corrispondenza*, vol. 2 (spanning the period from April 17, 1977 to March 12, 1984), and vols. 177–183 in the PCCICR Archives.

44. On the cover of the folder pertaining to the sessions in which he was involved, there is simply this note: "Fanno parte del 'Parvus coetus' *i Consultori*: Sabattani, Pinto, Ciprotti, Dordett, O'Connell, Maida, *Gordon* e Damizia" (emphasis added). A small handwritten note (in pencil) at the front of the folder likewise lists these names—the first six in a bolder script seemingly written by one person, the last two in smaller script, seemingly written by another. See PCCICR Archives, *vol. 181: XI. De processibus, Series II*, *Sessio I*, *diebus 3–8 aprilis 1978 habita*, "Lettera circolare N. 4251/78 del 26 gennaio 1978…," first folder. See also PCCICR Archives, *vol. 182, XI. De processibus, Parvus coetus (5–7 martii 1981)*, first folder.

generally throughout that publication), the anonymous reference identified the contributor as a consultor.

He would thus participate in sessions taking place April 3–8, May 15–20, October 23–28, November 20–25, and December 11–16, 1978; March 26–31, May 14–19, and June 11, 1979; February 26, 28, and 29, 1980; and March 5–7, 1981.[45] He was also entrusted with the important task of offering a *votum* on a special question discussed by the fathers of the code commission in their *Congregatio plenaria* held October 20–21, 1981.[46]

11. – On December 12, 1984, His Eminence Rosalio Cardinal Castillo Lara, the president of the Pontifical Commission for the Authentic Interpretation of the Code of Canon Law, proposed Father Gordon's name to the Cardinal Secretary of State for appointment as a consultor, together with several others.[47] On December 14, 1985, Pope St. John Paul II appointed him as a consultor to the Pontifical Commission, for a five-year period.[48] This was communicated to him on December 21, and he responded with gratitude to the Holy Father on February 6, 1986.[49] However, his role was not confirmed with the expiration of that period[50] "for health reasons."[51] He was thanked in a letter from the then-Pontifical Council for the Interpretation of Legislative Texts on August 5, 1991.[52] When he died eleven years later, the Pontifical Council for Legislative Texts declared: "The Superiors of the Pontifical Council for Legislative Texts recall with affection and gratitude in prayer the Very Reverend Father IGNACIO GORDON S.J. who

---

45. Cf. *Communicationes* 10 (1978) 209–272; 11 (1979) 67–162, 243–296; 12 (1980) 188–200; 43 (2011) 441–467.

46. See "Votum de revisione sententiae."

47. PCCICR, letter, prot. n. 353/84 December 12, 1984, and the attachment entitled "Proposta di nuovi Membri e Consultori della Pontificia Commissione per l'interpretazione autentica del Codice di Diritto Canonico," in PCLT Archives, *Ufficio I. Consultori, Cons./I,* Sc. I, C/760, I/CON./I/2. To these is also attached some brief notes about certain proposed individuals. There we read: "Il Rev.do P. Gordon Ignacio, S.I., formò parte del Gruppo di studio per la revisione dello Schema 'De processibus.'"

48. "Diarium Romanae Curiae. Segreteria di Stato: Nomine," *AAS* 78 (1986) 131; *Communicationes* 17 (1985) 316. The prot. n. of the Secretary of State is 146.100; that of the Pontifical Commission is 788/85 (see PCLT Archives, *Ufficio I. Consultori, Cons./I,* Sc. I, C/760, I/CON./I/2).

49. Ignacio Gordon to Pope St. John Paul II, letter, February 5, 1986: in PCLT Archives, *Ufficio I. Consultori, Cons./I,* Sc. I, C/760, I/CON./I/2.

50. Cf. *Communicationes* 23 (1991) 131–132.

51. PCLTI, letter, prot. n. 2800/91, April 21, 1991: PCLT Archives, *Ufficio I. Consultori, Cons./I,* Sc. I, I/Cons./I/1: "Per motivi di salute non sono in grado di continuare a svolgere questo loro incarico: il P. Ignacio GORDON CUVILLO, S.I. . . ."

52. PCLTI, letter, prot. n. 3012/91, August 5, 1991: in ibid., I/Cons./I/5.

with so much promptness and competence collaborated in the work of revision of the preceding Code of Canon Law."[53]

12. – After searching its archives, I discovered not one *votum* written by Father Gordon for the Pontifical Commission/Council pertaining to procedural law in the post-1983 period while he was a consultor.[54] And only one time, it seems, was he solicited formally as a consultor, in regard to the question of active legitimation of a group of the faithful to propose hierarchical recourse. On February 26, 1987, he was invited to take part in a collegial study of the question, including the problem of how to formulate the *dubium iuris* to be proposed to the plenary session of the Pontifical Commission.[55] However, he was not asked to submit a written *votum*; he simply offered his opinion *viva voce* at the session of the consultors.[56] He was available for those five years, but in fact, by the time of his appointment, he had already been significantly reducing his scholarly activity—which was at its highest level in the late 1960s and early 1970s.

C. Priest

13. – What can likely be confirmed by anyone who studied under or otherwise knew Father Gordon is that he was known by many to be a kind soul. Former students and other associates of his spontaneously described him to me as "*molto gentile,*" "gentle," "a gentleman," "a very dear man," and "*un gran sacerdote.*"

The Reverend Father Augustine Mendonça, who was his student in 1979–1980, explains how "he inspired me with his personal simplicity, holiness and seasoned wisdom. . . . Whenever I met him by myself he was extremely kind to me."[57] The Reverend Monsignor Roch Pagé, who had been his student, said he was "beloved by students" and that "he taught always with a smile on his face."[58]

---

53. See PCLT, necrology, December 6, 2002: in ibid., I/Cons./I/8.

54. Cf. PCLT Archives, *Responsiones. Codex Iuris Canonici, II. Liber VII (cann. 1400–1752),* II/RL. VII, sc. XII and XII/bis; ibid., *Tribunali. Supremo Tribunale della Segnatura Apostolica, Rapporti,* III/STSA, sc. I.

55. PCCICAI, letter, prot. n. 1248/87, February 26, 1987: in PCCICAI Archives, *Consulta VII (3 marzo 1987),* VII/1987/1. *Vide infra* Chapter IX, no. 29.

56. Cf. "I. Foglio d'ufficio" and "Consulta (3 marzo 1987). Relazione," in PCCICAI Archives, *Consulta VII (3 marzo 1987),* VII/1987/1; "Iº. Parere della consulta," in PCCICAI Archives, *Plenaria VIII (29 aprile 1987),* I Dubium.

57. Augustine Mendonça to William L. Daniel, letter, May 19, 2018.

58. Roch Pagé, conversation with William L. Daniel, June 25, 2018, at The Catholic University of America, Washington, DC. It was my honor and pleasure to be a student, in turn, of both Fr. Mendonça and Msgr. Pagé during the second cycle of my canonical studies (2004–2006).

Father Aidan McGrath, OFM, whose doctoral dissertation he directed, seemed grateful for the opportunity to record his recollections, because "I realized just how much I owe to Fr. Gordon." "He was a great man." Despite some personal hesitations, it was Father Gordon's "gentleness and kindness [that] convinced me that I could go forward and study Canon Law."[59]

The late and great Cardinal Zenon Grocholewski, who was his student in the middle and late 1960s and personal collaborator in the university and at the Signatura, underlines his "*authentic humility*. I think that anyone who had had contact with him was due to become aware of this quality. Everyone felt at ease with him. He never spoke of his accomplishments. This humility was the foundation of the gentleness, understanding and respect with which he treated his students."[60]

The renowned Professor Gianfranco Ghirlanda, SJ, who was his student in the middle to late 1970s and lived in the same community as Father Gordon for about twenty years, described him as "humble" and a "lovely" person. He was serious and did not immediately display a social openness, but the depth of his warmth was revealed after a brief time of coming to know him. And in fact he was notably approachable by students, colleagues, and fellow religious alike.[61]

The noted author, scholar of jurisprudence, and revered judicial vicar of the Lombardo Regional Tribunal, Monsignor Paolo Bianchi, kindly shared with me several technical contributions of Father Gordon, based on his interactions with him as a student. And he adds: "But the most vivid recollection that I have of him is his discreet, calm, serene, and subtle features, full of humility and wisdom, joined with a sobriety of a really exemplary life."[62]

14. – "What was striking about Father Gordon was the fact that his commitment [to being a professor and scholar of canon law] was sustained by *a remarkable spiritual life*."[63] This was evidenced by the many fruits reported here. One could catch glimpses of it throughout his writings, including but not limited to his custom of placing at the beginning of some unpublished writing or letter a

---

Retrospectively, I can affirm that Fr. Gordon's influence was reflected in the zeal for the study of jurisprudence for which the former is famous, and in the latter's method of teaching procedural law, from which I benefitted (*pars statica/pars dynamica*).

59. Aidan McGrath to William L. Daniel, letter, August 22, 2018.

60. Grocholewski, 361–362, no. 3.

61. Gianfranco Ghirlanda, conversation with William L. Daniel, May 19, 2018, at the Pontifical Gregorian University, Rome.

62. Paolo Bianchi to William L. Daniel, "Ricordo di padre Ignacio Gordon," private correspondence, May 6, 2019.

63. See Grocholewski, 364, no. 7.

notation in honor of our Lord: "Ihs" (*Iesus hominum salvator*, or his name in Greek: *Ihsus*). At the beginning of his *dispensa* on the *pars statica* of procedural law, he begged God to bless it: "May God grant that these notes reach their intended goal."[64] He found one student's inability to publish his dissertation defended in 1964 until after the Second Vatican Ecumenical Council to be "providential" due to the doctrinal and normative developments that could now be taken into account.[65] One of his former students and later colleagues testifies beautifully: "I never saw him annoyed or vexed with anyone; when a situation became trying, I remember him quietly exclaiming '*Santa pace!*' He never spoke to me directly about matters spiritual; but, in his office at the Jurisprudence Course, when the Angelus sounded at midday, he would interrupt conversation to pray, without any exaggeration or excessive piety; the prayer was as natural to him as saying hello."[66] Another, who had the occasion to visit him during his years of retirement, "found him wholly dedicated to prayer and to the offering up of his suffering."[67]

15. – His priestly spirit was demonstrated also in his consistent, charitable attentiveness to others in the midst of and through his work. Several examples serve to illustrate this.

A student whose doctoral dissertation he directed ended its preface "giving thanks especially to the Very Reverend Father Ignacio Gordon, who suggested this thesis . . . to us and constantly helped us with his precious advice and with great patience, understanding, and love."[68] He had suggested a particular topic to another student as well and, "in spite of serious illness, continued to guide my research with unfailing enthusiasm and interest."[69] Another was moved in

---

64. See *Pars statica*, 1.

65. Cf. Ignacio Gordon, "Presentación" (October 15, 1970), in Rafael Figueroa Campos, *La "persona standi in iudicio" en la legislación eclesiástica*, Analecta Gregoriana 179 (Rome: Università Gregoriana Editrice, 1971) v–vi.

66. Aidan McGrath to William L. Daniel, "Fr. Ignacio Gordon S.J. – Some personal memories," private correspondence, August 22, 2018, 3. On a personal note, he states: "Fr. Gordon was one of the greatest influences on me as a religious, as a priest, and as a canonist" (ibid.).

67. Giuseppe Versaldi to William L. Daniel, "Father Ignacio Gordon, S.J.," private correspondence, September 26, 2018, 2.

68. See Nikola Škalabrin, *De vaginismo et inconsummatione matrimonii in decisionibus rotalibus (1945–1975)*, Dissertatio ad Doctoratum in Facultate Iuris Canonici Pontificiae Universitatis Gregorianae (Diacovo: CertisaK, 1987) 5.

69. Aidan McGrath, *A Controversy concerning Male Impotence*, Dissertatio ad Doctoratum in Facultate Iuris Canonici Pontificiae Universitatis Gregorianae (Rome: Pontificia Universitas Gregoriana, 1988) 6.

the same context "to express my recognition and my profound respect" for Father Gordon.[70] Still another expressed his gratitude to all the professors of the faculty, "especially the Very Reverend Father Ignacio Gordon, who with great charity, patience, and humanity continually assisted me and directed me in creating this work."[71]

He was not only helpful to those who were under his direction. One student of canon law writing a thesis in the area of the *munus docendi* declared in his acknowledgements: "I am also grateful for the encouragement and help, in many quiet ways, of Fr. Ignacio Gordon, S.J."[72] Monsignor Paolo Bianchi likewise benefitted from Father Gordon's counsel, even though he was not the director of his doctoral thesis.[73] It seems unlikely that these are the only students Father Gordon assisted in an informal and quiet way.

16. – The same applies to his rapport with those taking part in the *Cursus* events. He wrote a brief letter to a prospective participant from Rockford, Illinois, encouraging him to come to Rome for the 1975 *Cursus*. And he added at the end: "I hear that your mother does not have good health these days. I am praying to God so that your mother may quickly recover and be well."[74] A participant in the first *Cursus* expressed in a letter to him "my deep gratitude to you for your constant kindness and your devoted work."[75] Another called him "the soul of the *Cursus*" since he gave so much of himself and his teaching to the participants.[76] "It can be said that he gave everything of himself in these" *Cursus* events.[77] Another offered a prayerful wish that "the Lord may reward all the labors which

---

70. See Anne Bamberg, *L'impuissance organique de la femme d'après la jurisprudence rotale récente (1970–1981)*, Excerpta ex dissertatione ad Doctoratum cum specialisatione in iurisprudentia in Facultate Iuris Canonici Pontificiae Universitatis Gregorianae (Luxembourg: [no publisher], 1982) 7.

71. See Andrea Henrisoesanta, *De probatione per documenta in processu canonico*, Excerpta ex dissertatione ad Lauream in Facultate Iuris Canonici Pontificiae Universitatis Gregorianae (Rome: Pontificia Universitas Gregoriana, 1966) 7.

72. William V. Millea, *The Doctrinal Authority of Theologians in Late Medieval Controversy*, Excerpta ex dissertatione ad Doctoratum in Facultate Iuris Canonici Pontificiae Universitatis Gregorianae (Rome: Pontificia Universitas Gregoriana, 1989) v.

73. Paolo Bianchi to William L. Daniel, "Ricordo di padre Ignacio Gordon," private correspondence, May 6, 2019.

74. See Ignacio Gordon, letter, September 17, 1975: in FICPUG Archives, *Archivio del quinto corso per giudici (3 nov. – 12 dic. 1975)*, Appendice, 30.

75. Cyril Murtagh, letter, January 20, 1972: in FICPUG Archives, *Archivio del primo corso per giudici (1971–1972)*, V.23.

76. See Gabriele Salvati, letter, December 10, 1971: in ibid., V.23.

77. Grocholewski, 364.

you do to form good priests."[78] Another expressed gratitude "for the edification which your dedication, your zeal, and your tireless amiability have brought us."[79]

17. – The Reverend Monsignor Frederick Easton relates a story that further illustrates how attentive Father Gordon was to individual participants, which would be emblematic of his general attentiveness to others. As is discussed below, a major highlight of the *Cursus* was the audience with the Holy Father.[80] At a certain point during the event, Father Gordon would announce the date and time for the audience, together with instructions for attending it. When hearing this announcement, Monsignor Easton could see immediately that he would not be able to attend it the year he participated in the *Cursus*, because he had already arranged to collect his mother and some friends at the airport the same day as the audience; they had planned a trip to Rome before he went there for the *Cursus*. This naturally left Monsignor Easton disappointed. He explains: "However, the next morning when the English speakers were in a room discussing a case from the Roman Rota, there was a knock at the door and it was Father Gordon who summoned me out into the hallway and said that he noted that when he announced the date and time for the papal audience, my face changed. That really was a big statement about how attentive he was to all of his students." When Monsignor Easton explained the situation, Father Gordon encouraged him to try to make it to the audience nevertheless. He met his mother and friends, and, with a little urging of the taxi driver, they arrived at the place for the papal audience. "When we got just outside the door of the Sala Clementina, Father Gordon spied me and waved me up with the other three where he had four seats reserved in the second row." Mingled with the joy of experiencing the papal audience and meeting Pope St. John Paul II was the deep impression that it was "Father Gordon who really made it happen."[81]

18. – Father Gordon himself drew attention to these qualities in others. For instance, in his *commemoratio* of then-Father Urbano Navarrete, he not only praised all the scientific accomplishments of that canonist but also underscored

---

78. See Ivo Reali to Ignacio Gordon, letter, December 2, 1971: in FICPUG Archives, *Archivio del primo corso per giudici (1971–1972)*, V.23.

79. Édgar Franca to Ignacio Gordon, letter, December 16, 1972: in *Archivio del secondo corso per giudici (5 nov. – 15 dic. 1972)*, FICPUG Archives, V.23.

80. *Vide infra* Chapter II, no. 8.

81. Frederick C. Easton to William L. Daniel, "Remembrances and reflections upon the experience of participating in the *Cursus Renovationis* at the Pontifical Gregorian University in the fall of 1981," private correspondence, May 1, 2018.

his generosity and self-sacrifice as a priest and colleague, as well as his courage in persevering in this service even when afflicted with an illness. Father Gordon comments: "Perhaps this Christian courage is to be called his greatest lesson, of indeed a higher teaching authority, which Fr. Navarrete discreetly offers us in this year of his retirement."[82]

19. – As the official obituary of the University puts it, he was a "gift [from] the Lord," "not only as a scholar but above all as an exemplary priest of the Society of Jesus."[83] Father Gordon's teaching and research were not merely his areas of work; they were also modes of expression of his priestly and religious vocation. As one of his former students testifies: "I could not but admire his humility and spirit of service in the total self-giving to his academic endeavor which everyone recognized in him. His readiness for dialogue with his students, along with the clarity of his teaching, made him a point of doctrinal reference and an example of self-giving to the service of the Church."[84] That meant, in part, that he strove for them not to be satisfied with mediocrity in their own scholarly work but had an "insistence on excellence throughout" their work of research and studies.[85]

20. – He was not formally entrusted with the full care of souls. However, what has already been said makes it immediately evident that he cared for many souls *lato sensu*, but ever also as a priest. Moreover, there were in fact a number of explicit expressions of priestly ministry carried out by him. Father Ghirlanda explains that Father Gordon had the long practice of giving spiritual direction after a full day's work. This was largely a matter of speaking on the telephone with religious sisters who sought his spiritual counsel. Also, on Sundays he regularly heard confessions at the Church of San Saba in Rome from 8:00 a.m. until 1:00 p.m.[86]

---

82. See Ignacio Gordon, "R.P. Urbani Navarrete triginta et duo anni Magisterii apud Pontificiam Universitatem Gregorianam feliciter commemorantur," *Periodica* 79 (1990) 20.

83. See Pontificia Università Gregoriana, *Liber Annualis, Roma 2003 – Univ. 450º* (Rome: Pontificia Università Gregoriana, 2003) 379.

84. Giuseppe Versaldi to William L. Daniel, "Father Ignacio Gordon, S.J.," private correspondence, September 26, 2018, 1.

85. Thomas E. Molloy, *The Document of the National Conference of Catholic Bishops of the United States on Due Process in the Light of American and Canon Law* (Rome: Catholic Book Agency, 1980) x.

86. Gianfranco Ghirlanda, conversation with William L. Daniel, May 19, 2018, at the Pontifical Gregorian University, Rome. Cardinal Grocholewski also writes in passing: "We also knew that he was a spiritual director valued by many persons" (see 364, no. 7).

Surely the extent of this dimension of Father Gordon cannot be documented. But it is interesting to note also that for a month (July 12–August 19, 1974), he went to Zaire for the third time to carry out the sacred ministry complementing a particular medical apostolate of an Italian dentist. The money to fund the project was contributed by Father Gordon himself.[87] It is not known how many times he did this in total,[88] but this alone reveals something of his apostolic zeal.

D. Further Illustrations

21. – In the final analysis, there is no sharp distinction in Father Gordon's activities as professor, jurist, and priest. They were each part of his identity during his most active years as a canonist. One further illustration of this is the manner in which his goodness is revealed throughout his writings.

For example, he recognizes that his proposals of reform come from his simplicity or plainness.[89] This is revealed also in his methodological humility, to be explored below, according to which he draws ample attention to the thought of others, without exaggerating the importance or novelty of his own opinions. Additionally, he was humane and sympathetic, for example, in regard to how a judge traveling to collect proofs in order to speed up the instruction of a cause may cause him "no little weariness." It is a good solution when it can be done "without grave expense of health and money."[90]

22. – His critiques were frequently made with an understanding and positive spirit. For example, even while questioning the contemporary inadequacy of the norm that, as it were, allowed a trial to extend for three years (1917 *CIC* c. 1620), he recognized the good efforts of tribunals to act within such parameters, seeing that they had "overcome not minor difficulties and not without great sacrifice."[91]

In treating the unfortunate problem of civil lawyers presuming to enjoy expertise in canon law, he displayed a deferential and respectful attitude toward

---

87. Cf. *Informazioni a cura del Segretariato Relazioni Studenti PUG* 6/50 (1 novembre 1974) 9–10.

88. There is an indication in another place that he had the intention to be in Zaire from November 15, 1982 until January 6, 1983. See Ignacio Gordon, letter, July 6, 1982: in FICPUG Archives, "Professorum Adunationes," at 3.V. Also, at the end of his article "La renovación de la Signatura Apostolica," he indicates that it was written from "Luabo (Zaïre) 15 de agosto de 1972" (610).

89. See "De nimia processuum matrimonialium duratione," 493, no. 4: "ex nostra tenuitate"; ibid., 645, note 1: "cum plena propriae [i.e. meae] tenuitatis conscientia."

90. See ibid., 539, no. 74.

91. See ibid., 499, no. 12.

their professors. Such lawyers were known to assume the patronage of ecclesiastical causes after having just one introductory course in canon law—such as a canon law student might receive in civil law. Such a course is obviously not sufficient to argue a cause on the basis of the canonical system "notwithstanding the knowledge and expertise of the professors" who teach that one course.[92]

He was modest in his critiques of others. In one cause pending before the Apostolic Signatura, he was illustrating the complexity of interventions of an advocate who, in his defense, was not receiving decisions from the Roman Rota at the pace and in the manner that he had expected. Whatever merit the advocate's principal petitions to the Supreme Tribunal may have had, Father Gordon gently observed that "he also requested other marginal ones, which do not seem to be of good sense."[93]

23. – In the context of his just and pointed critical examination of the proposals of the Reverend Monsignor Stephen J. Kelleher,[94] he displayed deep personal respect for him.[95] This is demonstrated in the first place by the seriousness with which he examined the reasoning and conclusions of Kelleher. Additionally, Father Gordon's disposition toward Kelleher lacked any harshness. We read in a footnote: "Once the present article had already been prepared for print, we were honored by a visit from Msgr. Stephen Kelleher, who very kindly conversed with us concerning his own opinion about procedural law." Father Gordon wished to debate Kelleher "in the same spirit of sincerity and humility" seen in Kelleher's writings; and this was an effort at "continuing the conversation, focused solely on the truth and the good of souls."[96]

Although Kelleher's proposals were outrageously divergent from the Church's teaching and discipline, Father Gordon perceived that the real diffi-

---

92. See ibid., 546, note 12.

93. See Ignacio Gordon, *votum* ("De recursu ad S.Tribunal Signaturae Apostolicae contra decretum Decani S.R.Rotae dierum 21–25 octobris in una [X]"), prot. n. 715/68 CG, July 7, 1969: in SSAT Archives, 6, no. 17. Without dwelling on it, he would also describe one of the advocate's lines of reasoning as "very formalistic and superficial" (ibid., 14, no. 45).

94. *Vide infra* Chapter III, nn. 10–18.

95. More generally, one person testifies that, while Fr. Gordon was clearly expressing displeasure with the American Procedural Norms, "his criticism was neither negative nor condemnatory: instead, he pointed out the advantages of a streamlined process, while highlighting the possibility of abuses" (Aidan McGrath to William L. Daniel, "Fr. Ignacio Gordon S.J. – Some personal memories," private correspondence, August 22, 2018, 3).

96. See "De nimia processuum matrimonialium duratione," 645, note 1. Among the articles examined was one still unpublished manuscript "quod nobis ipse auctor amice donavit" (ibid., note 3).

culties experienced by people in especially delayed trials "upset Msgr. Stephen J. Kelleher's priestly and human sensibility"; he "acted with undoubted zeal toward unhappy couples, but 'not with right knowledge' (Rom. 10:2)." He was "led by a sincere desire to console the unhappiness from which many spouses suffer."[97] It is therefore not surprising that Kelleher was able to react in a cordial way to Father Gordon, as he did in his August 12, 1970 letter to the latter, in which he stated that he had "intended for a long time to tell you how much I appreciated your articles in '*Periodica*.' While we disagree in some of our views I was delighted with the very fair and just way you presented my opinions."[98]

---

97. See ibid., 659–660, no. 144 and note 1.

98. See "La soppressione dei tribunali ecclesiastici," 751, note 62. Fr. Gordon reprinted this letter from Msgr. Kelleher in a footnote in order to demonstrate the accuracy of his presentation of Kelleher's writing, which was being baselessly denied by Fr. Peter Huizing (see ibid., 751).

CHAPTER II

The Ongoing Formation of Ministers of Justice

SUMMARY — A. The Need for Ongoing Formation (nn. 1–
2). ▪ B. The *Cursus renovationis canonicae pro Iudicibus et
Tribunalium administris* (nn. 3–10). ▪ C. The *Laurea in Iure
Canonico cum specializatione in Iurisprudentia* (nn. 11–13).

A. The Need for Ongoing Formation

1. – What would eventually become the renewal course for judges and later the specialization in jurisprudence had been the object of Father Gordon's reflection since 1968 at the latest. His perception that people were assuming judicial functions without adequate preparation weighed upon him as a matter of grave concern. There had to be an academic solution to this problem. In the first place, he initially envisioned a specialization in procedural law (*licentia specializata in iure processuali*), which would prepare future canonists for the ministry of justice. Later it would become clear that this had to have a predominantly substantive character, as will be discussed below. Apart from this, bearing in mind the inability of some bishops to support financially a canonical education for those to be entrusted with offices in the tribunal, there was to be a diploma in judicial and especially matrimonial matters (*Diploma peritiae in re iudiciaria*).[1]

2. – The preparation and ongoing formation of ministers of justice is a theme about which Father Gordon wrote with eloquence in 1969.[2] Reflecting on the gravity of the administration of justice, especially the duties of the judge, and on the lack of insistence in the general legislation that ministers of justice be endowed with a degree in canon law, he outlined certain elements of formation that he thought ought to belong to "the good formation of the judge and ministers" of justice.

---

1. "De specializatione iudiciaria in nostra Facultate Iuris Canonici," in FICPUG Archives. This document is five pages in length and explains the curriculum, the mode of holding lectures and examinations, and the like. At the upper right side of the first page, this typed inscription appears, followed by Fr. Navarrete's signature: "Schema elaboratum a P. Gordon a. 1968."
2. "De nimia processuum matrimonialium duratione," 529–531, no. 58.

First, at least a licentiate in canon law should be earned by all officials of the tribunal, while the judicial vicar ought to have earned a doctorate. Second, beyond such core degrees, it is fitting that there be "specific theoretical preparation for judicial matters," both the norms of procedural and substantive matrimonial law and Rotal jurisprudence.[3] This could even take the form of a "specialized degree" or courses at the *Studium Rotale* or other institutes. Third, instruction in "procedural praxis" could be completed by the more concrete training of ministers of justice, including notaries. This would include direction on how to examine a cause and write the various kinds of acts that are placed in a cause,[4] as well as by mock trials ("per modum ficti exercitii") and even internships in tribunals ("'in vivo' apud aliquod Tribunal") as aids to notaries or assistants to judges. And he adds this fourth point, perhaps having in mind his aspiration to institute the *Cursus renovationis canonicae pro Iudicibus*: "But if in this way which we have described or in a similar manner judges are instructed seriously and continually, steps can finally be made toward the foreseen establishment of a judicial career (*cursus*) or order in the Church."

Even clerics who are not ministers of justice need some knowledge of procedural and substantive law. Those entrusted with the care of souls regularly have some role in their parishioners' engagement in trials. For this reason, Father Gordon saw courses in tribunal activity, and the manner of judicial instruction in particular, as beneficial in the ongoing formation of clergy.[5]

B. The *Cursus renovationis canonicae pro Iudicibus et Tribunalium administris*

3. – These were not mere reflections or detached proposals on Father Gordon's part. He was in fact designing such a formation program. It would be the Course of Canonical Renewal for Judges and Ministers of Tribunals, or the *Cursus*. The *Cursus* began in 1971 and was for the most part an annual event until 1977. After that, it took place only on the odd years (1979, 1981), the last being held in 1981.[6]

---

3. Cf. *DC* art. 35 §§2–3.

4. In the cited passage written in 1969, he described this as a "progressive initiation in the function of judging, from the reading, study, and discussion of causes, to the drawing up of *vota* (e.g., in favor of the bond), to the interrogation of some witness and making the relative written act (*verbalizatio*), finally to writing out some sentence in a simpler matter."

5. See "De nimia processuum matrimonialium duratione," 538, no. 73.

6. See "Septimus Cursus pro Iudicibus," 164, no. 3.

Its foundation was announced by the Dean, Prof. Jean Beyer, SJ, on June 11, 1971, as an initiative of the Faculty of Canon Law.[7] It was immediately praised by the Apostolic See and would be also in subsequent years.[8] The same Dean made many public announcements about the *Cursus*, since it was a work of the Faculty of Canon Law. However, the director and principal contact person for the faculty was Father Gordon,[9] who was authoritatively identified by Dino Cardinal Staffa as "its author and promoter."[10]

4. – The *Cursus* had various elements. Naturally, it included lectures by experts especially in matrimonial and procedural law, as well as in administrative law and psychology. In 1979, there were also lectures on missionary law, since not a few participants were from mission lands, and on the Billings method of natural family planning.[11] Beginning in 1976, there was an intention

---

7. See the letter in the FICPUG Archives, where one also finds the original handwritten French draft of an announcement made to certain Cardinals in the Roman Curia.

8. See Sacred Congregation for Catholic Education (SCCE), letter, prot. n. 719/71/3, June 22, 1971: in FICPUG Archives, *Archivio del primo corso per giudici (1971–1972)*, I.2; Sacred Congregation for Religious and Secular Institutes, June 26, 1971, ibid.; Secretary of State (SS), letter, prot. n. 186472, July 6, 1971, ibid. See also SCCE, letter, prot. n. 719/71/5, July 11, 1972: in FICPUG Archives, *Archivio del secondo corso per giudici (5 nov. – 15 dic. 1972)*, I.2; SS, letter, prot. n. 238017, July 2, 1973: in FICPUG Archives, *Archivio del terzo corso per giudici (4 nov. – 15 dic. 1973)*, I.1–2; SCCE, letter July 5, 1973, in ibid.; SCCE, letter prot. n. 719/71/12, June 19, 1974: in FICPUG Archives, *Archivio del quarto corso per giudici (3 nov. – 14 dic. 1974)*, V.23.

9. For example, in several letters pertaining to the enrollment of the 1974 *Cursus*, he identifies himself as "Director Cursus" (*Archivio del quarto corso*, Appendix.30). He is listed as "Director" in Pontificia Universitas Gregoriana, *Liber annualis, Roma 1980 Univ. 427º* (Rome: Universitas Gregoriana, 1980) 114. See also "Cursus renovationis canonicae. Cursus pro Iudicibus et Tribunalium Administris," pamphlet, in *Archivio del primo corso*, I.3 at 3: "Epistolae mittantur ad I. Gordon, S.I., Piazza della Pilotta, 4 - 00187 Roma." At the bottom of the "Schema inscriptionis" we read: "*Schedam* mitte, quaeso, ad I. GORDON, S.I., Piazza della Pilotta, 4. 00187 Roma; ab eoque informationes circa cursum peti possunt" (ibid., I.5). "Alter Cursus renovationis canonicae pro Iudicibus et Tribunalium Administris," pamphlet, in *Archivio del secondo corso*, I.3: "Epistolae pro inscriptionibus faciendis, notitiis petendis, etc. mittantur ad: *I. Gordon, S. I. 'Cursus pro Iudicibus', P.zza della Pilotta, 4. - 00187 Roma.*" The same indications are used also in subsequent years (cf. FICPUG Archives, *passim*). At the *Cursus*, there would often be some marketing of recently published canon law books, whose purchase was somehow facilitated through the *Cursus*. The small order forms from one year bore this heading: "P. Gordon (Aggiornamento Giudici)" (*Archivio del secondo corso*, IV.22). See also "Notificatio III 7a, 2-VI-1974," in *Archivio del terzo corso*, I.11, at 3, no. 4.

10. See "Em.mi et Rev.mi Card. Dini Staffa verba introductoria in IV Cursum pro Iudicibus," in *Archivio del quarto corso*, II.12: "Magno cum animi mei gaudio quartum cursum auspicor renovationis canonicae; et gaudium meum ex eo etiam oritur, quod huius felicis incepti partem ab initio cepi, cohortando pro viribus auctorem eius promotoremque: Rev.mum P. Gordon et, cum eo, totam hanc adeo sollertem facultatem...."

11. See "Octavus Cursus pro Iudicibus," 735–736.

to devote more time than in the past to the jurisprudence of the Roman Rota, with the examination of several causes of nullity of marriage judged by that apostolic tribunal.[12]

5. – It was also meant to be interactive. In 1975, Father Gordon identified the interactive element as "general conversations" that took place on Thursdays, "at which participants could propose questions, difficulties, etc. to the Professors, and in this way begin a dialogue on a particular point."[13] There was also a decidedly practical component initiated by then-Archbishop Aurelio Sabattani, the secretary of the Apostolic Signatura, whereby sample causes were distributed to all the participants, who decided them and drafted mock definitive sentences. These were then examined by the professors, whose critical observations were communicated to each author.[14]

The distribution of sample cases seems to have undergone some evolution, so much so that Father Gordon would comment that they gave the *Cursus* "a new appearance and made themselves more accommodated to renewing judges in canonical jurisprudence." Indeed, at the seventh *Cursus*, in 1977, there were distributed sample cases of nullity of marriage, non-consummation, presumed death of a spouse, and contentious-administrative recourse. The professor would instruct the participants to study them privately and draft sample decisions. Then, a few days later, they would gather in language groups to share their opinions, resulting in a group decision or split decisions, with an indication of the motives supporting each decision. Finally, in the assembly of all the participants, the professor would introduce the cause, the secretary from each group would present the decisions from its group, and the professor would give his own opinion. There would then follow a dialogue between the participants and the professor.[15] The highly instructive dynamic that this created would be decisive for the institution of the specialization in jurisprudence to be discussed below.[16]

---

12. See Jean Beyer, letters, May 31 and June 18, 1976: in FICPUG Archives, *Archivio del settimo corso per giudici (3 Nov. – 14 Dic. 1977)*, I.1.

13. See "Paulus PP. VI alloquitur," 5, no. 1.

14. Cf. ibid.

15. Cf. "Septimus Cursus pro Iudicibus," 160–162, quotation *in fine*.

16. Cf. "Septimus Cursus pro Iudicibus," in FICPUG Archives (this is a hard copy—with Fr. Gordon's own handwritten corrections—of the text published in *Periodica*, cited in the previous footnote). Because this modest title does not do justice to this 14-page document, Fr. Navarrete made this notation: "Ratio cur instituenda sit Laurea specializata in iurisprudentia. Relatio P. Gordon."

6. – Another interactive element was the series of visits made to various dicasteries of the Roman Curia for gaining some understanding of how particular questions deferred to it are handled, especially pertaining to marriage and the clerical state.[17] This seems not to have been part of the firm program of the *Cursus* when it was being advertised. However, during the first *Cursus*, Fr. Gordon had arranged with the Sacred Congregation of the Sacraments for participants in groups to observe live sessions of the commissioners of the dicastery entrusted with examining individual petitions for the dissolution of a non-consummated marriage.[18]

Over the years, the participants paid the most visits to the Sacred Congregations for the Doctrine of the Faith, for the Discipline of the Sacraments, and for the Clergy.[19] Later the Sacred Congregation for Bishops was added,[20] whose Prefect gave a lecture "on Bishops and on the function of judging."[21] There were also visits or lectures with the president of the Pontifical Commission for the Revision of the Code of Canon Law[22] and with officials of the tribunals of the Apostolic See.[23] The Apostolic Signatura was always well represented from the beginning of the *Cursus* by virtue of the fact that its Prefect, Dino Cardinal Staffa and later Pericle Cardinal Felici, gave the inaugural lectures. Moreover, there were regularly experiences also at the tribunal of the Vicariate of Rome.[24]

7. – There are detailed statistics and data about the participants in these *Cursus* events in the archives at the Gregorian University. Father Gordon himself publicized much of this information in the faculty's journal *Periodica*.

---

17. For the response to Fr. Gordon indicating the willingness of the Prefect of the Congregation for the Clergy to receive the participants in the 1973 *Cursus*, signed by the Prefect's personal secretary, then-Reverend Donald W. Wuerl, see letter, December 1, 1973, in *Archivio del terzo corso*, I.15.

18. "Esercitazione del Vicariato e della S.C. dei Sacramenti," in *Archivio del primo corso*, II.15.

19. See, e.g., "Alter Cursus renovationis canonicae pro Iudicibus et Tribunalium Administris," pamphlet, in *Archivio del secondo corso*, I.3 at III.A; "Tertius Cursus renovationis canonicae pro Iudicibus et Tribunalium Administris (4 nov. – 14 dec. 1973)," pamphlet, in *Archivio del terzo corso*, I.3 at III.A; "Octavus Cursus renovationis canonicae pro Iudicibus et Tribunalium Administris (2 nov. – 15 dec. 1979)," pamphlet, in FICPUG Archives, *Archivio dell'ottavo corso per giudici (2 Nov. – 15 Dic. 1979)*, I.3 at III.1.

20. "Quartus Cursus renovationis canonicae pro Iudicibus et Tribunalium Administris (3 nov. – 14 dec. 1974)," pamphlet, in *Archivio del quarto corso*, I.3 at III.A.

21. "Kalendarium-Programma. Pars 1a (4–23 nov.74)," in ibid., I.3.

22. Ibid.

23. Cf. "Quintus Cursus renovationis canonicae pro Iudicibus et Tribunalium Administris (3 nov. – 12 dec. 1975)," pamphlet, in FICPUG Archives, *Archivio del quinto corso per giudici (3 nov. – 12 dic. 1975)*, I.3 at III.A.

24. Cf. "Septimus Cursus renovationis canonicae pro Iudicibus et Tribunalium Administris (3 nov. – 14 dec. 1977)," pamphlet, in *Archivio del settimo corso*, I.3 at III.1.

Father Gordon's statistical skills and interests[25] led him to observe that there were 72 participants in 1971, 78 in 1972, and 73 in 1973, and that the fourth took place in 1974 from November 4 until December 13, at which there were 82 participants from 31 nations.[26] The fifth took place in 1975, from November 3 until December 12.[27] Jean Beyer described this last as "particularly 'missionary,'" since the participants were from 31 nations, including six African nations and seven Asian.[28]

The would-be sixth *Cursus* did not take place according to the ordinary program. Rather, "at the request of many, it was substituted with the International Convention of Canon Law held on February 14–19, 1977 at the Pontifical Gregorian University in commemoration of the first centenary of the Faculty of Canon Law."[29]

The seventh took place in 1977, from November 3 until December 14, at which there were 92 participants from 35 nations.[30] Father Gordon notes that, from 1971 until 1977, the *Cursus* had 465 participants from 61 nations.[31] The eighth took place in 1979, from November 2 until December 14, at which there were 70 participants from 29 nations.[32] The ninth and last took place in 1981, from November 3 until December 12, at which there were 78 participants from 30 nations.[33] Across the span of the nine courses, there would be 611 participants from 71 nations.[34]

8. – The first three years, the group of participants in the *Cursus* received a special papal audience.[35] In 1974, while this was not possible, the pope addressed

---

25. Throughout the archives, there are computation sheets that display the breakdown of participants according to academic degree (*iuxta tit. academ.*), function or office (*iuxta munera*), and homeland (*iuxta nationes*).

26. Cf. "Paulus PP. VI alloquitur," 5, no. 1.

27. See ibid., 11, no. 5.

28. See Jean Beyer, letter, November 18, 1975: in *Archivio del quinto corso*, II.17.

29. See "Septimus Cursus renovationis canonicae pro Iudicibus et Tribunalium Administris (3 nov. – 14 dec. 1977)," pamphlet, in *Archivio del settimo corso*, I.3, at 1 in the note marked with an asterisk (*).

30. "Septimus Cursus pro Iudicibus," 159, no. 1.

31. Ibid., 164, no. 3.

32. "Octavus Cursus pro Iudicibus," 733; cf. "Septimus Cursus pro Iudicibus," 170, no. 4.

33. "Computationes IX Cursuum pro Iudicibus," in FICPUG Archives, *Archivio del nono corso per giudici (3 Nov. – 12 Dic. 1981)*, I.7.

34. Ibid.

35. Paul VI, discourse to the 1st *Cursus pro Iudicibus*, December 13, 1971: *AAS* 64 (1972) 23–24; idem, discourse to the 2nd *Cursus pro Iudicibus*, December 13, 1972: *AAS* 64 (1972) 780–782; idem, discourse to the 3rd *Cursus pro Iudicibus*, December 14, 1973: *AAS* 66 (1974) 10–12; Jean Beyer, letter, December 9, 1971: in *Archivio del primo corso*, I.4; Prefect of the Papal Household,

the group in a personal and somewhat lengthy way at the general audience on December 4, 1974.[36] He also acknowledged and addressed them in a general audience on December 7, 1977, "among other beautiful details," comments Father Gordon, "honor[ing] the Gregorian University with the description 'our'" (*Nostra Universitas Gregoriana*)—a detail that deeply moved him.[37] In 1979, it seemed not to be possible to hold an audience for the *Cursus*, since the pope was scheduled to visit and give a speech at the Gregorian University the day after the conclusion of the *Cursus*. However, after Father Gordon implored the Prefecture of the Papal Household, the group was granted a special audience on December 13, 1979—the day before the end of the *Cursus*.[38]

9. – Father Gordon was not only the principal organizer of the event but also, naturally, one of the instructors. The first year, 1971, he lectured on the influence of the American Procedural Norms upon promulgation of the motu proprio *Causas matrimoniales*, which introduced reforms of the marriage nullity process for the whole Latin Church.[39] He also treated the process for obtaining a dissolution of a non-consummated marriage and certain functions of the *Sectio prima* of the Apostolic Signatura in relation to matrimonial causes.[40]

During most of the *Cursus* (viz., those held 1972–1975, 1977, and 1979), he treated the forms of marriage nullity trials, their complete evolution (or *iter*), the non-consummation process and its instruction in particular, the Apostolic Signatura (in regard especially to regional tribunals), and the process used before the *Sectio altera* of the Signatura.[41] As his bibliography reveals, these themes were

---

December 12, 1971: in ibid., II.17: "Sua Santità riceverà in udienza i Docenti e i Partecipanti al Corso di Aggiornamento Canonico per Giudici, Avvocati e Addetti ai Tribunali Ecclesiastici nel giorno di domani, lunedì, alle ore 12, 15"; Jean Beyer, letter, November 14 or December 11, 1972: in *Archivio del secondo corso*, I.5 and II.17; Prefect of the Papal Household, December 12, 1972: in ibid., II.17. For the last special audience, see Prefect of the Papal Household, December 4, 1981: in *Archivio del nono corso*, II.15.

36. Cf. "Paulus PP. VI alloquitur," 6–9, nn. 2–3. There is even an audio cassette tape of the papal audience in *Archivio del quarto corso*.

37. "Septimus Cursus pro Iudicibus," 166–167. See Ignacio Gordon, letter to Cardinal Felici, December 11, 1977: in *Archivio del settimo corso*, II.15.

38. Cf. "Octavus Cursus pro Iudicibus," 736, no. 5.

39. Cf. *Adnotationes in m.p. "Causas matrimoniales,"* 247, no. 3.

40. "Cursus renovationis canonicae. Cursus pro Iudicibus et Tribunalium Administris," pamphlet, in *Archivio del primo corso*, I.3 at 2–3.

41. "Alter Cursus renovationis canonicae pro Iudicibus et Tribunalium Administris," pamphlet, in *Archivio del secondo corso*, I.3; "Tertius Cursus renovationis canonicae pro Iudicibus et Tribunalium Administris (4 nov. – 14 dec. 1973)," pamphlet, in *Archivio del terzo corso*, I.3; "Quartus Cursus renovationis canonicae pro Iudicibus et Tribunalium Administris (3 nov. – 14 dec. 1974),"

central to his research. In 1973, he also addressed certain procedural questions, such as whether the obligation of the defender of the bond to appeal a sentence declaring nullity of marriage should be suppressed.[42] In 1979, he also addressed Paul VI's reforms of the Roman Curia, especially as regards vigilance over the correct administration of justice, as well as the procedure for the removal of pastors.[43] And in 1981 he gave lectures on "the structure of the new book on processes,"[44] that is, what would be Book VII of the Code of Canon Law, which would enter into effect two years later.

10. – The *Cursus* was being enthusiastically received by those who attended it, as Father Gordon explained in his presentation about it on March 21, 1972 before the Italian regional tribunal of Abruzzo.[45] Participants were continuously reporting back to him various good fruits that their attendance at a *Cursus* had borne, including the issuance of more sentences, better instruction of non-consummation petitions, and the erection of new regional tribunals. And he attributed all such good fruits to the Lord God: "May God grant that these fruits mature for the good of the Church and be multiplied in time and abroad."[46]

C. The *Laurea in Iure Canonico cum specializatione in Iurisprudentia*

11. – An academic initiative that grew out of the *Cursus* was a new doctorate in canon law with a specialization in jurisprudence (*Doctoratus* or *Laurea in Iure Canonico cum specializatione in Iurisprudentia*), whose first class matriculated in

---

pamphlet, in *Archivio del quarto corso*, I.3; "Quintus Cursus renovationis canonicae pro Iudicibus et Tribunalium Administris (3 nov. – 12 dec. 1975)," pamphlet, in *Archivio del quinto corso*, I.3; "Septimus Cursus renovationis canonicae pro Iudicibus et Tribunalium Administris (3 nov. – 14 dec. 1977)," pamphlet, in *Archivio del settimo corso*, I.3 at II; "Octavus Cursus renovationis canonicae pro Iudicibus et Tribunalium Administris (2 nov. – 15 dec. 1979)," pamphlet, in *Archivio dell'ottavo corso*, I.3 at II.

42. "Notificatio III, 4a," in *Archivio del terzo corso*, I.11.

43. Cf. *Adnotationes in m.p. "Causas matrimoniales*," 242–243, no. 1c; "Octavus Cursus renovationis canonicae pro Iudicibus et Tribunalium Administris (2 nov. – 15 dec. 1979)," pamphlet, in *Archivio dell'ottavo corso*, I.3 at II.F.

44. "Nonus Cursus renovationis canonicae pro Iudicibus et Tribunalium Administris, sub luce Schematum novi Codicis I. C. (3 nov. – 12 dec. 1981)," pamphlet, in *Archivio del nono corso*, I.3 at II.D.10. The relative *dispensa* no doubt would have been *Processus nullitatis matrimonii*.

45. "Cursus Renovationis Canonicae pro Iudicibus et Tribunalis Administris, Notificatio 10a," May 8, 1972: in *Archivio del primo corso*, I.11, no. 2.

46. See "Paulus PP. VI alloquitur," 6, no. 1.

the 1978–1979 academic year.[47] It was described in an inaugural lecture (of the rector of the university, it seems) as "a fruit of the seven Renewal Courses which were held in the preceding years in the Faculty."[48] At the same time, its beginning seemed to constitute a kind of eclipsing of the *Cursus*.[49]

As was noted above, as early as the fifth *Cursus*, the faculty was beginning to reform its approach with the goal of imparting knowledge of the matrimonial jurisprudence of the Roman Rota. This had an immediate impact on the "curriculum" within the *Cursus*, but it would also evolve into the creation of this new initiative, which would demand so much effort that the faculty would eventually discontinue the annual *Cursus*. It seems safe to conclude that the inspiration and promotion of this specialization in jurisprudence likewise came from Father Gordon himself. Indeed, at the top of one unattributed and undated Italian account of the specialization's inception, there is a handwritten note by Father Navarrete: "Fr. Gordon's project" ("*Progetto del P. Gordon*").[50]

12. – That being said, its creation was highly collaborative in nature. Documents from planning meetings of the program's future professors testify to this.[51] Father Gordon had a great vision of an academic initiative that would protect marriage, the family founded on marriage, and the correct administration of justice. Being a proceduralist, his academic contribution principally concerned the process itself. Originally, he taught classes on lower-level tribunals and the matrimonial and contentious-administrative processes.[52] And for some years, with collaborators, he taught a course entitled *De Trib. inferioribus et processibus* (lower-

---

47. "Septimus Cursus pro Iudicibus," 162, no. 2.

48. See lecture [*incipit: Anno academico 1977–1978 ad finem vergente*], in *Archivio dell'ottavo corso*, II.12. No author is named, but such lectures were given, it seems, by the rector of the university or sometimes the Dean of the faculty.

49. In the customary letter of the Dean promoting the eighth *Cursus*, the most prominent paragraph describes and promotes the doctorate with specialization. Cf. Urbano Navarrete, letter, June 5 (Latin, Spanish, Portuguese and English), June 12 (French), June 15 (German), 1979: in *Archivio dell'ottavo corso*, I.1.

50. "Progetto di Dottorato in Diritto Canonico specializzato in giurisprudenza," in FICPUG Archives. Another document of the same kind has this notation with Fr. Navarrete's signature: "*Primo progetto del P. Gordon*" ("Laurea. Per una Laurea specializzata in Giurisprudenza Canonica," in ibid.).

51. "De Doctoratu in Iure Canonico cum specializatione in Iurisprudentia. Sessio Professorum Iurisprudentiae, Brescia 8 VI 1978," [Romae] August 1, 1978: in FICPUG Archives. Other such sessions were held on June 4, 1981 and February 1, 1983 (see "Professorum Adunationes," in ibid.).

52. See *De Doctoratu in Iure Canonico cum specializatione in Iurisprudentia (Roma 1978–1979)*, pamphlet: in FICPUG Archives, on back cover.

level tribunals and processes).[53] He drew upon the expertise of others to impart knowledge in substantive law, especially each *caput nullitatis*, and the defects of consent in particular.

13. – Its faculty was to be composed both of Gregorian University professors and of Rotal auditors and canonists from other nations. It was to have no more than ten or fifteen students, so that there could be a more effective common study of jurisprudence. Regarding this principal aim of imparting matrimonial jurisprudence, we read: "*The goal* of this new academic degree would be to encourage the study of jurisprudence in Rome, with the twofold purpose of contributing to the formation of judges for various nations and to the unity of jurisprudence in the Church."[54] Additionally, it instructed students about the apostolic tribunals, the judicial process related to diverse kinds of causes, the deontology of the judge, and the dialogue brought about by judicial instruction.[55] Courses in these subjects were given during the first year, and a doctoral dissertation was to be written within the next year. Matriculating students had to hold at least a licentiate of canon law; if they had already earned a doctorate, they were not expected to write another doctoral dissertation.[56]

---

53. See, e.g., *Cursus ad Doctoratum in Iure Canonico cum specializatione in Iurisprudentia obtinendum (Roma 1979–1980)*, pamphlet: in *Archivio dell'ottavo corso*, I.3, on back cover; *Liber annualis, Roma 1980 Univ. 427º*, 112, at J29; Pontificia Universitas Gregoriana, *Liber annualis, Roma 1990 Univ. 437º* (Rome: Universitas Gregoriana, 1990) 133.

54. "Laurea. Per una Laurea specializzata in Giurisprudenza Canonica," in FICPUG Archives.

55. A volume collecting documents of procedural law was published expressly with students of this doctorate in mind (cf. *DR* 2:5–6).

56. Cf. "Septimus Cursus pro Iudicibus," 163, no. 2a-c; *Cursus ad Doctoratum in Iure Canonico cum specializatione in Iurisprudentia obtinendum (Roma 1979–1980)*, pamphlet: in *Archivio dell'ottavo corso*, I.3.

CHAPTER III

Procedural Law in the Context of the Life of the Church

SUMMARY — Introductory remark (no. 1). ▪ A. The
Ministry of Justice as Ecclesial Service (nn. 2–6). ▪ B. Procedural
Law and the Good of Souls (nn. 7–8). ▪ C. The Judicial Protection
of Marriage (nn. 9–18). ▪ D. Conclusion (no. 19).

1. – The branch of canonical science called procedural law is one of particular technicality and complexity. For this reason, it might seem somewhat foreign to the life of the Church, which is both a visible society of believers living in space and time and a spiritual community mystically wedded to Christ and animated with the Holy Spirit. The ecclesial character of procedural law thus demands specific reflection and emphasis in order to understand its place in the order of salvation within the New Covenant.

A. The Ministry of Justice as Ecclesial Service

2. – Father Gordon was such a man of the Church and so dedicated a priest[1] that he "wanted with all his strength to contribute, with his work, to the qualitative increase of the life of the Mystical Body of Christ."[2] The ecclesial dimension of procedural law was something he underscored frequently. He intuitively framed his treatment of procedural questions within the broader ecclesial context. He believed that the study and implementation of procedural law indeed was advantageous "pro bono Ecclesiae."[3] This was founded on a deep respect for the pastors of the Church, which was expressed, for example, in how he was moved by the presence of two diocesan bishops at the *Cursus* of 1974. He remarked: "The assiduous engagement in the work by both of them, their vigilant attention

---

1. *Vide supra* Chapter I, nn. 13–20.
2. See Grocholewski, 362, no. 4. To illustrate, the author relates how Fr. Gordon recommended him for service in the Apostolic Signatura, but he turned the invitation down for his own reasons. At this, Fr. Gordon rebuked him, saying, "In doing this you think only of yourself and not the good of the Church."
3. *Pars statica*, 23, no. 28.

to juridico-pastoral problems, and their relaxed manner of conversing with the other participants was not only edifying for everyone but also an eloquent testimony to the importance that local Churches rightly attribute to the ministry of the administration of justice."[4]

3. – Also, he reflected on the role and importance of the ministry of justice within the social life of the Church. He held that solutions to any difficulties in providing suitable ministers of justice are to be found "after taking into account the diminishment of priestly vocations and the multiplication of pastoral responsibilities."[5] Thus, the collaboration of lay people is rightly sought out as a suitable remedy, albeit within certain parameters.

From the perspective of the faithful at large, those who benefit from the ministry of justice in the Church are ordinarily the lay faithful whose marriages have suffered a rupture. And so, it is necessary that the faithful be given reason to trust the tribunals of the Church. "For if the people are mistrusting, they will not request the ministry of judges, and therefore the administration of justice, at least in contentious matters, will be practically inactive." Such trust is cultivated by "the correct and swift administration of justice."[6] This trust is weakened by, among other things, the abuses of advocates seeking immodest financial gain in illegitimate ways. That is something to be rooted out "so that the Church may appear before the people of God to be a lover of the poor and of poverty."[7]

4. – The ministry of justice, or the authoritative resolution of controversies by the judiciary, is ever to be in harmony with the doctrine of the Catholic faith. When trying to find solutions to problems among the people of God, it is best "to attend to the Magisterium of the Church so as to avoid grave errors." Canonists in particular should "go along a strictly scientific path and not give in to sensationalism."[8] Reforms of law, for example, are to be in continuity with canonical tradition and norms of justice, and never based on merely contemporary movements in social life. Likewise, individual judges faced with complex jurisprudential problems are ever to bind themselves to fidelity to the Church's consistent teaching.

---

4. See "Paulus PP. VI alloquitur," 5, no. 1.
5. See "De Tribunalibus Regionalibus," 580.
6. See "De nimia processuum matrimonialium duratione," 506, no. 24.
7. See ibid., 551, no. 92.
8. See ibid., 660, note 1.

5. – Father Gordon took to heart the direction of Pope St. John Paul II in art. 75 of the apostolic constitution *Sapientia christiana*, according to which faculties of canon law were instructed to study canonical institutions "in light of the law of the Gospel" (*in lumine legis evangelicae*).[9] With regard to the administration of justice, Father Gordon therefore recalled "those words and illustrations with which the Lord demands, on the one hand, the reconciliation with a brother who may have been offended before bringing a gift to the altar" and "on the other, permits one who has been unjustly offended to try to obtain due reparation, even through the involvement of the competent authority."[10] The service of justice is done in the Lord and indeed finds confirmation in his own teaching.

This evangelical light shines forth more clearly when the ministry of justice is treated as something sacred. The use of the oath during the judicial instruction, for example, is of great importance "so that the parties (and in turn the witnesses, experts…) may perceive the *sacredness* both of the administration of justice and of the duty that they have to collaborate in the discovery of the truth."[11]

6. – Because of the "ecclesiality" and sacredness of the administration of ecclesiastical justice, ministers of justice should apply themselves to it as a service for the good of the whole Church. Because of this conviction, it is not surprising that Father Gordon derived much inspiration from the example of the eighteenth century referendaries of the Signatura of Justice. For their "labor was made more beautiful and still more evangelical thanks to the splendor of its gratuitousness. For it was proper to the referendaries that, accepting no stipend, they accepted whatever labors in proposing, examining, and supporting commissions [i.e., requests for judicial favors] solely out of devotion for the Apostolic See."[12]

B. Procedural Law and the Good of Souls

7. – One natural consequence of the ecclesial dimension of procedural law is its correspondence with the Church's end: the salvation of souls. Father Gordon saw the deep study of procedural law to be "a true service to the Church"[13] because

---

9. John Paul II, apostolic constitution *Sapientia christiana*, April 15, 1979: *AAS* 71 (1979) 494, art. 75.

10. See "Origine e sviluppo," 5–6; "De obiecto primario competentiae," 509.

11. See *Pars dynamica*, 32, no. 136.

12. See "De referendariorum ac votantium dignitate," 202, no. 2.

13. Cf. Ignacio Gordon, "Presentación" [October 15, 1970], in Rafael Figueroa Campos, *La "persona standi in iudicio" en la legislación eclesiástica*, Analecta Gregoriana 179 (Rome: Università Gregoriana Editrice, 1971) vi.

of its role in contributing to the good of souls. He believed that the effective implementation of procedural law in tribunals contributes especially to the good of the souls of the parties involved in a trial. "The faithful, timely, and effective administration of justice greatly contributes to the peace of the faithful, for 'the work of justice is peace!'"[14]

The grave work of issuing suitable procedural legislation is obviously a prerequisite in pursuing this goal of the ministry of justice. The legislator therefore has to design the procedural norm so that it gives due order to the judicial process and is in harmony with the real human conditions of those who approach the Church's judiciary. For example, weighing the importance of the collegial character of the office of judge, he could see that an absolute insistence upon it would negatively impact the availability of tribunals to the faithful and the timely administration of justice in causes touching upon matters of conscience. Thus, Father Gordon described the concession of no. V §2 of *CM*, allowing conferences of bishops to permit a single clerical judge, in these terms: "The legislator is constrained to establish this norm on account of the good of souls and the anguish of persons."[15]

8. – Because so many causes pertain to fractured matrimonial relationships, the souls of the spouses are to be given particular care by ministers of justice. The latter are always to "have compassion on marital tragedies with human sensibility and Christian charity."[16] The cases of marriage examined by a tribunal "are not simply a problem of canon law but above all a sorrowful human drama."[17] Marriage nullity trials in particular "so profoundly affect a person's human and supernatural life." Conversely, certain "evils frequently follow" from defects in judicial praxis, especially those that cause undue delays in the progression of trials, that "certainly do not derive from the slow development of civil processes."[18]

Undue delays occur "not without the grave harm of souls," since, in matrimonial trials, "it is not uncommon that a cause of nullity supposes two or even four persons, who are not living according to conscience."[19] This can be understood in different ways. The petitioner and the respondent, who may be essentially bound to one another, may have wrongly abandoned their marriage, if it is valid. If it is invalid or even if it is valid but not established as such in the external

---

14. See *Pars statica*, 23, no. 27.
15. See *Adnotationes in m.p. "Causas matrimoniales,"* 277, at 2.1a.
16. See "De nimia processuum matrimonialium duratione," 662, no. 150.
17. See "Dichiarazione di nullità," 150.
18. See "De nimia processuum matrimonialium duratione," 500, no. 14.
19. See "De Tribunalibus Regionalibus," 592, including note 44.

forum, the petitioner and his partner living in an irregular union are living contrary to the sixth commandment of the Decalogue. And this is multiplied if both the petitioner and the respondent are living in irregular unions. In any case, it is usually a matter of persons who are trying, to some degree, "to order [their lives] according to the precepts of the Lord" and arrive "at peace with God." Undue delays create an occasion "to lead them into despair and make recourse to entering a civil marriage or simple concubinage."[20]

C. The Judicial Protection of Marriage

9. – The faithful, incorporated into the Church by baptism, all find their origin in the sacred covenant of marriage (at least in some way) and belong to a human family. The Church's stable life among men thus depends upon the existence and health of marriage and the family. As a result, her sacred discipline eloquently provides for the protection of marriage, including its judicial protection. This goal of matrimonial procedural law thus contributes to the service of the Church and of souls by promoting its stability and the discipline that is a consequence of the truth of its indissolubility.

The judicial protection of marriage is founded on the juridical presumption of the validity of each marriage: "'Marriage enjoys the favor of the law.'[21] However, this favor is not some generic principle, whose application is left to the free inspiration of judges or administrators. On the contrary, the legislator himself takes care to determine in the law itself concrete ways in which this favor is to be understood, both in substantive law and in procedural law."[22]

Some may challenge this based on a certain relativism. Nevertheless, "the argument based on the diverse culture and morals of certain peoples does not hold" the Church to weaken her judicial protections of marriage. "For otherwise, many demands of the Christian life should be set aside since they may be contrary to the mentality of 'this age.' But the Church cannot neglect all of those things that contribute to a greater extent to the indissolubility of the matrimonial bond."[23]

---

20. See "De nimia processuum matrimonialium duratione," 504, no. 20. On this doctrine, see Giuseppe di Mattia, "Collegio giudicante e decreto di rinvio a procedimento ordinario nel motu proprio 'Causas matrimoniales,'" in *Studi di diritto canonico in onore di Marcello Magliocchetti* (Rome: Catholic Book Agency, 1975) 2:473.

21. See 1917 *CIC* c. 1014; 1983 *CIC* c. 1060.

22. See Ignacio Gordon, *votum* ("De recursu contra Congressus decisionem latam in quaestione de iure appellandi"), prot. n. 2120/71 CG, April 3, 1973: in SSAT Archives, 17–18, no. 73.

23. See PCCICR Archives, *vol. 181. XI. De processibus. Sessio VI⁺ Series II 'diebus 26–31 martii 1979 habita. Relatio,* 190; *Communicationes* 11 (1979) 266.

10. – A series of proposals that occupied considerable attention from Father Gordon were those made by Monsignor Stephen J. Kelleher[24]—onetime minister of justice (1943–1960) and later *officialis* (1962–1968) of the Archdiocese of New York, as well as a consultor in the Pontifical Commission for the Revision of the Code of Canon Law.[25] It would seem to have been Kelleher's developed and radical proposals as well as his potential for influence that motivated Father Gordon to address them. For he proposed that matrimonial tribunals be eliminated, that the decision about the nullity of marriage be left to the personal decision of either or both spouses, and that some commission be established in each diocese before which the spouses would appear to state their reasons for declaring their marriage null and receive the commission's recommendation. Canonical doctrine widely recognizes Father Gordon's confrontation of Kelleher's proposals.[26]

---

24. Cf. Stephen J. Kelleher, "The Dignity of Persons in a Marriage and the Dignity of Their Marriage," *The Jurist* 26 (1966) 243–245; idem, "The Problem of the Intolerable Marriage," *America* 119/7 (September 14, 1968) 178–182; idem, "Canon 1014 and American Culture," *The Jurist* 28 (1968) 1–12; idem, "A Suggested Method of Procedure in the *Recognitio* of the Fourth Book of the Code," *The Jurist* 29 (1969) 78–84; idem, "Dignitas personae et dignitas communitatis," in *Acta conventus internationalis canonistarum, Romae diebus 20–25 maii 1968 celebrati*, ed. Pontificia Commissio Codici iuris canonici recognoscendo (Vatican City: Typis Polyglottis Vaticanis, 1970) 307–310.

Fr. Gordon's examination of Msgr. Kelleher's proposals is also published in an abbreviated form in Italian. See "La soppressione dei tribunali ecclesiastici." He treats it in summary form, too, in *Adnotationes in m.p. "Causas matrimoniales,"* 242, no. 1b.

25. See *Communicationes* 1 (1969) 21.

26. Carlo Gullo, "Celerità e gratuità dei processi matrimoniali canonici," in *La giustizia nella Chiesa: fondamento divino e cultura processualistica moderna*, Studi Giuridici 45 (Vatican City: Libreria Editrice Vaticana, 1997) 239: "Il matrimonio è un atto sociale; non è quindi pensabile che si possa risolvere il problema della validità o meno dei matrimoni, rimettendolo al responsabile giudizio delle parti e, dunque, in definitiva, trasformandolo in un mero problema di coscienza. [*Footnote:*] Espone il punto con molta chiarezza e risponde adeguatamente a certe proposte provenienti sopratutto dagli USA, GORDON (["De nimia processuum matrimonialium duratione,"] 648–668). On Fr. Gordon's engagement with the problem, see also, e.g., Francesco D'Ostilio, "La durata media delle cause matrimoniali," *Monitor Ecclesiasticus* 114 (1989) 219, note 222; Gianpaolo Montini, "Dall'istruzione *Provida Mater* all'istruzione *Dignitas connubii*," in *Il giudizio di nullità matrimoniale dopo l'Istruzione "Dignitas connubii." Parte Prima: I principi*, Studi Giuridici 75, ed. Piero Antonio Bonnet and Carlo Gullo (Vatican City: Libreria Editrice Vaticana, 2007) 28–32; Piero Antonio Bonnet, "Le prove (artt. 155–216)," in *Il giudizio di nullità matrimoniale dopo l'Istruzione "Dignitas connubii." Parte Terza: La parte dinamica del processo*, Studi Giuridici 77, ed. Piero Antonio Bonnet and Carlo Gullo (Vatican City: Libreria Editrice Vaticana, 2008) 245–246, notes 358–359; idem, *Il giudizio di nullità matrimoniale nei casi speciali*, Studia et documenta iuris canonici IX (Rome: Catholic Book Agency, 1979) 31, note 76; Carlos M. Morán Bustos, "El proceso canónico de nulidad matrimonial: *ratio* y valoración a los 30 años de su entrada en vigor," in *El Código de derecho canónico de 1983: balance y perspectivas a los 30 años de su promulgación*, ed. José Luis Sánchez-Girón and Carmen Peña García (Madrid: Universidad Pontificia Comillas, 2014) 331–332.

11. – Father Gordon wisely perceived that Monsignor Kelleher's proposals were so serious because they pertained "not only to procedure."[27] More than some minor point of procedural law was at stake in such proposals. For they were motivated by certain notions sustained by Kelleher that are a matter of substantive law. In particular, Kelleher saw the marriage nullity trial as depending upon (for him) regrettable notions or emphases in the Church's teaching and discipline on marriage—namely, the contractual nature of marriage (i.e., the efficacy of consent between the baptized), the physical concept of (non-)consummation (as distinct from consummation coming about through the achievement of "a substantial, full personal relationship"), and the indissolubility of a marriage that is *ratum et consummatum*.[28] For him, the sole reason for declaring a marriage null is the so-called incapacity of the spouses to live as husband and wife, "in which the whole theory of Kelleher concerning the incapacity to consummate marriage psychologically seems to be hidden."[29] Accordingly, the abolition of the marriage nullity process is really tantamount to, or based upon, a rejection of the correct doctrine on holy matrimony. It also seems to bring about "the gravest evil of restoring *clandestine marriages* in the Church."[30] The integrity of the Church's teaching about marriage necessitates its judicial protection, lest it be consigned to the private arena where it is vulnerable to the caprice of individuals.

12. – Father Gordon identified and responded to certain premises underlying Monsignor Kelleher's proposals, since they seemed to lack foundation and stand contrary to sacred tradition and the consistent discipline of the Church.[31] One premise concerns the legitimacy of the concept of the so-called "intolerable marriage"—that is, one deemed by either or both spouses to be so "unhappy" that one could not be expected to remain in or resume it. Father Gordon challenges the very legitimacy and usefulness of this concept of the intolerable marriage: "Since it includes also unhappy marriage for merely psychological reasons, it is equivocal from a juridical perspective." For, according to an American canonist who also served in the New York Tribunal, the concept does not distinguish whether a marriage is valid, doubtfully valid, or invalid. "It therefore includes all of them, provided that it concerns an unhappy marriage."

---

27. See "De nimia processuum matrimonialium duratione," 646, no. 121.

28. Cf. ibid., 653–654, no. 133.

29. See ibid., 666, note 17, *sub* B).

30. See ibid., 666, no. 158. On the new clandestine marriage, *vide infra* no. 16.

31. For the teaching in this no. 12, see "De nimia processuum matrimonialium duratione," 647–648, 660–661 at nn. 124–125, 145–147.

Another premise of Kelleher was that there must be some solution in the Church for such a marital situation. Father Gordon, however, affirmed "that a remedy cannot be offered by means of a new marriage for all intolerable marriages, if in fact such a remedy would sometimes involve a new concept of consummation contrary to the consistent teaching of the Church. Or rather, it would be contrary to the divine law prohibiting the dissolution of a ratified and consummated marriage."

Yet another premise underlying Kelleher's proposals is that the Church's procedural law is meant to address the problem of such a marital situation. Father Gordon declares "that intolerable marriages are not the object of an ecclesiastical trial." The object of the marriage nullity trial is to examine whether the alleged nullity of marriage is proven; it is "not for deciding which marriages are intolerable." "Much less is the tribunal a 'hospital' or a 'clinic' for healing unhappy marriages."

13. – More broadly, Father Gordon denied that "*all* those problems [of intolerable marriages should] be resolvable before God and the Church."[32] By including "before God" in this brief statement, he seems to imply the whole teaching of Christ about his disciple's call to take up the cross and follow him. God alone is sufficient, and he is omnipotent. At the same time, the example of the martyrs and of the very crucifixion of his beloved Son reveal that it is not his will to deliver his children from all suffering on earth. On the contrary, he permits our suffering and promises to remain ever close to us. The person who is in a marriage that he cannot easily tolerate ought in the first place to depend upon God. How much more is this true when it is a question of a sacramental marriage, when all that the spouses do, especially all that they suffer, contributes to their sanctification and that of their children and of the whole family. The Church supports those who suffer in different ways, but this support does not primarily entail or even necessarily include removal of the cause of suffering. The marriage nullity process offers a reminder of these difficulties related to the mystery of suffering and thus protects the true image of marriage in its whole earthly reality.

14. – Father Gordon writes in one place: "In the face of the drama of an unhappy marriage, the Church, Bishops, and judges are to diligently examine all the circumstances that might have made it null; but if this examination does not demonstrate nullity, the Church respects the uncontested validity of this unhappy

---

32. See ibid., 662, no. 149.

marriage as parents respect that breath of life that their deformed newborn has."[33] The Church is not necessarily equipped to repair what is broken but offers the greatest support and aid to those who suffer from their own sins or illness and the sins or illnesses of others: "Nor must it be forgotten that the spouses of a valid but unhappy marriage can find a most efficacious aid and comfort for a sorrowful situation in prayer, in the frequent reception of the sacraments, and in carrying out works of charity for others who are suffering."[34] The wholesale persuading of those in broken marriages to introduce causes of nullity of marriage without regard for the facts of the particular marriage "is gravely abusive and indirectly fosters divorce."[35] Thus there is wisdom in the pre-judicial investigation described in the 2015 motu proprio *Mitis Iudex*, insofar as it both helps prepare parties for intelligent and effective engagement in the trial while also helping them see whether it is even opportune to introduce a cause.[36]

15. – Contrary to Monsignor Kelleher's ideas, the protection of marriage in the Church demands, among other things, the existence of the marriage nullity process and the exclusive competence of the judicial authority of the Church. If the process sometimes constitutes an unfortunate occasion for spouses to experience injustices (such as by delays, silence, or cold treatment), the solution is not "that tribunals be abolished but only that they be reformed." Spouses are by no means qualified to judge the possible nullity of their own marriage: "no one is a good judge in his own cause," and "parties do not for the most part have the preparation needed for making a prudent judgment about the validity of their own marriage." By giving spouses this authority in the Church because many are already making an autonomous decision to divorce and enter illegitimate unions, "the way would be opened for canonizing any evil whatsoever." And the composition and manner of deciding and proceeding on the part of some diocesan commission is "totally arbitrary." Moreover, it would happen that "in cases—probably very infrequent ones—in which the commission would decide in the negative, it can be presumed that a spouse or the spouses, who requested the judgment of the commission, would still use their proper and supreme decision in favor of liberty."[37] The whole proposal, therefore, undermines the due protection of marriage in the Church.

---

33. See "Dichiarazione di nullità," 145, §4,3.
34. See ibid., 146.
35. See *Pars dynamica*, 4, no. 6.
36. *MI, Ratio procedendi*, artt. 2, 4–5.
37. See "De nimia processuum matrimonialium duratione," 662, 664, 665, at nn. 148, 152, 155, 157.

16. – Obviously disturbing to Father Gordon was the practice, testified to by Monsignor Kelleher himself, of subsequent unions being entered by spouses bound in a prior marriage with the informal approval of some priest. He analyzes this grave violation of marriage in these juridical terms:

> Now, new unions made by these Catholics, after making a private decision about the nullity of the prior marriage, even if . . . they are not to be called *subjectively* concubinary (since they are entered at the suggestion and perhaps with the presence of a priest and therefore, it can be presumed, in good faith), they are certainly *objectively "clandestine."* It is also true that all of this is done without the knowledge—at least by law—of the bishop or the pastor or his delegate, and so just as the diocesan and parochial registers never make reference to the *nullity* of a prior marriage, so they do not mention the *celebration* of the subsequent one. Now, anyone can see how many evils follow from these unions both for children and for the faithful and therefore for the Church.[38]

17. – Another proposal of Monsignor Kelleher's that Father Gordon confronted was that according to which the standard for examining whether nullity of a marriage is established be change from moral certitude to "a preponderance of evidence."[39] This would practically replace the canonical system's *favor matrimonii* with a *favor libertatis* within the judicial process itself. As Father Gordon reports, this was motivated by "the greater ease that"—in the judgment of Kelleher—"must be granted so that unhappy marriages may have a remedy, especially taking into account the dignity and rights of persons." Father Gordon could appreciate these latter goals, while also insisting that they be placed in a proper context: "The dignity and rights of the human person, as well as the proposal of making their protection easier before tribunals, are undoubtedly highly Christian and positive values. Nevertheless, they are not *absolute* but only relative, and so they must be coordinated with the common good to which pertains the protection of the stability of marriage." In fact, the proposed replacement of the standard of moral certitude, together with the elimination of other procedural protections to marriage (e.g., reservation to a college of judges, the obligation of the defender of the bond to appeal a decision *pro nullitate*), do not protect the stability of marriage. "For the whole dynamic of Kelleher's system related to canon 1014 consists

---

38. See ibid., 667–668, no. 158.

39. This was promoted in general ways, but Kelleher's own articulation and promotion of it seems to have been consistent and clear, as is documented in ibid., 702, note 1.

in systematically eliminating all procedural protections of the presumption in favor of marriage. However, it does not aim at any coordination between the rights of spouses and the stability of marriage but, on the contrary, sacrifices this stability for them."[40] And even though the eventually approved text of Norm 21 of the APN employs the term "moral certitude," he maintained with others that it was used improperly since its real meaning was equivalent to "a greater probability."[41]

18. – The judicial standard of moral certitude in matrimonial trials is the theoretical safeguard of the *favor matrimonii* particularly in relation to the presumption of validity of each marriage. For, when a doubt abides about the alleged nullity of a marriage, moral certitude is not attained and the judge yields to what is favored by law.[42] Thus, the presumption of validity of every marriage in fact exists "in order to protect marriage."[43]

This presumption flows from common sense, "since, when people do something, they make sure to do it validly." It also flows from the good that is marriage, since it fosters the Church's "protection of children and continence as well as the stability of the institution of marriage."[44] The legislator therefore demands that these goods may only be legitimately compromised when they lack foundation in a valid marriage. In other words, it is the truth about the marriage that determines whether such a foundation exists. Such certitude is explicitly required in the context of procedural law in order for the judge to declare a marriage null, and it is implicit in the positive formulation of the presumption of law: "The genuine meaning of the third assertion of canon 1014 [of the 1917 *CIC*] ('Until the contrary is proven') is . . . 'until the contrary is *certainly* proven.'"[45] Liberation from marriage when there is merely a greater probability of its nullity but no certitude "would be contrary . . . to the judicial protection which is generally due to matrimonial causes on account of their gravity."[46]

---

40. See ibid., 709–710, no. 256.

41. Cf. *Adnotationes in m.p. "Causas matrimoniales,"* 252–253, I,2).

42. 1917 *CIC* c. 1869 §4; 1983 *CIC* c. 1608 §4.

43. See "De nimia processuum matrimonialium duratione," 694, no. 223, 2). The historical origin of several elements of the marriage nullity process clearly reveals the goal of protecting marriage (cf. ibid., 709, no. 254).

44. See ibid., 721, nn. 278–279.

45. See ibid., 717, no. 271.

46. See ibid., 724, no. 286.

D. Conclusion

19. – In the pages that follow (and precede) this one, the ecclesial character of Father Gordon's reflections on procedural law are to be kept ever in mind. For they seem to have continually motivated his labors for the Church, for the university, and for his students. His concentration on particular themes—especially the ongoing formation of canonists, the effective celerity and collegiality of judicial activity, the requirement of the double conformity of sentences, and the dignity of contentious-administrative jurisdiction—express his solicitude for the good of the Church and of souls and the protection of marriage.

CHAPTER IV

His Scientific Method

SUMMARY — Introductory Remark (no. 1). ▪ A. Objective
Analysis (nn. 2–6). ▪ B. Theoretical Foundations (no. 7). ▪ C.
Juridical Realism (nn. 8–11). ▪ D. Scholarly Apparatus (nn. 12–
13). ▪ E. Scientific Deontology: Humility and Service (nn. 14–15).
▪ F. A *Vademecum* for Causes of Nullity of Marriage (nn. 16–17). ▪
G. Teaching Procedural Law (nn. 18–22). ▪ H. The Distinction
between the *Pars statica* and the *Pars dynamica* (nn. 23–27). ▪
I. The Reform of Procedural Law (nn. 28–34).

1. – The ensemble of Father Gordon's scholarly writings in the area of procedural law reveal several consistent aspects of his scientific method—that is, the
manner of arriving at principles and conclusions and the forms of examination
and reasoning used in his technical work. These will be illustrated throughout
the chapters that follow, but some firm and clearly deliberate elements of his
method merit their own attention.

A. Objective Analysis

2. – There is a common, though not necessarily unique, element of Father
Gordon's method that stands out and displays a sense of objectivity, humility,
and balance. And this is his practice of explaining, with citations and quotations,
the diverse opinions sustained by authors on a particular question prior to proposing his own analysis and argument. He in fact was quite deliberate in supporting his account of other authors' views by "giv[ing] in a note, in their original
language and with precise references to the sources, lengthy passages" from
authors, especially those he was disputing.[1]

For example, he first cites authors who lay blame for the excessive length of
matrimonial trials on the ineffectiveness of individuals and then those who attrib-

---

1. Cf. "La soppressione dei tribunali ecclesiastici," 751. One author refers to Fr. Gordon as
offering in one case "the best synthesis of the different opinions" (see Bassiano Uggé, *La fase preliminare/abbreviata del processo di nullità del matrimonio in secondo grado di giudizio a norma del can.
1682 §2*, Tesi Gregoriana – Serie Diritto Canonico 60 (Rome: Editrice Pontificia Università Gregoriana, 2003) 120, note 82).

ute the problem to the alleged inadequacy of the law itself. He then explains his conviction that both explanations have a certain legitimacy—that a complex of practical, human factors are the primary reason for the problem and that the law itself, too, needed some reform.[2]

3. – His confrontation of Monsignor Stephen J. Kelleher's proposals is highly exemplary in this regard.[3] For—to cite one example—in twelve and a half pages, he patiently exhibits the premises to and the content of the radical proposals of that canonist (the three *theses Kelleherianae*). He then refutes the premises and proposals, one after the other, in about nine pages.[4]

4. – He takes various approaches in presenting diverse doctrinal positions. Sometimes he presents the common doctrine on a particular question, which may correspond with his own position; then he carefully explains a minority view and offers several responses to it.[5] Other times, he does the opposite.[6] In one case, in which there were significant differences among authors, he presents the opposing arguments first, even though those arguments' adherents "have neglected to demonstrate [them] positively." He then presents the counterarguments, with which he was sympathetic.[7]

Even when he was firmly convinced, he was often deferential to those having the opposing view. For example, after stating a strong argument for why the judicial instance (*instantia*) begins once the citation has been completed, he proceeds to identify a strong argument "in consideration for the contrary opinion."[8]

5. – His presentation and objective analysis of diverse doctrinal opinions was imparted to his students as well. He modeled it for them in his own *dispense* and even explained his motivation for it: "We have not omitted to cite abundantly the authors

----

2. Cf. "De nimia processuum matrimonialium duratione," esp. 507–508, nn. 26–27; 641–642, no. 114. For other illustrations of this approach, see "De iustitia administrativa ecclesiastica," 290–295, 305–307; "De appellationibus," *passim*; *Pars statica*, *passim* (e.g., 69–76, nn. 105–114; 222–225, no. 340; 316–320, nn. 463–466); "De obiecto primario competentiae," 522–531.

3. *Vide supra* Chapter III, nn. 10–18.

4. Cf. "De nimia processuum matrimonialium duratione," 644–668, which include some introductory orientations.

5. Cf. "De appellationibus," 288–292. In this case, the question was quite settled and the minority opinion quite weak.

6. Cf. ibid., 293–299. In this case, the minority opinion was supported with stronger arguments and more prominent authors.

7. Cf. "De obiecto primario competentiae," 521–536.

8. See *Pars statica*, 64.

themselves and, in questions of greater importance, to offer a nearly panoramic view of the different opinions with their argumentation, adding also our own opinion." This he did "so that, recognizing the complexity of things, students may learn to refrain from lighter and ill-advised solutions and be able to develop their own opinions under the guidance of the excellent authors."[9] In turn, he would praise them for doing this themselves. For example, in his prefatory remarks to some dissertations that he directed, he underlines above all the ability of the students to present the diversity of doctrinal opinions and finally to declare and defend their own view. Though he praises their research of the sources, the medieval doctrine, other legal systems, and the records of legislative drafting, the presentation and critical evaluation of the current doctrine was what he found to be of most importance.[10]

6. – One can easily detect his influence in this regard on his students, who themselves could objectively articulate adverse arguments and then propose responses to each argument. Two examples are sufficient to illustrate this: one from a doctoral dissertation, another from a licentiate thesis.

In his doctoral dissertation, Father Michael R. Moodie, SJ presents three "reasons opposed to the establishment of interdiocesan administrative tribunals": "administrative tribunals would undermine the relationship between the bishop and the faithful," "administrative tribunals are an unnecessary assumption of a formalistic civil law structure," and "administrative tribunals would place undue material burdens upon the local churches." And subsequently he offers his own individual responses to each objection,[11] which are notable for their balance and objectivity.

In his licentiate paper (*tesina*), then-Father Raymond Leo Burke examines the double conformity of sentences in causes of nullity of marriage. After explaining its history and its regulation in the legislation at the time of writing, he addresses proposals for eliminating its requirement. First, he identifies the three

---

9. See ibid., 46, no. 75.

10. See, e.g., Ignazio Gordon, "Presentazione," in Emilio Ghidotti, *La nullità della sentenza giudiziale nel diritto canonico* (Milan: Giuffrè Editore, 1965) xi: "Il valore, intanto, dell'opera del dr. Ghidotti...sta...nell'aver compiuto un esame ampio e completo delle sentenze offerte dai canonisti nel dibattuto problema e averle criticate a fondo"; idem, "Presentación" [October 15, 1970], in Rafael Figueroa Campos, *La "persona standi in iudicio" en la legislación eclesiástica*, Analecta Gregoriana 179 (Rome: Università Gregoriana Editrice, 1971) v: "Sin embargo, el punto de más relieve científico—y a la par de mayor actualidad—es el capítulo que se ocupa de las distintas soluciones elaboradas por los Doctores para resolver el problema planteado por la respuesta de 1946."

11. See Michael R. Moodie, *The Constitution and Competence of Interdiocesan Administrative Tribunals according to the 1980 Schema of the Code of Canon Law*, A dissertation in partial fulfillment of the requirements of the degree Juris Canonici Doctor [unpublished] (Rome: Pontificia Universitas Gregoriana, Facultas Iuris Canonici, 1984) 337–345.

principal "arguments against retention of the requirement," namely, (1) that the requirement shows excessive favor to the public good against the private good and dignity of persons, (2) that it attributes greater value to caution than to the efficient handling of causes of nullity of marriage, and (3) that it is based on a dated social situation that no longer exists. In response, he argues quite in line with the thought of his master. (1) The dignity of persons is protected by respecting their ability to approach the tribunal and to receive a response in accord with the truth, to which they have a right. There really is no contradiction between the public and private good in this regard. The seriousness and subtlety of the object of such causes demand that they be examined by the superior tribunal. (2) The insistence on super-efficiency incorrectly presupposes that the tribunal exists so that those in broken marriages may receive a solution. A proper efficiency demands certain cautions so as to guarantee a just and true decision. A balance is achieved by retaining the requirement while allowing for a shorter appellate process. (3) The historical situation is different, but the protection of marriage is no less necessary. In fact, the prevalence and protection of divorce in secular law makes it all the more urgent for the truth and dignity of marriage to be protected before the Church's tribunals.[12]

B. Theoretical Foundations

7. – The scientific work of Father Gordon exemplifies the importance of theory and general principles when seeking solutions to practical problems or examining practical proposals. For example, prior to the promulgation of the 1983 code, authors and prelates of the Church were beginning to propose that non-clerics be eligible for appointment to the office of judge. Prescinding from his own convictions about this, he illustrates the importance of treating this question with a solid understanding of the true nature of ecclesiastical power.[13] Some likewise were suggesting the implementation of diverse forms of decentralization in the area of procedural law. His own treatment of this matter begins with clear reflections on the meaning of decentralization in general, in the Church, and in the area of the administration of justice in particular.[14]

---

12. Cf. Raymond Leo Burke, "*Duplex sententia conformis*: Still a Guarantee of Truth and Justice in Causes Regarding Nullity of Marriage?" (JCL Thesis, Pontifical Gregorian University, 1982) 40–60. It bears this inscription on the cover page: "Opus scriptum ad Licentiam praesentatum Rev. P. Ignacio GORDON, S.I. a studente Rev. D. Raymond Leo BURKE. Romae, die 22 Februarii 1982."
13. Cf. "De nimia processuum matrimonialium duratione," 514–518, nn. 38–41.
14. Cf. ibid., 671–672, nn. 165–169.

In his "De Tribunalibus Regionalibus," he takes as the impetus for his presentation an observation made in a broader ecclesial discussion—namely, a *votum* from the coordinating commission of the Second Vatican Ecumenical Council. That *votum* expressed aspirations for "a simplified procedure of matrimonial processes" and "precise rules for assuring the choice of competent judges." It is in this context that he places his subject matter: regional tribunals. After an introductory presentation on the institute of the regional tribunal, he offers an orderly series of replies to two questions: "Do Regional Tribunals contribute to the selection of judges?" and "Do Regional Tribunals contribution to the abbreviation of the process?" This method of posing questions bears the mark of objectivity and detachment and invites the reader or audience into a reflection, with him as guide. It also situates structural-juridical questions on the proper ecclesial foundations.

C. Juridical Realism

8. – Related to his method is the realism that marked his examination of various questions. He was thus readily able to distinguish that which is effective or useful in principle from that which sometimes really occurs in practice.

9. – For example, he applies the principle *ius sequitur vitam* in a sound and realistic way when he observes the need for a reduction in the duration of a trial proposed by the legislator. Over the ages, one observes such reductions in the great bodies of legislation: in Justinian's code, a civil trial was to be concluded in three years and a criminal trial in two years; in the Decretals of Gregory IX, the first instance of a trial was to be completed in three years, and second instance in one, unless necessary and clear reasons demanded up to two years; the Council of Trent stipulated two years for first instance and one for second instance. About two centuries after that Council, causes of nullity of marriage were necessarily lengthened by the requirement of a double conformity of sentences, always demanding at least one appellate process, and sometimes two.[15] Still, one might have expected in the next revision of procedural law a further reduction in the length of the instances, but the 1917 *CIC*, in canon 1620, in fact repeats the norm of the Council of Trent on the matter, while urging that causes be ended as quickly as possible without prejudice to justice ("quamprimum, salva iustitia").

---

15. Benedict XIV, constitution *Dei miseratione*, November 3, 1741: *Codicis iuris canonici fontes*, ed. Pietro Gasparri (Rome: Typis Polyglottis Vaticanis, 1926) 1:695–701, at §8.

Father Gordon's realism and attentiveness to the circumstances of life led him to see that such wide temporal parameters (two years in first instance, one year in second instance) were "very long, especially with regard to matrimonial causes, in view of the speed of modern life." Nor did it seem realistic to him to make those hoping for a subsequent marriage to wait potentially three years for a decision in the matter—and that being only a legislative standard, to say nothing of how long a trial might really last in a particular case. This would be "too hard" (*durissimum*) for most people. The wide parameters of law are "greater than people of our age can bear."[16] He thought it better to expect the first instance to last no longer than one year, and three months for further instances.[17] Trials beyond that length become unduly difficult for people to bear. At the same time, the efforts of some tribunals "to make law and canonical praxis adequate for human reality," while not completing their work in a just minimum length of time, are to be praised.[18]

10. – This realism is detected, too, in his reflections on implementation of the model of the regional or interdiocesan tribunal. He recognized that that structure is something that "by its nature" fosters the selection of suitable judges, while acknowledging that "in practice, for various reasons, many regional tribunals do not meet expectations." One reason is the fact that there may not in reality be an equal distribution of causes; that problem demands that the reconfiguration of territories pertaining to an individual tribunal be enacted.[19]

11. – It also led him to appreciate reasonable differences of opinion about the binding force of certain norms. For example, he maintains that the motu proprio *Causas matrimoniales* derogated from the American Procedural Norms. However, since there was a letter from the secretary of the United States conference of bishops telling the bishops the contrary, seemingly based on a judgment of the Apostolic See, "in practice, since that letter has so much authority, the Most Excellent Ordinaries can safely act according to its tenor."[20]

---

16. See "De nimia processuum matrimonialium duratione," 497–498, nn. 8–9.

17. Cf. *Pars statica*, 326, no. 471d, at 2).

18. See "De nimia processuum matrimonialium duratione," 499, no. 11.

19. See "De Tribunalibus Regionalibus," 587, 594.

20. See *Adnotationes in m.p. "Causas matrimoniales,"* 248, no. 3. On an insert to the *dispensa*, he humbly documents that in fact the question had become a moot point, since the American norms had been confirmed by the Apostolic See until the coming into effect of the revised code (cf. "I. GORDON. Adnotationes in M.P.," at I.247–248).

D. Scholarly Apparatus

12. – Another part of his scientific method, which he includes "for the convenience of the reader,"[21] is the inclusion of large appendices of documentation frequently cited or of special value to the topic being treated in a given work. A rather notable example of this is his treatise on the excessive length of matrimonial processes, to which he attaches nine appendices spanning thirty-three pages.[22]

In other articles, one finds, for example, five appendices spanning fourteen pages[23] and one multifaceted appendix spanning ten pages.[24] In a *dispensa* from the 1979 *Cursus*, he gives three appendices furnishing responses and decisions from the Apostolic See pertaining to *CM*, a supplemental bibliography, and three sample decrees pertaining to the *processus brevior* of *CM*.[25] In his *dispensa* on the marriage nullity process based on the schemata on procedural law, he inserts three appendices spanning twenty-three pages, reprinting the text of cited draft canons and demonstrating for readers the evolution of the canons from the 1917 *CIC* to the schemata.[26] He does this even in some of his *vota* for the Apostolic Signatura, as in the case of one to which he attaches two documents that entered into or were the basis for his observations,[27] and in another he included a bibliography of the many sources he cited.[28]

It can safely be asserted, as he said of another's work, that Father Gordon deemed detailed bibliographies "to constitute a singular work aid for canonists and judges."[29] And he was a model of this kind of aid offered to readers. One author presents an extensive bibliography on a particular question, concluding with a work by Father Gordon at which he notes parenthetically, "where a still more complete bibliography can be found."[30]

---

21. See "De nimia processuum matrimonialium duratione," 496, no. 7.

22. Ibid., 562–594.

23. "De Curia Romana renovata," 103–116.

24. "Decisio Signaturae Iustitiae," 201–210.

25. *Adnotationes in m.p. "Causas matrimoniales,"* 16–24.

26. *Processus nullitatis matrimonii,* 117–139.

27. Ignacio Gordon, *votum* ("De decreto generali Conferentiae Episcoporum [N] circa instrumenta iuridica conciliationis"), prot. n. 15781/83 VT, May 20, 1989: in SSAT Archives. The attachments are the 9-page general decree itself and a 3-page document entitled "Versione italiana di alcune osservazioni del Votante e risposte della [X]."

28. Ignacio Gordon, *votum alterum circa causas [X] et [Y] et aliarum,* prot. n. 270/70 CG, October 24, 1970: in SSAT Archives, 36–37.

29. See *DR* 2:6, no. 3.

30. See Alessandro d'Avack, "Questioni concernenti l'appello," in *Il motu proprio "Causas matrimoniales" nella dottrina e nell'attuale giurisprudenza,* Studia et documenta iuris canonici VIII, Annali

13. – He drew scientific data from a broad collection of sources. For example, he examines not only the legislation and canonical doctrine but also jurisprudence,[31] discussions from the revision of the code and from the Synod of Bishops, and even from private correspondence[32] and statistical analysis.[33] In examining a particular question, he prudently traces the "historical evolution of opinions" expressed in the 1967 Synod of Bishops, among authors, and within the code commission, and he then carries out a careful analysis of them.[34] Also, the literature from which he draws was so expansive and multilingual as to be truly representative of the global discussion.[35]

Another source from which he drew in some matters is the secular juridical science. He held that it is "useful to research civil laws and juridical orders" in which canon law in some ways shares, especially in the area of contentious-administrative jurisdiction.[36] Hence, in his annotations to the *NS*, he cites several sources of secular legislation as useful for understanding the contentious-administrative trial.

E. Scientific Deontology: Humility and Service

14. – What is clear from many particular aspects of Father Gordon's method is that the scientific goal of his academic work was to seek the truth and the right solution to problems, not himself. This led him to strive for a sound balance between firm conviction and intellectual humility. His Eminence Giuseppe Car-

---

di dottrina e giurisprudenza canonica (V), ed. Angelo di Felice (Rome: Catholic Book Agency, 1979) 57, note 17.

31. See, e.g., Ignacio Gordon, *votum* ("De recursu contra Congressus decisionem latam in quaestione de iure appellandi"), prot. n. 2120/71 CG, April 3, 1973: in SSAT Archives, 15–19, nn. 58–78; "De appellationibus," *passim* but esp. 298–299.

32. Cf. "De nimia processuum matrimonialium duratione," 498–499, no. 10, *et passim*.

33. Cf. ibid., 502, note 15; 555, no. 103; 556–557, nn. 105–106; 560, nn. 111–112; "De diverso regimine appellationum," 716–718, no. 2. See also his numerical illustration of the various possible *turni* of the Roman Rota in *Pars statica*, 275–276, no. 398.

34. "Votum de revisione sententiae," 111–124.

35. See the lengthy bibliographic note 12 in "De nimia processuum matrimonialium duratione," 494–496, where he lists doctrinal material in French, German, Spanish (including works written by a Hollander translated into Spanish), Italian, and English. In a similar vein, see "De Tribunalibus administrativis," 605–606, notes 10–11. For other proofs of this, see, e.g., "De nimia processuum matrimonialium duratione," 641–643, nn. 114–116; "De appellationibus," 285–287, note 3; *Adnotationes in m.p. "Causas matrimoniales,"* 244–246, no. 3, and 18–19 [Appendix II]; *Pars statica*, 29–32; "Normae speciales," 75–76, note 1 and 111–113, nn. 93–94, completed, in a sense, in "De iustitia administrativa ecclesiastica," 304, note 5.

36. Cf. "Normae speciales," 110, no. 89.

dinal Versaldi describes Father Gordon—his former professor—in these terms: "While remaining faithful to the canonical tradition, [he] demonstrated great intellectual openness and innovative courage."[37]

This is corroborated by His Eminence Zenon Cardinal Grocholewski, who recalls that Father Gordon was in the middle of a certain writing project concerning some procedural question, and he shared a draft of his work with his students, among whom was Grocholewski, so that they could have a discussion about it. Father Gordon could see that Grocholewski was unsettled about some aspects of the draft, and he pressed him to explain his concern. He relates: "To my great surprise, Father Gordon, simply in front of everyone, immediately admitted that what I said made sense. At that moment, Father Gordon increased much in my eyes, demonstrating that he was a person who seeks only the truth and what is just, not himself." Father Gordon's research and discussions about canonical questions consistently reflected this disposition.[38]

15. – As an academic proceduralist, he strove to be at the service of his students and of practitioners, as should not be at all surprising in light of his character as described above.[39] A particular discussion held by the *coetus studiorum de processibus* highlighted this, which Father Gordon's subsequent scientific activity bore out. One unidentified organ that had been consulted suggested that, in place of the ordinary contentious process, the marriage nullity process be presented as the model for all trials. Five consultors rejected this proposal for many persuasive technical reasons. Father Gordon, though, "tenaciously defended the fittingness of assenting to the proposition of the new systemization." And why? "Because," he says, "it is urgently requested by those who work in tribunals."[40]

---

37. Giuseppe Versaldi, "Father Ignacio Gordon, S.J.," private correspondence, September 26, 2018, 1.

38. See Grocholewski, 361, no. 2.

39. *Vide supra* Chapter I, nn. 5, 13–17, 19.

40. See PCCICR Archives, *vol. 181. XI. De processibus. Sessio III ≐ Series II ^diebus 23–28 octobris 1978 habita. Relatio,* 82; *Communicationes* 11 (1979) 80–81, at 81: "Gordon [Consultor quidam] mordicus defendit opportunitatem accedendi propositioni novae systematicae, quia, dicit ipse, instanter id petitur ab illis qui in tribunalibus agunt." One consultor agreed with him, but the advice of another was ultimately agreeable to all: retain the current systematization but strive "to order the evolution of the institutes and norms so that it may be more useful in the praxis of tribunals for the conducting of matrimonial processes."

F. A *Vademecum* for Causes of Nullity of Marriage

16. – Though he did not prevail in this latter intervention, Father Gordon was still sure to present the marriage nullity process in a complete manner to his students and those participating in the subsequent *Cursus* events. He prepared a booklet in 1981 (and a revised version in 1983) that present the annotated canons governing the marriage nullity process, rationally interweaving the norms on trials in general and on the ordinary contentious trial with the special norms on causes of nullity of marriage.[41] It is "an aid (*subsidium*) for work, not a scientific commentary,"[42] inasmuch as it displays the law in a clear manner and offers brief explanations in the footnotes. He described his effort in these terms in 1981:

> In the new code, as in the code promulgated in the year 1917, the process of matrimonial nullity was formed by appropriately substituting and inserting the specific canons of the nullity process among the canons on the contentious process in general. In the present booklet, we have taken care to bring about this substitution and insertion for the convenience of ecclesiastical judges, so that, in a single sequence of canons, they may be able to have in view everything and solely the things that pertain both to the presuppositions of the matrimonial process and to its pathway (*iter*), from the *libellus* all the way to the execution of the last sentence.[43]

The canons concerning the *pars statica* are arranged in logical order and those concerning the *pars dynamica* in the chronological order of the trial, efforts being made to preserve the order of the canons.[44] This chronological approach of presenting canons "exclusively pertaining in any way to the matrimonial process of nullity" is taken "since it is more useful for judges."[45]

17. – These booklets constitute, as it were, his own, private revised version of *Provida Mater Ecclesia* (*PME*) and a twenty-two year anticipation of the instruction *Dignitas connubii* (January 25, 2005). Indeed, in the 1983 version, he hails the utility of *PME* and expresses expectations that a new *PME* will be issued

---

41. *Processus nullitatis matrimonii* (1981); *Novus processus nullitatis matrimonii* (1983). The latter received the necessary authorizations about three months after the promulgation of the *CIC*, and his preface indicates that it was finalized on the Feast of the Nativity of the Blessed Virgin Mary.

42. *Novus processus nullitatis matrimonii*, iv, *sub* 2.

43. See *Processus nullitatis matrimonii*, iii.

44. Cf. ibid.

45. *Novus processus nullitatis matrimonii*, iii–iv.

in due course:[46] "No one versed in judicial affairs is unaware of how useful the aforementioned instruction was for judges exercising their function. And so we do not doubt that the Dicastery of the Roman Curia now competent in this matter will take care to prepare a similar aid for the convenience of judges." Of his 1983 booklet he says that "we have in the meantime ventured provisionally to prepare this substitution and insertion of canons." At the same time, he recognizes that his indications of the enduring efficacy or utility of certain provisions of *PME* is sure but "exceeds the capacity of a private man."[47]

G. Teaching Procedural Law

18. – From a technical point of view, the object of university instruction in the discipline of procedural law was, for him, "the doctrine and procedural praxis of administering justice in the ecclesiastical forum."[48] The study of procedural law—which law is itself a "school of prudence and discretion"—is also effective for imparting on students an ability to make a "correct evaluation of things and persons" and to make a "sound judgment."[49]

19. – As he approached retirement, he had an abiding concern for students' ability to grasp procedural law. It was his impression, testifies one of his colleagues who wished to remain anonymous, that "for students who have not worked in a tribunal, procedural law is very difficult and abstract"; they should thus be taught

---

46. We read in the preamble to *DC* (Vatican translation): "After the Code was promulgated in 1983, there appeared a pressing need to prepare an instruction which, following the footsteps of *Provida Mater*, would be helpful to judges and other ministers of tribunals. . . . The Instruction then has been drafted and published with the intention that it be a help to judges and other ministers of the tribunals of the Church, to whom the sacred ministry of hearing the causes of nullity of marriage has been entrusted" (13 [§3], 17 [§1]).

47. *Novus processus nullitatis matrimonii*, iii. As one author wrote about this work at that time: "Un valido e quanto mai utile lavoro di comporre in una sintetica visione tutti i canoni del nuovo Codice riguardanti il processo matrimoniale è stato già compiuto dal Prof. I. Gordon." Cesare Zaggia, "*Iter processuale* di una causa matrimoniale secondo il nuovo Codice di Diritto Canonico," in *Il matrimonio nel nuovo Codice di Diritto Canonico. Annotazioni di diritto sostanziale e processuale* (Padua: Libreria Gregoriana Editrice, 1984) 206, note 1. See also Craig Arthur Cox, *Procedural Changes in Formal Marriage Nullity Cases from the 1917 to the 1983 Code: Analysis, Critique and Possible Alternatives*, Canon Law Studies 528 (Washington, DC: The Catholic University of America, 1989) 263–264.

48. See *Pars statica*, 1.

49. See ibid., 23, no. 28: "Omnes autem auditores invenient in iure processuali scholam prudentiae et discretionis, apud quam addiscent rectam rerum et personarum aestimationem, adeoque sanum iudicium efformare."

"in a simple way the important things" in the code on the topic.[50] Father Gordon described his concern and his approach in these terms:

> The main difficulty [for students] is based on the subtlety, multiplicity, and interdependence of procedural laws. Added to this is the newness that students usually experience on this subject, together with the fact that this area of canon law is usually unknown to them up to this point. But we face this difficulty by explaining procedural law gradually, moving from questions that are simpler to those that are more difficult and, as is it were in a cyclical way, with subtler argumentation, so that by successive explanations they are entered into in a more orderly and deep manner.[51]

20. – A methodological or pedagogical consequence of this philosophy is that he offered a brief introductory treatment of all aspects of the *partes statica et dynamica*.[52] In other words, he explained in broad strokes everything that he was about to teach them in detail throughout the whole course. Applying the principle *repetitio mater studiorum*, the student would already have some familiarity with each element of procedural law when it came time to examine it in detail. Moreover, each particular element under examination would be, in the student's mind, more easily situated within the broader context of the tribunal and the trial.

21. – Another insightful idea of his was to encourage students to read the acts or definitive sentence of a contentious, non-matrimonial cause, since it could more simply illustrate the elements of the trial. He writes: "In order that these elements [of the trial] may be still more easily and almost intuitively perceived, we highly recommend that students attentively read first a summary of some judicial cause." And he comments in the footnote: "In particular, it will be very useful to read a contentious cause which pursues not the mere declaration of a right but the definition of a controverted right. For in such a cause the proper nature of the trial will be better perceived."[53]

Indeed, causes of nullity of marriage, while being the most common in the Church's judiciary in our time, have some peculiar elements: the judge is to have a more proactive role, the opposing party (the defender of the bond) is public and institutional, and the decision is purely declarative. The prototypical form of

---

50. Private letter, June 25, 2018.
51. See *Pars statica*, 21, no. 25.
52. Cf. ibid., 32–44, nn. 48–72. On these concepts, *vide infra* section H.
53. See *Pars statica*, 33–34, no. 48, including note 59.

the trial, on the other hand, involves two parties who have an extrajudicial interest in the controversy; they stand equally before the impartial judge, whose decision establishes certain rights and obligations for them.

22. – His method for imparting the procedural discipline of the Church seemed to be something that he had mastered, as is evidenced in the apparent receptivity of his students demonstrated above (e.g., Chapter I, no. 5). Quite relevant in particular is the account of another student from 1979–1981: "Over the two years of the License that followed, I came to enjoy Fr. Gordon's lectures on procedures. At that time, I had never been near a marriage tribunal but I came to have a very clear idea of the outline of the canonical process, the principal figures involved, and the essential elements of each stage of the procedures."[54] Another found his approach to teaching procedural law to be "charming," as is seen in the incident below about the controversy over the watch.[55]

H. The Distinction between the *Pars statica* and the *Pars dynamica*

23. – One approach to the teaching of and research on procedural law for which Father Gordon seems to be well known is to emphasize the distinction between the *pars statica* and the *pars dynamica* of the judicial process. This distinction can easily be seen as innate to the discipline of procedural law, since it refers to the stable realities of judicial institutes and the practical realities involved in the concrete manner of proceeding. It is not a distinction that Father Gordon invented, since it already was employed by secular proceduralists. He himself expressly cites in particular Francesco Carnelutti who, in his *Istituzioni del nuovo processo civile italiano*, teaches that the study of the process is a complicated matter, but it is possible with clear methodology. Carnelutti teaches:

> The method that is followed herein is now tried by long scientific and didactic experience, but its foundations and importance have only recently been clarified. It is developed by way of a distinction between two aspects of the structure of the process, as in general of any other juridical institute. These correspond to the concepts of what is *procedurally static* and *dynamic* or, in general, what is *juridically static* and *dynamic*. This is not an indispensable

---

54. Aidan McGrath, "Fr. Ignacio Gordon S.J. – Some personal memories," private letter, August 22, 2018, 1.

55. James Conn, private letter, June 4, 2018; *Pars statica*, 35, no. 52, 2º. *Vide infra* Chapter VI, no. 45.

method, but it is certainly very useful for the scientific discovery of the phenomena of the process and of law.[56]

Carnelutti explains that the *pars statica* "studies the process outside time . . . at a stop." It examines the process as "a *situation,* or better, *an ensemble of situations in which the process is broken up.*" These situations are elements (parties, defenders, the judicial office, competence, proofs, goods that are the object of a trial), procedural juridical relationships (the powers and duties of the judge, the public ministers, the parties, their defenders, and third parties), and the abstract contents of the process (the unity or plurality of the object of litigation, the unity or plurality of the processes themselves). He further explains that the *pars dynamica* studies "the process in time, that is, in its movement or development." It examines the process as "an *event,* or better, *an ensemble of the events that form it.*" These events are acts (understood extraprocedurally or procedurally; classified in terms of capacity, suitability of object, legitimation, form, intention, cause, place, time, and condition; and considered in terms of possible defects and remedies for defects) and procedures (*procedimenti*) within the process (investigation, execution, and special procedures such as those injunctive, cautionary, and voluntary).[57]

24. – And so while Father Gordon is not the originator of this distinction, he seems to be the canonist that introduced it most influentially into canonical doctrine and pedagogy. Proceduralists commenting on the 1917 *CIC* largely followed what Lega called "the legal order of the canons and titles" of Book IV.[58] And this was not surprising since such was prescribed by norms of the Apostolic See: the exegetical method was to be followed in the teaching of canon law and in final examinations, and professors were to lecture and write in their field according to the order of the titles and canons of the code.[59]

---

56. See Francesco Carnelutti, *Istituzioni del nuovo processo civile italiano,* 4th ed. (Rome: Società Editrice del "Foro Italiano," 1951) 1:103, no. 98. The original Italian is difficult to translate into English without rendering "procedural" and "juridical" as adverbs while retaining the words "static" and "dynamic," or rendering "static" and "dynamic" as nouns (e.g., procedural staticity and dynamism). In the original (with these emphases), the author identifies "i concetti della *statica* e della *dinamica processuale* o, in genere, della *statica* e della *dinamica giuridica.*" The sense here is "procedural/juridical establishment and dynamism": respectively, those things that are firmly stable or permanent, and how they operate in practice.

57. See ibid. and 105, 280–281, 385–396, nn. 99–100, 280.

58. See Michele Lega and Vittorio Bartoccetti, *Commentarius in iudicia ecclesiastica iuxta Codicem iuris canonici* (Rome: Anonima Libraria Cattolica Italiana, 1950) at 1:xvii.

59. Cf. Sacred Congregation for Seminaries and Universities, general decree *Cum novum,* August 7, 1917: *AAS* 9 (1917) 439; idem, general decree *Legum canonicarum,* October 31, 1918: *AAS* 11 (1919) 19.

The proceduralist in the era of the 1917 *CIC* who was the most innovative while being at the same time among the most influential was Francesco Roberti. Among his many influential teachings was his characterization of the distinct parts of procedural law, which would prepare for Father Gordon's distinction between the *partes statica et dynamica*. He distinguished the presuppositions of the process (*praesupposita*) from the evolution of the process (*evolutio*) or the process of investigation (*processus cognitionis*), which was followed by the process of execution (*processus exsecutionis*).[60]

These were the principal models of instruction and scholarship in canonical procedural law under the regime of the 1917 *CIC*. Unless I am mistaken, the distinction between the *partes statica et dynamica* was not expressly or influentially used prior to Father Gordon.

25. – As Father Gordon taught, the static part of the trial includes the whole theory of rights (*iura*), action (*actio*), and the trial (*iudicium*), as well as all the persons and structures involved in a trial. These are the elements of the trial in a state of "rest" (*quiescientia*). The dynamic part treats the same elements "in motion," that is, "in the evolution of the process."[61] He even suggested that the part of what would become Book VII of the 1983 *CIC* on the contentious trial in general ought to have been called "*De evolutione processus*," since that part was the body of norms on the *pars dynamica*.[62] These two parts could also be thought of, respectively, in terms of the presuppositions of the trial (*praesupposita*), or those things that have to be in place before there can be a trial (cf. Roberti), and the pathway or journey (*iter*) through the trial itself.[63]

26. – These designations have made their way into the common parlance of canonical proceduralists and ministers of justice. And since they were not used in canonical procedural doctrine before him but were used after his introduction

---

60. Francesco Roberti, *De processibus* (Vatican City: Pontificium Institutum Utriusque Iuris, 1956) 1:28–29, which seems to have influenced, e.g., Fernando della Rocca, *Canonical Procedure. Philosophical-Juridic Study of Book IV of the Code of Canon Law*, trans. John D. Fitzgerald (Milwaukee: The Bruce Publishing Company, 1961) 36–48, nn. 20–26.

61. Cf. *Pars statica*, 33, no. 49: "pars *dynamica* eadem elementa in motu seu in processus evolutione contemplatur." See also ibid., 45, no. 73. For these designations, see also *Processus nullitatis matrimonii*, 1, 21; *Novus processus nullitatis matrimonii*, 1, 13.

62. Cf. PCCICR Archives, *vol. 181. XI. De processibus. Sessio III⁑ Series II˄diebus 23–28 octobris 1978 habita. Relatio*, 83; *Communicationes* 11 (1979) 82.

63. Cf. *Processus nullitatis matrimonii*, iii. Here he also mentions the *processus dynamica*. In another context, he cited elements of "…la 'statica' del processo" ("Elementi innovativi nei processi," 8).

of them, this seems to be thanks to him. This influence is expressly recognized by some.

One of his former students, then-Father Thomas J. Green, as a professor writing in 1978, adopted this terminology and noted: "The terms 'static' and 'dynamic' in reference to the different parts of the procedural law corpus are borrowed from Gordon's class notes in procedural law at the Pontifical Gregorian University in Rome."[64] And in the manual written just before he became a judge of the Roman Rota, Monsignor Pio Vito Pinto wrote: "We, too, with Gordon, shall call Part I the *pars statica* of the process . . . while Part II is the *pars dynamica*. . . ."[65]

27. – The procedural literature bears out this distinction even further, even when it does not mention Father Gordon or his method. Some examples help to illustrate the breadth of its use.

The most extensive collection of research in the area of canonical procedural law yet published in the twenty-first century follows this model: the first volume is on general principles (similar to Fr. Gordon's *Introductio*), the second on the *pars statica*, and the third on the *pars dynamica*.[66] Monsignor Grzegorz Erlebach's thorough examination of causes of nullity of the sentence likewise treats the material according to this same distinction.[67]

Other authors use the distinction without dwelling on it, practically presuming its meaning. For example, the revised, multi-volume manual of Father Francisco Ramos, OP, who taught at the Pontifical University of St. Thomas in Rome, is entitled *Diritto processuale canonico: volume 1: Parte statica, volume 2/1–2: Parte*

---

64. Thomas J. Green, "Marriage Nullity Processes in the Schema *De Processibus*," *The Jurist* 38 (1978) 317, note 17.

65. See Pio Vito Pinto, *I processi nel Codice di diritto canonico: Commento sistematico al Lib. VII* (Vatican City: Pontificia Università Urbaniana, Libreria Editrice Vaticana, 1993) 20–21, no. 8: "Anche noi con Gordon, chiameremo la Pars I *parte statica* del processo [. . .]. Mentre la Pars II è la *parte dinamica*...."

66. *Il giudizio di nullità matrimoniale dopo l'Istruzione "Dignitas connubii." Parte Prima: I principi,* Studi Giuridici 75, ed. Piero Antonio Bonnet and Carlo Gullo (Vatican City: Libreria Editrice Vaticana, 2007); *Il giudizio di nullità matrimoniale dopo l'Istruzione "Dignitas connubii." Parte Seconda: La parte statica del processo,* Studi Giuridici 76, ed. idem (Vatican City: Libreria Editrice Vaticana, 2007); *Il giudizio di nullità matrimoniale dopo l'Istruzione "Dignitas connubii." Parte Terza: La parte dinamica del processo,* Studi Giuridici 77, ed. idem (Vatican City: Libreria Editrice Vaticana, 2008).

67. Grzegorz Erlebach, "Le fattispecie di negazione del diritto di difesa causanti la nullità della sentenza secondo la giurisprudenza rotale: criteri generali e parte statica," *Monitor Ecclesiasticus* 114 (1989) 495–556; idem "Le fattispecie di negazione del diritto di difesa causanti la nullità della sentenza secondo la giurisprudenza rotale (parte dinamica)," *Monitor Ecclesiasticus* 115 (1990) 387–433; idem, *La nullità della sentenza giudiziale "ob ius defensionis denegatum" nella giurisprudenza rotale,* Studi Giuridici 25 (Vatican City: Libreria Editrice Vaticana, 1991) 203, 239.

dinamica.[68] Similarly, Father Manuel Jesús Arroba Conde, a leading proceduralist in the first decades of the twenty-first century, follows Roberti's distinction between presuppositions of the process and the acts, or steps, of the process; but he divides his manual between the *pars statica* and the *pars dynamica.*[69] In another manual, the terminology is not used but is mirrored by a distinction between "the general part" of procedural law and "the treatment of different processes."[70] The *dispense* of the great proceduralist and jurist Monsignor Gianpaolo Montini—a kind of successor to Father Gordon at the Gregorianum—are subtitled *pars statica* and *pars dynamica.*[71] This terminology is also used in general commentaries on the *CIC.*[72]

I. The Reform of Procedural Law

28. – Father Gordon exhibited due respect for the norm of law in force when offering solutions to practical problems. Regarding scientific and forensic aspira-

---

68. Francisco J. Ramos and Delfina Moral Carvajal, *Diritto processuale canonico: volume 1. Parte statica,* 3rd ed. (Rome: Angelicum University Press, 2013); Francisco J. Ramos and Piotr Skonieczny, *Diritto processuale canonico: volume 2/1. Parte dinamica,* 3rd ed. (Rome: Angelicum University Press, 2014); idem, *Diritto processuale canonico: volume 2/2. Parte dinamica,* 3rd ed. (Rome: Angelicum University Press, 2014).

69. Manuel Jesús Arroba Conde, *Diritto processuale canonico,* 5th ed. (Rome: Editiones Institutum Iuridicum Claretianum, 2006).

70. See Carmelo de Diego-Lora and Rafael Rodríguez-Ocaña, *Lecciones de Derecho procesal canónico. Parte general* (Pamplona: EUNSA, 2003) 20. Similarly, Joaquín Llobell divides the material in terms of 1) presuppositions (jurisdiction, pastoral care, procedural law), 2) protagonists (tribunals, officials, parties), and 3) processes; see his *I processi matrimoniali nella Chiesa,* Subsidia Canonica 17 (Rome: EDUSC, 2015).

71. Gianpaolo Montini, *De iudicio contentioso ordinario. De processibus matrimonialibus. I. Pars statica* (Rome: GBPress, 2016); idem, *De iudicio contentioso ordinario. De processibus matrimonialibus. Pars dynamica,* 3rd ed. (Rome: Editrice Pontificia Università Gregoriana, 2012); idem, *De iudicio contentioso ordinario. De processibus matrimonialibus. II/2. Pars dynamica addenda post Litteras Apostolicas motu proprio datas "Mitis Iudex Dominus Iesus"* (Rome: Editrice Pontificia Università Gregoriana, 2018).

72. See, e.g., Juan Luis Acebal, "Parte II. Del juicio contencioso," in *Código de Derecho Canónico. Edición bilingüe comentada,* 11th ed. (Madrid: Biblioteca de Autores Cristianos, 1992) 738; Luigi Chiappetta, *Il Codice di diritto canonico. Commento giuridico-pastorale,* ed. F. Catozzella et al., 3rd ed. (Bologna: Edizioni Dehoniane, 2011) 3:92, no. 5343; Craig A. Cox, "Part II. The Contentious Trial [cc. 1501–1670]," in *New Commentary on the Code of Canon Law,* ed. John P. Beal, James A. Coriden, and Thomas J. Green (New York/Mahwah: Paulist Press, 2000) 1655; Gianpaolo Montini, "Pars I. De iudiciis in genere," in *Codice di Diritto Canonico commentato,* ed. Redazione di *Quaderni di diritto ecclesiale,* 3rd ed. (Milan: Àncora, 2009) 1117. See also Mario F. Pompedda, "Diritto processuale nel nuovo Codice di diritto canonico. Revisione o innovazione?" *Ephemerides iuris canonici* 39 (1983) 206, 215, nn. 5, 13; Javier Ochoa, "I processi canonici in generale." *Apollinaris* 57 (1984) 195–222, at 198; John P. Beal, "The Ordinary Process According to *Mitis Iudex:* Challenges to Our 'Comfort Zone,'" *The Jurist* 76 (2016) 161.

tions to abbreviate the judicial process, he insisted that such aspirations are to be limited to the reduction of the time spent in handling a cause, rather than innovations aimed at simplifying the manner of proceeding. He believed that more fundamental change could come about only through a pontifical commission to revise the legislation. For there is a necessary complexity to some aspects of trials. In the particular context of regional tribunals, he said that such innovations "which are a matter of the *ius condendum*, remain outside (*vagantur*) the current possibilities." Legitimate practices may be implemented "while today's procedural law remains still intact. Moreover, before we think about new measures to be established for speeding up the process, it pertains to prudence to make diligent use of those that are already available now."[73]

29. – For the most part,[74] within his doctrinal activity[75] his own approach was not to suggest concrete reforms but rather to highlight just solutions proposed by other authors, prelates, or authoritative sources. In this way, especially when there was some foundation in existing law, jurisprudence, or praxis, he seemed to favor certain reforms that would promote the celerity of the process. Examples of these include the following.

30. – He thought that the competent forum could be broadened to include the domicile of the petitioner, though he argued in favor of the prior hearing of the respondent himself. This was based on his impression that it would not give rise to obvious abuses. However, he would later see abuses arising in the praxis of American tribunals' broad acceptance of the residence of either party, without condition.[76]

---

73. See "De Tribunalibus Regionalibus," 592; see also 579.

74. For an example of one of his own proposals, see "De nimia processuum matrimonialium duratione," 712–717, nn. 261–270, in which he demonstrates that the presumption of the law in favor of marriage is not absolute in canonical tradition and suggests that some nuance in this matter be "partially received into the new code" which was then being drafted (723–724, no. 285). Evidently, the exceptions to the *favor matrimonii* are specific (e.g., when there is a total non-observance of canonical form) and do not compromise the general orientation of the canonical system articulated in *CIC* c. 1060 and *CCEO* c. 779. Another example was his unsuccessful proposal that was contrary to the prevalent reading of the January 11, 1971 authentic interpretation. He proposed that the *Sectio altera* of the Apostolic Signatura be attributed the primary and single competence for making judgments about the alleged violation of subjective rights on the part of administrative authorities, and that the competence to judge the alleged illegitimacy of singular administrative acts be suppressed (cf. "De obiecto primario competentiae," 537–540).

75. Obviously, in carrying out his consultative activity within the *Coetus studiorum de processibus*, he readily fulfilled his charge of proposing changes, as is illustrated *passim* herein.

76. Cf. "De nimia processuum matrimonialium duratione," 682–683, nn. 193, 195–196; "El M. P. '*Causas matrimoniales*' y las normas americanas," 199, b) and 200. Cf. *MI* c. 1672, 2º.

31. – The decree of admission or rejection of the *libellus* could be included within the competence of the *officialis* (judicial vicar) or presiding judge instead of being reserved to the college of judges.[77] The 1917 *CIC* had identified the "judge or tribunal" as the authority competent to admit or reject the *libellus* (c. 1709 §1), while *PME* seemed to reserve this to the college of judges for causes of nullity of marriage (artt. 61–62).[78] Father Gordon, though, perceived general utility in a response given by the Sacred Congregation for the Sacraments to the Archbishop of Milan, who questioned whether this always had to be the college or whether the *officialis* could also do it. The Congregation stated:

> This Sacred Congregation holds that the *Officialis* can, with a *motivated* decree, reject a *libellus* when it is *evidently* established either that the accusation is deprived of juridical foundation, or that the petitioner is unable to accuse the marriage, or that the tribunal is incompetent. Against such a decree, though, *recourse* can be made, but *exclusively to the College*, which will proceed *ad juris tramitem*. Express mention of the right to make recourse to the College will be made in the decree of the *Officialis*. It is to be well understood that if the College should confirm the rejection of the *libellus*, the party still has the right to make recourse to the superior Tribunal according to the norm of canon 1709 §3.[79]

This particular proposed reform to the universal law, as well as this source, is notably interesting at the present time. For it is a precursor to an alteration introduced by Pope Francis, whereby not only can the *Officialis* or judicial vicar admit or reject the *libellus*, but it is reserved to him (*MI* c. 1676 §1).[80]

32. – Several reforms that he supported, including those just described, were directed especially at the acceleration of certain moments in the trial. Three more

---

77. Cf. "De nimia processuum matrimonialium duratione," 683–685, nn. 197–199; *Pars dynamica*, 6, no. 14.

78. "Art. 61. - Tribunal . . . debet quantocius libellum aut admittere aut reiicere. . . . Art. 62. - Si *tribunalis collegialis* decreto libellus reiectus fuerit ob vitia quae emendari potest, actor novum libellum rite confectum potest eidem *tribunali* denuo exhibere; quod si *tribunal* emendatum libellum reiecerit, novae reiectionis rationes exponere debet. . . ." (emphasis in original).

79. See *Il monitore ecclesiastico* 50 (1938) 217, VIII), which he cites also in *Processus nullitatis matrimonii*, 24, b, and *Novus processus nullitatis matrimonii*, 15, note c.

80. On this theme, the question of recourse to the college, and related matters, see my "The Reservation to the Judicial Vicar of the Introductory Stage of the Ordinary Marriage Nullity Process," in *A Service Beyond All Recompense. Studies Offered in Honor of Msgr. Thomas J. Green*, ed. Kurt Martens (Washington, DC: CUA Press, 2018) 165–180.

of these could be mentioned by way of illustration. (1) The *contestatio litis*, in any kind of cause, should occur ten days after admission of the *libellus*, regardless of whether the respondent is contumacious.[81] (2) The *contestatio litis* could either be consolidated with the interrogation, or it could be accomplished between the judge, defender of the bond, and procurator-advocate(s).[82] And (3)—as would be established by *CM*—the ordinary appellate process could be abbreviated, such that, after the appeal of the defender of the bond, the superior college of judges would decide only whether to confirm the sentence or to have the cause examined according to the ordinary method.[83]

Two other reforms promoted the reduction of formalism in the interest of discovering the truth. (1) Even when a respondent is declared contumacious, all acts should be communicated to him in hopes of drawing him into the trial.[84] And (2) the confession of one spouse could prove the nullity of marriage, when the person is judged credible and there are no contrary elements.[85]

33. – He supported the modernization of procedural law, since some of its components in the Pio-Benedictine code were rooted in a period when there was more concurrent jurisdiction between the Church and civil society, and that code was promulgated before a greater separation between Church and state and the secularization of civic life were clearly anticipated. Accordingly, he noticed within the 1976 schema *de processibus* certain proposed norms that would govern actions introduced because of the announcement of some new work in the Church or in order to seek the reparation of damages. When weighing the utility of these norms, he suggested their suppression since such cases "are so rare in our tribunals that it becomes useless to arrange in the law the procedural evolution of such specific actions, when the general principle is sufficient that 'every right is supported by an action'"[86] (1917 *CIC* c. 1667; 1983 *CIC* c. 1491). He similarly suggested the suppression of the norms on possessory actions (*de spolio*). While this was

---

81. Cf. *Pars dynamica*, 21, nn. 82–83, as well as 87–88, no. 375.

82. Cf. "De nimia processuum matrimonialium duratione," 685–686, nn. 201–203. We read at no. 203: "Utralibet solutio bona nobis videtur."

83. Cf. ibid., 724–727, nn. 287–293.

84. This was a proposal of certain German canonists, which Fr. Gordon deemed "a better method" than what was in c. 1845 of the 1917 *CIC* (see *Pars dynamica*, 88, no. 378).

85. Cf. "De nimia processuum matrimonialium duratione," 687–694, nn. 204–222. Cf. *CIC* 1983 c. 1679; *DC* art. 180; *MI* c. 1678 §1.

86. Cf. PCCICR Archives, *vol. 181. XI. De processibus. Sessio III ÷ Series II diebus 23–28 octobris 1978 habita. Relatio*, 77; *Communicationes* 11 (1979) 76. This proposal was accepted, ultimately, by all.

not entirely accepted, the canon remitting the ecclesiastical law to local civil laws, proposed by himself and then-Archbishop Sabattani, was accepted.[87]

34. – In general, though, he modeled and encouraged continuity within canonical tradition in the area of procedural law, and in matrimonial procedural law in particular. Thus, even while unequivocally accepting legitimate legislative innovations, he wisely characterized derogated procedural norms (*PME* in particular) in terms of being "prescripts . . . which must not be forgotten."[88]

---

87. PCCICR Archives, *vol. 181. XI. De processibus. Sessio III*·*- Series II*·*diebus 23–28 octobris 1978 habita. Relatio, 81; Communicationes* 11 (1979) 79–80.

88. See *Processus nullitatis matrimonii*, iv. What he writes has the tone almost of a rule of law, substantially echoing cc. 6 §2 and 21 of the 1983 *CIC*: "sed plura alia adhuc sunt [praescripta], quorum memoria oportet ne pereat."

CHAPTER V

Introductory Notions of Procedural Law

1. – The principal scholarly contribution of Father Ignacio Gordon was in the area of canonical procedural law. He offered clear and influential teaching about various elements of the judiciary in itself (*pars statica*)[1] and about the distinct moments in the judicial process (*pars dynamica*).[2] In addition to these two fields of juridical reflection are a number of presuppositions to the judicial process, which he largely treated by way of introduction to the *partes statica et dynamica*. In this chapter, attention is drawn to some introductory notions that are more developed in his writings.

A. Procedural Law in General

1. The Nature of Procedural Law (*ius processuale*)

2. – Father Gordon defined procedural law in these terms: "Canonical procedural law (*ius processuale canonicum*) can be defined as that part of canon law that concerns the pathway to be followed in examining and expediting the questions

---

1. *Vide infra* Chapter VI.
2. *Vide infra* Chapter VII.

or affairs of the faithful."[3] Evidently, for him *ius processuale* is something quite broad, since there are many kinds of questions or affairs (*quaestiones aut negotia*) in which the faithful may be involved, including causes of canonization, various administrative procedures, and means for avoiding trials. Indeed, he held that the word *processus* means the series of steps followed in the exercise of either judicial or administrative (executive) power in the resolution of controversies. In an even broader sense, it is inclusive of procedures (*procedimenta*) used in all administrative activity.[4]

3. – One must therefore be clear about the area of canonical procedural law in which he is operating, lest—among other things—he violate "the principle of the non-intermingling of procedural pathways,"[5] failing to retain procedural purity. Father Gordon's area of concentration was on the law governing trials, which he calls in one place "ius iudiciale" (judicial law)—less a technical and more an explanatory expression, which is not commonly used, even by himself. It is "the principal part of procedural law" to which "the other parts look as their model," even to the point of imitating its forms. Stated otherwise, the law on trials (*de iudiciis*) is "the foundation of the whole procedural law of the code."[6]

2. Procedural Legislation (*leges processuales*)

4. – Procedural law has a complexity and can seem intimidating and formalistic in the context of the ecclesial society. However, each of its norms, with some reflection, can be seen to correspond to the demands of right reason, so that by their observance one can bring the right to a fair trial to realization and arrive at the just and correct decision.[7]

5. – Procedural laws, like penal laws, are adjectival (*leges adiectivae*); that is, they are added to laws that establish rights and obligations (substantive laws, *leges*

---

3. See *Pars statica*, 3, no. 1, as well as 36 and 58–59, nn. 54, 91. He demonstrates, however, that this is not the univocal opinion within canonical and perhaps especially secular doctrine (see ibid., 59–60, no. 92).

4. Cf. "De Tribunalibus administrativis," 612, no. 12, 3a.

5. Cf. "De iustitia administrativa ecclesiastica," 283, no. 45 ("principi[um] de non intermiscendis viis processualibus"). In that particular context, he was explaining the incoherence of introducing a judicial action against a bishop before the metropolitan and then challenging the decision of the latter by way of administrative recourse to a congregation of the Apostolic See.

6. See *Pars statica*, 3, 24–25, 32, nn. 2, 31–33, 48. He also uses the expression *ius iudiciale* in only the heading of a scholion: "De iure iudiciali sive canonico sive civitatum" (ibid., 20, no. 24).

7. Cf. ibid., 21, no. 26.

substantivae) in order to protect those rights and obligations. One's substantive right is attached to his person in accord with what is recognized in substantive law. His right to introduce an action is an adjectival right, since it is attributed to him for the protection of his substantive right.

Also, procedural laws are formal, instead of material, since they dictate the treatment of some matter. Penal laws are material laws, although there are penal procedural laws, which are formal, since they prescribe the manner in which a penal question is to be handled. Material laws determine the object of a trial, while procedural laws determine the steps and elements of the trial itself. However, there are some substantive norms in procedural law, such as qualifications for the office of judge (the object of an administrative provision) and judicial expenses (the object of legislation and of a judicial decision).[8]

6. – As regards the force of procedural laws, the law in force at the time of the trial is the one to be applied. For "the later law is deemed more apt for administering justice," which is presumably why the legislator would have issued it as a reform of the prior law. The matter is different in regard to substantive law: apart from penal causes,[9] the substantive law in force at the time of the event that is the object of the trial is the one to be applied, since it is what determined the rights and obligations in question.[10]

3. The Universality of Procedural Law

7. – Procedural law necessarily has a unitary and universal character in the Church. There may be latitude for some adaptations (or legislative decentralization) as regards the practical arrangements to be made at the local level; but a multiplication of procedural norms "undermin[es] the necessary procedural unity of matrimonial causes" in particular. This was witnessed by the Church in the early 1970s, leading to the growing aspiration among tribunals of different nations to determine which norms would be *theirs*.[11]

8. – "A unitary procedural legislation is demanded by the right of the faithful to make recourse to the Holy See." For the fundamental manner of administering

---

8. Cf. ibid., 26–27, 34, nn. 35–37, 50; "Discorso generale," 63.

9. Cf. *RJ* 49 in VI°; 1917 *CIC* c. 2226 §2; 1983 *CIC* c. 1313 §1.

10. Cf. *Pars statica*, 104, no. 149.

11. See "El M. P. '*Causas matrimoniales*' y las normas americanas," 196. On this problem and on Fr. Gordon's contribution, see, e.g., my "The Universality of the *Ordo iudiciarius* of the Church," *Studia canonica* 52 (2018) 407–441.

justice by the apostolic tribunals is that which belongs to the whole Church, and its manner of deciding causes sets the pattern for the whole Church. Without such unity (without restricted decentralization), two serious difficulties would arise. (1) The judges of the appellate tribunal would be ill-prepared to examine causes first treated at the local level, since the norms governing each tribunal would potentially be different. This problem would both complicate the administration of justice and retard the evolution of the individual trial. (2) This would naturally have substantive implications, especially with regard to the evaluation of proofs. There would thus be a double standard from one tribunal to the next or from one region to the next. For example, the declaration of a party might be considered to have the force of full proof in one tribunal but not in another. This would promote the search for a "more favorable tribunal" that would be more likely to decide in accord with the wishes of one party or the other. This would destabilize the administration of justice in the Church.[12]

9. – "What things are substantial in the process . . . must be the object of a unitary procedural law," while other matters and adaptations of substantial things may be regulated by particular law. Father Gordon lists the following as the elements pertaining to the substance of the process:

a) *The presuppositions of the process*: action, competence, representation, etc.
b) Its *quasi-anatomic structure*: the singular or collegial nature of the tribunal, the fundamental elements at the beginning, middle, and end of the process, the order or levels of functional competence, etc.
c) *The dynamic elements determining the evolution of the process*: the so-called "procedural forms" of greater importance (viz., whether the process is oral or written, secret or public, summary in certain cases or solemn), the headings and force of proofs, the regime of nullities, the system of *res iudicata* and challenges.[13]

10. – Other elements may be remitted by the supreme legislator to lower-level legislators, especially the diocesan bishop, who is the moderator of his tribunal, but even also the conference of bishops, as the case may be. When issuing norms pertaining to the protection of rights, bishops—whether individually or as a conference—are to be attentive to the universal norm of procedural law,

---

12. Cf. "De nimia processuum matrimonialium duratione," 676–679, nn. 178–184.
13. See ibid., 679–680, no. 187.

including the correct use of technical judicial terminology, lest "juridico-procedural unity be ruptured," such that "recourses, appeals, etc. within different dioceses and ecclesiastical provinces in the Church would be impossible."[14] Such terminological choices, leading to the distortion of concepts, would be an incorrect application of the notion of subsidiarity in the context of procedural law.[15]

B. The Nature of the Judicial Process or the Trial

1. Definition of the Trial (*iudicium*)

11. – A trial (*iudicium*) is a process carried out in the judicial forum (*in foro iudiciali*) or before the judge (*coram iudice*) for the definitive resolution of a controversy, or the discovery of the truth about it. It ends with the completion of the last instance.[16] The expression "'judicial process' (*processus iudicialis*) . . . expresses the same reality as 'trial' (*iudicium*), but with a different color: 'process' connotes a succession of steps; 'trial' [or 'judgment'] connotes rather the definition of a controversy."[17]

12. – Canonical tradition defines a trial in these still-useful terms: "Nomine iudicii ecclesiastici intelligitur controversiae in re de qua Ecclesia ius habet cognoscendi, coram tribunali ecclesiastico legitima disceptatio et definitio" (1917 *CIC* c. 1552 §1). That is: "The expression 'ecclesiastical trial' means the legitimate discussion and definition of a controversy before an ecclesiastical tribunal about a matter that the Church has the right to judge."

---

14. See Ignacio Gordon, *votum* ("De decreto generali Conferentiae Episcoporum N. circa instrumenta iuridica conciliationis"), prot. n. 15781-28/83 VT, May 20, 1989: in SSAT Archives, 2, *sub* "Arg. 1." In this regard, the *Congresso* observed for the Congregation for Bishops that the conference of bishops in question "non semper obtemperat principio generali quod omnes normae debent observare accuratam et praecisam terminologiam canonicam ad evitandas confusiones." It continues: "Haec Signatura Apostolica animadvertit iuxta mentem CIC Conferentias Episcopales non posse condere legem subsidiariam immutando sensum technicum vocabulorum aut institutorum processualium. Oportet ut Episcopi leges constituant quae systemati processuali Codicis Iuris Canonici cohaerent" (Supreme Tribunal of the Apostolic Signatura, *Animadversiones Congressus*, prot. n. 15781-28/83 VT, November 30, 1989: in ibid., 1, preamble at b and no. I.2).

15. Cf. Gordon, *votum*, prot. n. 15781-28/83 VT, *sub* "Art. 2."

16. Cf. *Pars statica*, 36–37, no. 54. In this context (37, nn. 55–56), he draws on authors to define related terms: *forum* (the territory, the location of the trial, the judge, judicial power itself; but see 108–109, no. 154, including note 4, where he omits territory and includes competence), *tribunal* (the place of the trial, the judge [alone or with the other ministers of justice; see also 163, no. 254], the level of jurisdiction), and *iudex* (the public person endowed with jurisdictional power). On the properly judicial sense of the term *tribunal*, see also "Normae speciales," 90, note 1.

17. See *Pars statica*, 59, no. 92, 1°.

Using philosophical categories, Father Gordon taught that the intrinsic causes of the trial are its matter, or the object of the controversy (*controversia*), and its form, which is the body of procedural norms to be observed (the *disceptatio et definitio* are each to be *legitima*). The extrinsic causes of the trial are the parties, the judge (both efficient causes), and the goal of the trial (the first cause). In other words, the trial is an orderly evolution of steps determined by law for the purpose of investigating and defining a particular controversy. A concrete trial comes into existence when particular opposing parties appear or are summoned before a competent judge for the purpose of finding a resolution to their own controversy. The extrinsic causes are not mentioned in the definition, but they are implicit, since it is the parties who bring into existence the matter of the trial, and the judge personifies and attributes its form.[18]

13. – Presupposing this definition is the public nature of the trial. It is public not merely in the sense of being known or knowable to people but in the technical sense of occurring within a society by and under the authority of those who govern and represent it. For the trial "proceeds from a public person, who is the judge," the authenticity of whose acts is publicly guaranteed by the assistance of a notary. And the administration of justice is a public good, even if the object of a trial may be a private good. Whether the object of the trial is public or private "depends on the nature of the parties." When they are "public persons acting as such [e.g., the promoter of justice accusing a marriage of nullity], . . . or at least one of them is public and acting as such, . . . the controversy is public and the trial about it is also public in every aspect." When they are "private persons or acting as private persons, . . . the controversy is private, but the trial is private in some aspect (in view of the parties' procedural relationship with one another) though public in another aspect (in view of the parties' procedural relationship with the judge)."[19]

---

18. Cf. ibid., 61–62, 65, nn. 92–96, 99. Citing this doctrine, e.g., is Juan José García Faílde, *Tratado de derecho procesal canónico*, 2nd ed. (Salamanca: Publicaciones Universidad Pontificia de Salamanca, 2007) 26.

In *Pars statica*, Fr. Gordon rehearses the doctrinal opinions about the principal purpose of the trial: while some say it is the protection of subjective rights, the majority of authors hold that it is the execution of laws (65–67, nn. 100–101). For an illustration of all these elements, see ibid., 69, no. 104. Following what was indicated in the 1917 *CIC*, he made these distinctions: the matter or object of the trial may be contentious or criminal and, among those contentious, petitory or possessory, real or personal; the form of the trial may be common or special, solemn or summary, ordinary or apostolic (ibid., 78–82, nn. 118–120).

19. See ibid., 76–78, nn. 115–117, quotation from 78, no. 117.

14. – All of these elements (intrinsic and extrinsic causes, publicity) constitute the general notion of the trial. Other elements of the definition situate it within the life of the Church: it is a question of the Church's jurisdiction (*res de qua Ecclesia ius habet cognoscendi*), and therefore the tribunal is an ecclesiastical one (*tribunal ecclesiasticum*). The legitimacy of the trial, then, demands observance of the procedural law *of the Church*.[20]

15. – Among the four main theories on the nature of the trial,[21] Father Gordon rejects two of them. 1) *Trial as contract* cannot be admitted since, despite historical precedents, it is clearly now understood to be an instrument of public power. 2) The theory of *trial as juridical position/situation*, sees the parties as having a series of advantages and burdens (not rights and obligations) in view of obtaining the desired outcome of the trial. The result is not some alteration or attribution of substantive rights; it is more of a contest resulting in the victory of one party and the loss of the other.

3) He favors the theory of *trial as juridical institution*, which is defined generally as a mutually connected ensemble of actions and omissions that effectively lead to a common end to which the agents in fact strive. The agents in a trial are the judge and the parties, who, through their procedural relationships, cooperate to achieve the application of the law to a concrete case.

4) He also thinks the theory of *trial as juridical relationship* is defensible, except for its neglect of the question of the finality of the trial. This theory sees the trial as fundamentally a complex of rights and obligations placing the judge and the parties in relationship with one another. This relationship has three qualities: it is autonomous from life outside the trial, it exists throughout the different stages of the trial, and it is public. The theory of trial as juridical institution perfects this last mentioned theory, since it entails the same juridical relationships.

2. *Actio*

16. – The term *actio* in procedural law has, one might say (though Fr. Gordon does not, explicitly), static and dynamic senses. Its first sense is as a pure subjective right: the right to introduce a cause before the competent judge. It is distinct from an exception, in that it is an expression of initiative taken when a right is challenged outside a trial, while an exception is an expression of response taken when a right

---

20. Cf. ibid., 62–63, no. 97.
21. Cf. ibid., 69–76, nn. 105–114.

is challenged within a trial.[22] An action in this sense is not a creation of the positive law but is in the nature of a subjective right which the society must protect.[23]

The second, more dynamic sense of *actio* is the exercise of that right, which gives rise to a judicial instance (*instantia*): "Action in this second step, with the correlative intervention of the judge and others, is called an instance." An action, as the exercise of a right, may be introduced at various levels of jurisdiction "until the sentence becomes entirely firm." Thus, there may be many instances carried out in the protection of some right.[24]

17. – While there are different kinds of actions, each action does not have its own form of trial. In the canonical system, any action is treated according to either the solemn/ordinary form or the summary form, possibly with some elements specific to a particular kind of action (a "special" process).[25]

3. The Purpose of the Trial

18. – As is illustrated below,[26] a major theme to which Father Gordon devoted his attention was the celerity of the process—that is, the treatment of any judicial controversy across an appropriate (and ideally brief) span of time. Still, he did not so exaggerate the principle of celerity as to lose sight of the proper purpose of the trial. He recognized that, throughout the history of the marriage nullity process in particular, various reforms have been made by the supreme legislator whose goal has been to remove obstacles to the timely treatment of such causes. This was the circumstantial rationale motivating certain reforms (*ratio legis*). Such reforms, however, are always presumed to be subordinate to the above-stated primary purpose of the process. "The brevity of the process is not a norm so primary . . . that all others must yield to it."[27] Indeed, "the principle of brevity and celerity is not absolute but is to be subordinate to the supreme

---

22. Cf. ibid., 353, no. 535; "Discorso generale," 63.

23. Cf. *Pars statica*, 355, no. 540.

24. See ibid., 36, no. 52, 3°. For recent use of this terminology of Fr. Gordon citing this very text, see Davide Salvatori, "La rinuncia all'(istanza di) appello dopo una sentenza *pro matrimonii nullitate* alla luce del M.P. *Mitis Iudex Dominus Iesus*," in *Studi in onore di Carlo Gullo*, Annales IV (Vatican City: Libreria Editrice Vaticana, 2017) 3:709, note 10.

25. Cf. *Pars statica*, 82, note 7. On the different kinds of actions and related principles, see ibid., 355–386, nn. 541–615. On the ordinary form of trial, *vide infra* nn. 24–26.

26. *Vide infra* nn. 27–32.

27. See "De appellationibus," 298. He continues: "Adde quod *ratio legis* nequaquam est cum ipsa *lege* confundenda, neque contra clarum legis tenorem ad legis rationem aut ad mentem legislatoris appellare se licet."

principle in the process, which is the acquisition of truth and justice."[28] The goal of celerity "rests on truth and justice," inasmuch as it is a matter of the more expeditious discovery and declaration of the truth.[29]

19. – Indeed, each procedural norm is like a notch, ridge or bit, shoulder, or contour in a key. Each one of them has its function in allowing the key to fit into the keyway and activate the lock mechanism. If the key lacks an essential component, the door will not unlock; but if all the essential components are intact, the door will unlock. Just so, the correct and equitable observance of each procedural norm regulating an essential element of the trial ensures the just discovery of the truth at issue in the cause. If any of them is neglected or violated, the truth will not be discovered, or not be discovered in a just or authentic manner. The trial, then, is the key to unlocking the door to the truth about the controverted matter.[30]

20. – In causes of nullity of marriage and any others pertaining to the *ratio peccati*, the pronouncement of the truth is particularly grave and urgent. For errors are not merely technico-juridical problems but affect the very moral life of the parties. "Any conflict between the external forum and the internal forum is to be avoided, since the same person must be either joined in marriage or free from marriage before the Church and at the same time before God, lest he must be torn apart by contradictory rights and obligations."[31]

C. Judicial Power

21. – The power of the judiciary (*potestas iudiciaria*) is clearly an aspect of that *munus regendi* that is integral to the *sacra potestas* entrusted to the Church by Christ, her divine Founder. It can be defined as "the right of proposing in an obligatory way which actions of the faithful (both of subjects and of superiors) are concretely in conformity with what is just (*ius*), which are in conflict with it, and the legitimate effects of this conformity or lack of conformity."[32] It may also be called contentious power (*potestas contentiosa*) since it is exercised within the

---

28. See "De diverso regimine appellationum," 720, *sub* "*Ad respondendum.*"

29. See "De appellationibus," 292, "*Ad secundum.*"

30. Cf. *Pars statica*, 22, no. 1/26.

31. See "De nimia processuum matrimonialium duratione," 689, no. 209.

32. *Pars statica*, 51, no. 79a: "Potestas *iudiciaria* seu contentiosa definiri potest tanquam ius proponendi modo obligatorio quaenam fidelium (sive subditorum sive superiorum) actiones in concreto sint iuri conformes, quaeque eidem difformes, et effectus legitimos huius conformitatis vel difformitatis."

contradictorium, or procedural dialectic, wherein parties to the contention may make mutual assertions and responses under the authority of the judge. This power of the judiciary (*potestas iudiciaria* or *iudicativa*) is either judicial (*iudicialis*) or administrative (*administrativa*), which is to say, respectively, that its object may be either a controversy between private parties or between an ecclesiastical authority and his subject.[33] In either case, the competent judge is, generally speaking, exercising judicial power. Administrative power (*potestas administrativa*) is exercised in the general governance of the Church outside the context of trials.[34]

22. – That being said, judges have not only judicial power but also "administrative power joined with judicial power" inasmuch as they are superiors within the tribunal. This is distinct from the administrative power over the tribunal enjoyed by the moderators of tribunals, such as the bishop moderator.[35] According to Father Gordon, examples of such acts placed in virtue of administrative power joined with judicial power are the correction and punishment of advocates, procurators, and others intervening in the trial, as well as the admission of a curator (1917 *CIC* cc. 1640 §2, 1651; cf. 1983 *CIC* cc. 1470 §2 and 1479). The judge may be said to exercise "coercive" power when he, for example, punishes negligent ministers of the tribunal, contumacious parties, and witnesses who refuse to appear (1917 *CIC* cc. 1625 §3, 1845 §1, 1766 §2). Moreover, "unless I am mistaken, *ordinatory* decrees proceed from power that is *administrative joined with judicial,*" finding support in Ochoa and Roberti. However, the gathering of proofs is either judicial or administrative insofar as it is carried out within judicial causes or administrative procedures; "it depends on the power from which they [proofs] arise and especially from the act to whose issuance they are directed."[36]

---

33. For some nuances in the public or private character of parties, *vide supra* no. 13.

34. Cf. *Pars statica,* 51–52, 53–58, nn. 79a–c, 80–83; "De Tribunalibus administrativis," 615–616, no. 18; "Normae speciales," 106, no. 77; "De iustitia administrativa ecclesiastica," 254, no. 5, 3).

35. See *Pars statica,* 178–179, nn. 284–285.

36. See Ignacio Gordon, *votum, Nullitatis matrimonii; Incid.: competentiae Signaturae Ap.,* prot. n. 19032/87 CG, March 22[?], 1988: in SSAT Archives. The controversy in which he offered this *votum* involved the character of a Rotal decree advising the Dean of the Rota to call a cause to the Rota's jurisdiction (*avocatio causae*)—a decree Fr. Gordon understood to have an administrative character, joined with judicial power. At the *Congresso* of January 26, 1988, he had been entrusted with drafting the *Congresso's* decree, which was the object of a debate between Fr. Ochoa and Fr. Gordon (see "Relazione," document no. 31, April 7, 1988: in ibid.). Fr. Ochoa gave a *votum* about the draft decree on March 21, 1988, to which *votum* Fr. Gordon was here replying in his undated *votum.* On March 22 the secretary of the Signatura, then-Bishop Zenon Grocholewski, decreed the intervention of the promoter of justice, then-Fr. Frans Daneels, O.Praem. (see document nn. 27–28 in ibid.).

23. – Delegated judicial power is among the traditional and practical aspects of the Church's judiciary. It includes, among other things, the fact that an apostolic tribunal can be constituted by delegation of the Holy See ("ex delegatione S.Sedis").[37] It had been Father Gordon's wish that, "for the sake of clarity . . . all judicial power, not excluding the delegated tribunal," be outlined in the 1983 *CIC*. In this he dissented from the rest of the consultors drafting the revision of the 1917 *CIC*, who favored the elimination of the canons on the delegated tribunal.[38] He had also wanted to preserve the ground of un-appealability of the sentence issued in virtue of delegation to which the clause "appellatione remota" is attached (1917 *CIC* c. 1880, 2º), but this was not accepted.[39] Still, he would point out that such a sentence was nevertheless un-appealable if that clause were added to the mandate, even if it was judged superfluous to state this in the law.[40]

D. The Object of the Judicial Process

24. – The object of the trial is, in general, the pursuit or vindication of rights or the declaration of a juridical fact on the one hand, or the declaration or imposition of a penalty on the other hand (1917 *CIC* c. 1552 §2; 1983 *CIC* c. 1400). This corresponds to the two kinds of trials: the contentious trial and the criminal or penal trial.

25. – The ordinary contentious trial is the "normal" form of the judicial process in the canonical system. It has much in common with the solemn form of the old Roman process, but in it "the legislator strives that this judicial process become briefer than the solemn trial, whose structure it imitates," even while it has "fewer formalities." There is also a summary process—the oral contentious trial—but it is "rarely used."[41]

The name of the part in the 1976 schema on the ordinary form of the trial was "On the contentious trial in general." This clearly distinguished it from the

---

37. *Pars statica*, 81, no. 120, 3º.

38. See PCCICR Archives, *vol. 181. XI. De processibus. Sessio IIˆ-Series IIˆdiebus 15–19 maii 1978 habita. Relatio*, 40; *Communicationes* 10 (1978) 244.

39. Cf. PCCICR Archives, *vol. 181. XI. De processibus. Sessio Vˆ Series IIˆdiebus 11–16 decembris 1978 habita. Relatio*, 148; *Communicationes* 11 (1979) 149.

40. Cf. *Processus nullitatis matrimonii*, 80, f; *Novus processus nullitatis matrimonii*, 45, note 6.

41. See *Pars statica*, 17, 81, nn. 22, 120, 2º. In fact, he even proposed that it be suppressed "since use of such a procedural track will be minimal in consideration of the prohibition to treat matrimonial causes with the oral contentious process" (PCCICR Archives, *vol. 181. XI. De processibus. Sessio VIˆ Series IIˆdiebus 26–31 martii 1979 habita. Relatio*, 166; *Communicationes* 11 [1979] 248).

criminal or penal trial, but Father Gordon wanted it to be clear that it was in fact "the basis for every kind of process." And so he thought it should be called "On the evolution of the process"—that is, the manner in which any judicial process is to be carried out. This intervention no doubt helped influence the decision to include the adjective "ordinary" to describe the contentious trial.[42] Once the code was promulgated, he repeated the teaching that the "ordinary contentious trial… is the process that is the basis for all specific trials, contentious or penal (cf. cc. 1691, 1710, 1728 §1)."[43]

26. – Father Gordon wrote little about the penal trial.[44] One teaching he would stress, though, is that the most basic material distinction of trials is between the contentious and the criminal or penal trial. All causes whose object is not the commission of some delict are contentious causes; but when the question of a delict is itself the object of the trial, it is a criminal or penal trial.

Also, while admitting that this is not stated in the *CIC*, Father Gordon in one place distinguished between a criminal trial and penal trial: the one (*iudicium criminale*) is an investigation into whether a delict exists; the other (*iudicium poenale*) is carried out when its existence is already established but the imposition of the punishment has to be accomplished.[45] Elsewhere, however, he seems to presume their synonymy.[46] It appears that this distinction in his doctrine is based on the equivocal language of the 1917 *CIC*, while not referring truly to two different kinds of actions or trials.

---

42. Cf. PCCICR Archives, *vol. 181. XI. De processibus. Sessio III⸺ Series II˄diebus 23–28 octobris 1978 habita. Relatio*, 83; *Communicationes* 11 (1979) 82.

43. "Elementi innovativi nei processi," 8. The first cited canon is now c. 1691 §3 in virtue of promulgation of *MI*.

44. Fr. Gordon, like Ciprotti, proposed his own draft of what would become c. 1720 of the 1983 *CIC* on the imposition or declaration of a penalty *per decretum extra iudicium*. His fellow consultors found it to be "too scholastic," though they did incorporate some of its components, such as the consultation of two assessors and the certainty of the delict. Cf. PCCICR Archives, *vol. 181. XI. De processibus. Sessio VIII⸺ Series II˄diebus 26, 28 et 29 februarii 1980 habita. Relatio*, 5; *Communicationes* 12 (1980) 192–193.

45. Cf. *Pars statica*, 84–85, no. 121.3. Therefore, a criminal action would be a judicial petition for the imposition or declaration of a penalty, while a penal action would be a judicial petition for the execution of a penalty already imposed or for a declaration of it. However, the latter would seem to be not judicial activity but administrative activity, whereby the interested party would ask the competent authority to carry out (or execute) what was established as a result of the criminal trial (cf. ibid., 385, no. 612, as well as 357, no. 545, at c).

46. "[In foro delicti] proponi possunt omnes actiones criminales seu poenales" (ibid., 138, no. 203).

E. The Celerity of the Process

27. – As was mentioned above, Father Gordon's extensive study on the excessive duration of marriage nullity trials in the praxis of tribunals was highly influential during the work of revision of Book IV of the 1917 *CIC, De processibus*.[47] His reflection on that ecclesial problem extended beyond that foundational study and was a theme to which he returned throughout his academic life. For these reasons, his doctrinal contribution to this practical problem is significant and is widely recognized by canonical doctrine.[48]

28. – Father Gordon taught that speed is not laudable *sic et simpliciter*, nor is it the principal goal of the judicial process.[49] On the contrary, it may in fact victimize the parties by the commission of injustice on the part of those who should be administering justice. Speed is a measure of time but not an intrinsic goal of the process. It constitutes the temporal measure of the administration of jus-tice, such that the Church "may more quickly and better provide for truth

---

47. *Vide supra* Chapter I, no. 8.

48. See, e.g., Romualdo Rodrigo, "Cur optata a m.p. 'Causas matrimoniales' celeritas haud semper obtinetur?" *Periodica* 62 (1973) 525; Charles Lefebvre, "De motu proprio 'Causas matrimoniales,'" *Periodica* 61 (1972) 401–402; Piero Antonio Bonnet, *Il giudizio di nullità matrimoniale nei casi speciali*, Studia et documenta iuris canonici IX (Rome: Catholic Book Agency, 1979) 30, note 68; Javier Ochoa, "La figura canónica del procurador y abogado público," in *Dilexit iustitiam. Studia in honorem Aurelii Card. Sabattani*, ed. Zenon Grocholewski and Vicente Cárcel Ortí (Vatican City: Libreria Editrice Vaticana, 1984) 279, note 72; Velasio De Paolis, "Il processo penale nel nuovo Codice," in ibid., 477, note 13; Francesco D'Ostilio, "La durata media delle cause matrimoniali," *Monitor Ecclesiasticus* 114 (1989) 185–236, *passim* (see 185, note 110); Piero Antonio Bonnet, "L'attuazione e il funzionamento dell'attività giudiziaria nella Chiesa. Verità e giustizia nel processo canonico," in *La giustizia nella Chiesa: fondamento divino e cultura processualistica moderna*, Studi Giuridici 45 (Vatican City: Libreria Editrice Vaticana, 1997) 105; Raúl Román Sánchez, "La duración de los procesos canónicos de nulidad matrimonial," in *Curso de derecho matrimonial y procesal canónico para profesionales del foro (XV)*, Estudios 220, ed. Federico R. Aznar Gil (Salamanca: Publicaciones Universidad Pontificia, 2000) 235–263, esp. 249, 253; Carlo Fantappiè, "La duplice sentenza conforme: biografia di una norma nel quadro della legislazione matrimoniale," in *La doppia conforme nel processo matrimoniale. Problemi e prospettive*, Studi Giuridici 60 (Vatican City: Libreria Editrice Vaticana, 2003) 50; Piero Antonio Bonnet, "Il principio della duplice decisione giudiziaria conforme ed il suo fondamento," in ibid., 87, 96; Bassiano Uggé, *La fase preliminare/abbreviata del processo di nullità del matrimonio in secondo grado di giudizio a norma del can. 1682 §2*, Tesi Gregoriana – Serie Diritto Canonico 60 (Rome: Editrice Pontificia Università Gregoriana, 2003) 20–29; Luigi Sabbarese, "Semplicità e celerità nel processo matrimoniale canonico," in *Il giudizio di nullità matrimoniale dopo l'Istruzione "Dignitas connubii." Parte Prima: I principi*, Studi Giuridici 75, ed. Piero Antonio Bonnet and Carlo Gullo (Vatican City: Libreria Editrice Vaticana, 2007) 270, note 36, *et passim*.

49. *Vide supra* no. 18.

and justice."[50] Speed is a legitimate ancillary goal extrinsic to the process, which can be pursued while also administering justice in a serious way.[51] This is enshrined in the adage, *quam primum, salva iustitia*, stated in the 1917 *CIC* in the context of the ideal maximum length of a trial: within two years in first instance and one year in second instance.[52] However, Father Gordon could agree that twelve months would be, while not always possible, "an ideal duration" for first instance.[53]

29. – A grave concern that Father Gordon expressed in his reflections about the duration of trials pertained to unnecessary delay. His own reflection on human life, as well as the statements of other scholars and the Church's pastors, led him to see that such delays can frequently cause spiritual damage, psychological frustration, irreparable consequences (e.g., losing the opportunity to marry a particular person or bear children), and mistrust of the Church's tribunals.[54] Such delay is a true injustice, but it is not primarily caused by the law itself, or a normative defect, as much as by practical problems in the administration of justice. "It is illusory to hope that by the reformation of the procedure *alone*, briefer duration of matrimonial causes, which is everyone's wish, will be achieved." What is "necessary above all is the removal of impediments," or human factors.[55] In his first published work in the area of procedural law, he explains succinctly:

> Experience teaches that the protraction of causes—which occurs not without the grave harm of souls—happens especially for two reasons: *the first* is

---

50. See "De appellationibus," 316.

51. "De Tribunalibus Regionalibus," 595: "Nec timendum est quod celeritas serietati iudicii noceat." He underlines that the goal of celerity was maintained from the earliest centuries of the Church's judicial activity (cf. *Pars statica*, 9, no. 12).

52. "Can. 1620. Iudices et Tribunalia curent ut quamprimum, salva iustitia, causae omnes terminentur, utque in tribunali primae instantiae ultra biennium non protrahantur, in tribunali vero secundae instantiae ultra annum." *Vide supra* Chapter IV, no. 9.

53. See "De nimia processuum matrimonialium duratione," 499, no. 10.

54. See ibid., 504–506, nn. 20–25.

55. See ibid., 735, no. 314, 1º. This was supported explicitly by the relator of the *coetus de processibus*, who declared: "Ignatius Gordon S.J. in suo recenti studio: 'De nimia processuum matr. duratione' (Periodica de re morali, etc., 1969, p. 491–594) invenit quinque causas huius mendae: [*vide infra* no. 30]. Conditores iuris processualis relatis incommodis providere nequeunt. Imo subscribo toto corde sequentia verba auctoris: '*breviata procedura, si illae causae non corrigantur, diuturnitas processuum fere ubique permanebit*' (ibid. p.508). Ideo—sicuti fere semper accidit—defectus, magis quam in lege, invenitur in hominibus." See "Relatio quam, supra vota Consultorum, apparavit *Aurelius Sabattani, Archiep. Iustinianen.*, Relator in eodem coetu," prot. n. 2037/69, October 13, 1969: in PCCICR Archives, *vol. 175, XI. De processibus, Sessio VIII^ diebus 20–25 octobris 1969 habita*, second folder, at 14, C.

because judges and ministers, prevented or distracted by other cares, neglect the responsibility of judging; therefore illegitimate delays are multiplied at the different steps of the process, from the examining of the *libellus* up to the publication of the sentence. *The second* reason is that judges, even if they work strenuously, are burdened with a multitude of causes which therefore cannot be decided within due time.[56]

30. – Additional research and reflection would later lead him to identify the following as the five main reasons for delays in the administration of justice: 1) insufficient numbers of ministers of justice, which is "the first and foundational reason," 2) insufficient remuneration of ministers of justice, 3) lack of preparation of many judges, 4) the negligence of parties and tribunal officials, and 5) delays caused by advocates. Added to this is 6) some elements of procedural law itself, specific reforms of which would reduce delays. These he described, respectively, as causes that depend upon persons and those that depend upon procedure.[57] He commented that Pope Paul VI addressed both dimensions—the reform of tribunal praxis and of procedural law itself—by means of both his reform of the Roman Curia (*REU*), in which he enhanced and directed vigilance over the administration of justice, and his simplification of the marriage nullity process (*CM*), especially in regard to the competent forum, the constitution of tribunals, and appeals.[58]

31. – The undue protraction of a trial causes frustration for anyone intervening in or affected even by a cause that does not immediately pertain to the *ratio peccati*. It is indeed unfortunate when "a cause which seems plenty clear in regard to the merits of the matter" is unnecessarily extended "due to a question that was ill placed from the beginning, due to delays employed by the Sacred Roman Rota"—speaking of a particular case—"and especially due to the multiplied requests of the advocate not immune from error," causing the trial to become "a true labyrinth."[59] Whatever the object of the trial, procedural law should anticipate

---

56. See "De Tribunalibus Regionalibus," 592–593.

57. Cf. "De nimia processuum matrimonialium duratione," esp. 508, no. 27 and 509, no. 28; 735, no. 314. For summary remarks on the duration of the process, see "Dichiarazione di nullità," 144, §4,1.

58. Cf. *Adnotationes in m.p. "Causas matrimoniales,"* 242–243, no. 1c.

59. See Ignacio Gordon, *votum* ("De recursu ad S.Tribunal Signaturae Apostolicae contra decretum Decani S.R.Rotae dierum 21–25 octobris in una [X]"), prot. n. 715/68 CG, July 7, 1969: in SSAT Archives, 1.

possible attempts of manipulation by an obstructionistic party, lest he be able to "paralyze the process or compromise the triumph of the truth."[60]

This concern led him to praise certain elements of the reform of the procedural law of the Papal States by Pope Pius VII in the year 1817. That reform, among other things, brought about "greater brevity and simplicity to the extent that they can be coordinated with the thoroughness of trials; the banishment of useless formalities; ... the omission of forensic subtleties with which one party's defenders detail the fulfillment of obligations, causing harm to the other party."[61]

32. – As is well known, it was highly anticipated during the first half of the revision of the 1917 *CIC* that a hierarchy of administrative tribunals would be established in the Church, including tribunals at the local level. This is something that Father Gordon theoretically favored,[62] but it did not come to fruition. One benefit he saw to the legislator's choice to exclude administrative controversies from the competence of ordinary judicial tribunals is the alleviation and speeding up of their work—or, perhaps better, burdening them less. This for him was something to be celebrated, since it could have the effect also of "bringing the peace of Christ more rapidly to the hearts of the faithful who become subject to matrimonial processes."[63]

F. Vigilance over Judicial Activity

33. – Those entrusted with judicial power in the Church are bound not only to exercise it effectively but also correctly. Ministers of justice and those who supervise them are thus always to see to the *good* or correct administration of justice (*bona iustitiae administratio*).[64]

34. – To this end, Father Gordon underscored the importance of the function of the "central organism" of government that exercises vigilance over the correct administration of justice. At the beginning of his academic life, this organism was

---

60. See "El M. P. '*Causas matrimoniales*' y las normas americanas," 204. In this context, he was siding with authors who thought requiring the consent of the parties prior to transferring a cause to another tribunal (*CM* IV §3) was excessive, since one could withhold consent for wicked ends. It would have been better to require a prior hearing of the parties.

61. See "Codificationes legum," 84.

62. *Vide infra* Chapter IX, no. 8; Chapter X, no. 2 (§4).

63. See "La renovación de la Signatura Apostólica," 610, no. 156.

64. Cf. "De Tribunalibus Regionalibus," 596; "De nimia processuum matrimonialium duratione," 732, no. 305.

the Sacred Congregation for the Discipline of the Sacraments; beginning in 1967, following the reform of Pope Paul VI, it was the Supreme Tribunal of the Apostolic Signatura.[65] Such vigilance bears a resemblance to that of a department of justice in secular government (a *Ministerium Iustitiae*, as he identified it). It offers a positive service that is "basically necessary so that . . . tribunals may proceed correctly in their praxis."

At the same time, he recognized that the particular supervision over the work of a tribunal "cannot be multiplied. . . , since some tension can be created" between the bishop moderator of the tribunal and the dicastery. And so, for example, while the dicastery is competent to confer offices on ministers of justice, this is probably not agreeable in practice. On the other hand, the local authority would unjustly undermine the service of the dicastery were he to make inopportune comments about the interventions of the Apostolic Signatura. This can have the regrettable effect of "neutraliz[ing] the efficacy of the Signatura's notification."[66] Avoiding tensions and misunderstandings, all involved should come to see the work of vigilance as an expression of "care" (*cura*), "special attention" (*specialis attentio*), and "protection" (*tutela*) over the sacred goods of the Church.[67]

G. Jurisprudence

35. – Vigilance over the correct administration of justice includes supervision over the correctness of jurisprudence.[68] This does not strive to achieve "the unification of jurisprudence, impeding a sound diversity of opinions in judicial sentences," but "to correct and suppress" whatever is found to be "false and arbitrary in the sentences of tribunals."[69] This kind of vigilance has a posterior and extrinsic character, and it is most useful. However, it needs to be complemented by the ministry of a superior apostolic tribunal (viz., the Roman Rota), which can exercise a "prior, positive, constant and, as it were, intrinsic influence." For it is in a

---

65. *REU* 105; *NS* art. 17 §1. At that time, it was part of the so-called first section (*Sectio prima*) of the Signatura, though now it is part of the informally termed *sectio tertia* of the same dicastery (cf. *LP* artt. 35, 106–121).

66. See "El M. P. '*Causas matrimoniales*' y las normas americanas," 195, note 13. The particular case in question was one in which certain abuses were identified and corrected by the Apostolic Signatura, which asked the president of the U.S. conference of bishops to transmit its letter to all the bishops of the nation. In so doing, the president was dismissive of the concerns, and Fr. Gordon found his remarks to lack objectivity and appropriateness.

67. Cf. "De Tribunalibus Regionalibus," 588–589, 591.

68. *NS*, art. 17 §1; *LP* art. 111 §§1 and 3.

69. See "La renovación de la Signatura Apostólica," 578, 579, nn. 25, 27.

position to influence and exercise jurisdiction over the very decisions of tribunals, thus judging (confirming or correcting, in whole or in part) the specific jurisprudence employed in the particular case.[70]

36. – Father Gordon underscored the important distinction between the jurisprudence of secular tribunals and that of the Church, and of the Roman Rota in particular. While the former often has the character of new law, this is not so in the Church. The Rota's "jurisprudence, especially since the seventeenth century, has exercised great influence over other tribunals, but it is not that it binds them to conform their sentences with Rotal decisions." This is due to the distinction of powers and the principle of the free evaluation of proofs. In other words, while "on the one hand, it effectively contributes to the necessary unity to be obtained in judging, . . . on the other hand, it recognizes the dignity and freedom of each judge, who in issuing the sentence is only bound by the acts and what is proven, which are to be evaluated in accord with the law and one's conscience." These sources (the *acta et probata*) are that from which the judge draws moral certitude or not. He does not have a dependence on jurisprudence, which itself sometimes contains conflicting criteria. And he "is never compelled" to act at the prompting of or in immediate conformity with it, especially with some particular decision.[71]

Because of these factors, the correct administration of justice can involve "a certain moderate disagreement in jurisprudence." In other words, a lack of perfect uniformity between tribunals or between an inferior tribunal and the Roman Rota is not inconceivable. Nevertheless, justice has been correctly administered only if "the disagreeing sentences are solidly founded."[72]

---

70. Cf. "De nimia processuum matrimonialium duratione," 732–733, no. 306.

71. See Ignacio Gordon, *votum* ("De quibusdam quaestionibus circa competentiam S. T. Signaturae Apostolicae"), *Nullitatis matrimonii*, prot. n. 35/70 CG, May 3, 1970: in SSAT Archives, 3–4, nn. 6–10.

72. See ibid., 5, no. 12.

CHAPTER VI

The *Pars statica*

1. – As is explained above,[1] the *pars statica* of the judicial process includes especially the institutions of the Church's judiciary viewed in themselves, from the extrajudicial perspective. It also includes the disciplinary rules of procedural law that apply to these institutions and to the trial in general. This chapter does not pretend to do justice to Father Gordon's full contribution to the *pars statica*, which is enshrined in his large *dispensa* treating it. Rather, let it suffice here to draw attention to those institutes to which he seemed to give particular emphasis or to offer a marked contribution.

A. Tribunals

1. The Hierarchy of Tribunals in General

2. – In principle, the hierarchy of tribunals is three-tiered; that is, there are necessarily three levels of jurisdiction: the first, second, and third. This is because,

---

1. *Vide supra* Chapter IV, nn. 23 and 25.

after the completion of the third level at most, there would ordinarily be a double conformity of sentences, the object of litigation thus becoming a *res iudicata*.[2] The norm of justice expressed in the institute of the appeal, classically understood to flow from the fallibility of human judgments, demands this:

> For in view of human fallibility, even judges can be wrong. And consequently, if only a single level [of jurisdiction] were given, the injury of a right inflicted by a sentence would become irreparable. It therefore pertains to the effective protection of rights that no *res iudicata* come about by a single sentence [unless a sentence is not appealed] but only by a double conformity, which contributes greater security from any human error.[3]

3. – The integrity of judging at each level demands both autonomy and subordination in different respects. On the one hand, ecclesiastical tribunals enjoy autonomy. This autonomy ensures that they may issue decisions without subordination to their superiors, who can only insist on observance of the law and the use of a correct jurisprudence.[4] And it is a judicial autonomy, which envisions juridical independence from superior tribunals in the treatment of causes; such tribunals as a rule—with only limited exceptions (e.g., ordering admission of a *libellus*)[5]—intervene in a cause only after it has entered their jurisdiction. On the other hand, tribunals always exist in a position of subordination. This subordination is administrative in nature, since it is in relation to their immediate superior (e.g., the bishop moderator of the tribunal) and the Apostolic Signatura.[6]

4. – It is somewhat ideal that an appellate tribunal would be exclusively an appellate tribunal, since it is thus given the opportunity to dedicate itself to a particular manner of examining causes. The question of whether a definitive sentence is to be confirmed or reformed—in whatever way is prescribed by law, such as by a decree of immediate confirmation or not, or by a definitive sentence after carrying out an ordinary appellate process—has a complexity that is best reserved to those specially trained and dedicated to it. The expertise that results from "the homogenous quality of the study to be completed by judges" and "makes the

---

2. Cf. *Pars statica*, 163, no. 255. For other references to the ascent of a cause through the three levels, see ibid., 164, 167, 280, nn. 256, 5°, 262, 404 (at b); "De Tribunalibus administrativis," 638, no. 42.

3. See "De Tribunalibus administrativis," 639, no. 46.

4. *Vide supra* Chapter V, nn. 33–35.

5. 1917 *CIC* c. 1709 §3; 1983 *CIC* c. 1505 §4.

6. Cf. *Pars statica*, 170–171, nn. 269–270.

work lighter" is in fact a service to the Church and especially to the parties, since it fosters "a notable increase of the celerity" of the process.[7] In other words, "the judges become more excellent in their specific function and work more freely and easily."[8]

2. Interdiocesan (Regional) Tribunals[9]

5. – Father Gordon sustained a firm conviction that regional tribunals foster the more expeditious administration of justice, in comparison to diocesan tribunals. For, stated simply, they allow for the accumulation not only of personnel but also of financial resources.[10] He writes: "An effective solution [to lengthy trials], unless we are mistaken, is the erection of regional tribunals. They can adjudicate and decide an even greater number of causes than now—that is, with a lesser number of priests and with great speed, namely, with that speed which today's rhythm of life and psychology demand."[11] This is "the optimal solution to . . . almost all difficulties which retard matrimonial causes";[12] such tribunals

---

7. See "De Tribunalibus Regionalibus," 595. He would reiterate this point when examining the draft decree of particular regional tribunals; see Ignacio Gordon, *votum* ("Tribunalia Regionialia in [X] erigenda"), prot. n. 437/70 VT, September 8, 1971: in SSAT Archives, 1–2, no. 3, 2º.

8. See "De nimia processuum matrimonialium duratione," 554, no. 99.

9. In 1972, he explained that he meant "regional" in a generic sense, including any kind of "super-diocesan" tribunal: interdiocesan, provincial, regional (i.e., of a "conciliar" or "pastoral" region), interprovincial, or interregional (see "La renovación de la Signatura Apostólica," 582, no. 41).

10. Cf. "De nimia processuum matrimonialium duratione," 522, no. 46 and 553, no. 97. For a recognition of Fr. Gordon's convictions in the matter, see, e.g., Romualdo Rodrigo, "Cur optata a m.p. 'Causas matrimoniales' celeritas haud semper obtinetur?" *Periodica* 62 (1973) 540–542; Thomas J. Green, "Marriage Nullity Processes in the Schema *De Processibus,*" *The Jurist* 38 (1978) 326, 330; Rinaldo Bertolino, *La tutela dei diritti nella Chiesa. Dal vecchio al nuovo Codice di Diritto Canonico* (Turin: G. Giappichelli Editore, 1983) 95; Cesare Zaggia, "I tribunali interdiocesani o regionali nella vita della Chiesa," in *Dilexit iustitiam. Studia in honorem Aurelii Card. Sabattani,* ed. Zenon Grocholewski and Vicente Cárcel Ortí (Vatican City: Libreria Editrice Vaticana, 1984) 122–123, 139.

11. See "De nimia processuum matrimonialium duratione," 560, no. 110. This was also his argument within the *Coetus de processibus* in response to the proposal of eliminating the necessary second examination of a matrimonial cause decided in the affirmative in light of the high number of causes, and difficulties in organizing and staffing tribunals. He stated that "the solution is available to all of establishing regional tribunals, at least for second instance, in order to satisfy contingent necessities with united efforts" (PCCICR Archives, *vol. 181. XI. De processibus. Sessio VI⸱ Series II ˆdiebus 26–31 martii 1979 habita. Relatio,* 190; *Communicationes* 11 [1979] 266–267).

12. See "De nimia processuum matrimonialium duratione," 735, no. 314, 3º. His attention to regional tribunals is observed also, e.g., in his intervention resulting in the exception stated in c. 1438, 1º (see PCCICR Archives, *vol. 181. XI. De processibus. Sessio IIˆ-Series IIˆdiebus 15–19 maii 1978 habita. Relatio,* 38; *Communicationes* 10 [1978] 242).

"practically constitute in many cases the ideal solution for the correct and swift administration of ecclesiastical justice."[13]

6. – Regional tribunals are rightly erected by the bishops whose causes will be judged by it. Thus, for example, if a regional tribunal encompasses only a portion of the dioceses in a nation, its approval is not given by the conference of bishops but only by the bishops involved.[14] However, they need the *recognitio* or approval of the Apostolic See. For this "clearly solves the problem of the origin of these tribunals' jurisdiction," which they acquire "by the intervention of the Roman Pontiff." It also ensures that there be general supervision over the undue multiplication of such tribunals "without need and with the dispersing of resources."[15] In theory, the Apostolic Signatura could erect such a tribunal itself, though this was (and is) exceptional.[16]

7. – As a rule, regional or interdiocesan tribunals are competent solely to treat the most frequently recurring causes introduced before the Church's tribunals, namely, causes of nullity of marriage: "The name 'regional tribunals' refers to the tribunals established by the Holy See for some territory or region, encompassing at least several dioceses, having ordinary jurisdiction to decide all causes concerning nullity of marriage which arise within the limits of that territory."[17]

Quite notable for Father Gordon, therefore, was the May 18, 1965 decree of the Sacred Congregation of the Consistory, approved by Pope Paul VI, which constituted the tribunals of Toulouse and Rodez as, respectively, a first and second instance interdiocesan tribunal, such that they would judge "all causes, whether contentious or criminal, which should be deferred to their competent forum in the common law."[18] For that decree concentrated the exclusive judicial

---

13. See "La renovación de la Signatura Apostólica," 583, no. 44.

14. Cf. Ignacio Gordon, *votum* ("Tribunalia Regionialia in [X] erigenda"), prot. n. 437/70 VT, September 8, 1971: in SSAT Archives, 2, no. 3, 4°: "Cum Tribunalia appellationis non sint nationalia sed *regionalia* tantum, non sunt approbanda ab omnibus Episcopis totius Nationis, seu a Conferentia Episcopali [X]." Nevertheless, he favored the competence of the conference of bishops to establish a regional first instance tribunal, presumably requiring the approval of the Apostolic Signatura (cf. PCCICR Archives, *vol. 181. XI. De processibus. Series II': Sessio I'diebus 3–8 aprilis 1978 habita. Relatio,* 28; *Communicationes* 10 [1978] 232).

15. See "Normae speciales," 147, note 4.

16. Cf. "La renovación de la Signatura Apostólica," 583, no. 43.

17. See "De Tribunalibus Regionalibus," 580; "De nimia processuum matrimonialium duratione," 552, no. 94.

18. See Sacred Congregation of the Consistory, *Tolosanae-Ruthenensis et aliarum,* decree *De causis agendis,* May 18, 1965: *AAS* 57 (1965) 1006–1007. On this decree, see also *Pars statica,* 259, no. 383.

competence of eleven territories in two judicial organs, leaving any diocesan tribunals "practically suppressed" in divergence from the norm of law according to which the diocesan bishop is the judge of first instance and is to constitute a tribunal.[19] This is different than the case of a regional tribunal endowed with limited material jurisdiction, since the bishop remains judge and can entrust causes to his tribunal; whereas in the case of these French tribunals, no diocesan tribunals existed.

With some concern, then, Father Gordon thought that, with that decree, "a way is opened which can lead to a profound transformation of the ordering of tribunals in the Church, or at least in some of her parts."[20] However, while at the time that arrangement seemed exceptional, it has in fact become the consistent praxis of the Apostolic Signatura, since those who regularly administer justice in an interdiocesan tribunal in causes of nullity of marriage are likely the ones best equipped to judge other kinds of causes that rarely occur.[21]

8. – That development led him to distinguish between regional tribunals that are *special* and *general*—that is, having jurisdiction over a particular kind of cause or over all causes.[22] Special could also have been considered "particular," but the chosen term is felicitous because, as was said, it is usually a matter of causes of nullity of marriage. Such causes are understood by doctrine to be "special" inasmuch as they are governed by their own norms, which somewhat diverge from the general norms of procedural law.[23]

9. – The examination of questions arising in regard to individual regional tribunals was the object of several of his *vota* written for the Apostolic Signatura. In one, the bishop moderator of a regional tribunal erected just prior to the coming into effect of *REU* was in doubt about the force of the norms governing the supervision of his tribunal by the Apostolic See. For the Signatura had issued its own norms after competence in this matter had been transferred to it by Pope Paul VI in 1967. Father Gordon maintained that this uncertainty of the bishops "has real

---

19. 1917 *CIC* cc. 1572 §1, 1573 §1; 1983 *CIC* cc. 391 §2, 1419 §1, 1420 §1.

20. See "De Tribunalibus Regionalibus," 585.

21. Cf. Raymond Leo Burke, "The Relation between the Apostolic Signatura and the Particular Churches," *The Jurist* 74 (2014) 16.

22. Cf. "De nimia processuum matrimonialium duratione," 553, no. 96; a general regional tribunal was presented by Fr. Gordon as a clear exception in his "De Tribunalibus Regionalibus" (586 and 585).

23. This is why the legislator offers a separate treatment "on certain special processes" in Part III of Book VII of the *CIC* 1983 (*De quibusdam processibus specialibus*).

foundation" since there was no derogating clause in the Signatura's norms. Accordingly, he advised that the Signatura request from the Roman Pontiff the faculty to derogate from the prior norms.[24] In fact, however, the reorganization of the tribunals in the nation in question was to take place immediately; and so Father Gordon later offered his *vota* on the decrees of erection proposed by the conference of bishops—a service that he would repeat with some frequency.[25]

3. The Supreme Tribunal of the Apostolic Signatura

10. – The Supreme Tribunal of the Apostolic Signatura is the tribunal at the "apex" or "summit of the hierarchy of tribunals."[26] For, even though it has special competence, this includes judicial competence in relation to the other tribunals, both the Rota and inferior tribunals. It is thus an important component of the treatment of the *pars statica* of procedural law. Nevertheless, its treatment in this work is reserved for its own chapter (Chapter VIII), since Father Gordon dedicated much doctrinal attention to its history and current structure.

4. The Tribunal of the Roman Rota[27]

11. – The Rota is the "permanently established judicial apostolic tribunal" to which the Roman Pontiff would ordinarily entrust judicial causes deferred to

---

24. Cf. Ignacio Gordon, *votum*, prot. n. 267/68 VT, in SSAT Archives, *Libro Cassa 1969–1980* (November 4, 1971) esp. 3, nn. 6–8. His view seemed to change on this point, since in 1972 he stated that the Signatura's norms derogated from most of those given by the Sacred Congregation for the Sacraments (cf. "La renovación de la Signatura Apostólica," 583, no. 45). He would later observe, however, that the Signatura's norms did not derogate from the particular norms internal to the regional tribunals themselves ("Responsio nonnullis quaestionibus," 640; cf. Zaggia, 149).

25. Cf. Ignacio Gordon, *votum* ("De schemate decreti erectionis quinque Tribunalium Regionalium in [X]"), prot. n. 267/68 VT (Cart.Spplem.), October 30, 1970: in SSAT Archives, *Libro Cassa 1969–1980*. He later offered another examination of the decree: *votum* ("Tribunalia Regionalia pro [X]. Alterum examen. decr. erectionis"), prot. n. 267/68 VT, February 16, 1972: in ibid. Other examples of his examination of draft decrees of erection include the following: *votum* ("De erectione Tribunalium [A] in [B]"), prot. n. 452/70 VT, November 19, 1970: in SSAT Archives; *votum* ("[Y]. Reorganizzazione Tribunali Ecclesiastici"), prot. n. 265/70 VT, May 28, 1971: in ibid. (which, despite its title, is written in Latin); *votum* ("Tribunalia Regionialia in [X] erigenda"), prot. n. 437/70 VT, September 8, 1971: in ibid.; *votum* ("Annotationes ad schema decreti pro erectione Tribunalium Regionalium in [Z]"), prot. n. 1743/71 VT, January 19, 1972: in SSAT Archives, *Libro Cassa 1969–1980*; *votum*, prot. n. 265/70 VT, June 30, 1972: in SSAT Archives.

26. See *Pars statica*, 167, 169, nn. 262, 266; "Normae speciales," 96, no. 44.

27. For a description of the Rota's history, name, structure, manner of proceeding, and competence, see *Pars statica*, 266–283, nn. 391–412.

him.[28] For this reason, "it is rightly considered the mightiest of all [tribunals] in the Church."[29] It is "a Tribunal for the first appeal," not for third instance only. And so its jurisdiction is "concurrent with" that of "ordinary appellate tribunals."[30]

12. – It might seem to enhance the celerity and simplicity of the process for all appeals to be potentially handled more locally without needing to rely on the Roman Rota, because that would mean that the judicial acts would not have to be transmitted to Rome and translated, and because there is a great familiarity with particular cultural factors in the nation where events pertaining to the object of the trial transpired.[31] However, the institution of regional or national third instance tribunals would severely compromise the unity of jurisprudence in the Church: "Decentralization of third instance would not only diminish the influence of the Sacred Roman Rota on making a unity of jurisprudence but even almost suppress it." Were such regional third instance tribunals to be established, the Roman Rota would examine fewer lower-level sentences, allowing local judges "more easily to indulge in their own opinions." In the end, the use of "more benign—dare I say lax!—tribunals" would bring about "a most grave detriment to the faithful and the Christian family."[32] There really "cannot be a place for decentralization in this matter."[33]

5. The Collaboration of Tribunals

13. – The institute of the rogatorial commission is stated in law as a right of each tribunal to call upon others for assistance, whether in the communication of some act, in the collection of some proof, or some other kind of service best carried out locally.[34] Conversely, "all tribunals have the duty to assist any tribunal requesting collaboration." Unfortunately, though, "in practice many tribunals very negligently satisfy this obligation, either because they are silent for long months or because they complete their task imperfectly such that the acts are to be treated as null."[35]

---

28. See "De Tribunalibus administrativis," 632, note 18. See also "Normae speciales," 95, "De 4º."

29. See "De obiecto primario competentiae," 526–527.

30. See "De appellationibus," 292.

31. "It happens not rarely before the Sacred Roman Rota" that a cause will suffer delay, even in making a preliminary decision about its admission. See Ignacio Gordon, *votum* ("De recursu ad S.Tribunal Signaturae Apostolicae contra decretum Decani S.R.Rotae dierum 21–25 octobris in una [X]"), prot. n. 715/68 CG, July 7, 1969: in SSAT Archives, 12, no. 38.

32. See "De nimia processuum matrimonialium duratione," 731–732, nn. 302–303.

33. See ibid., 733, no. 309.

34. See 1917 *CIC* c. 1570 §2; 1983 *CIC* c. 1418.

35. See "De nimia processuum matrimonialium duratione," 537, no. 72.

14. – Father Gordon taught that a rogatorial letter was to be sent not to the judicial vicar of the tribunal but its bishop moderator.[36] This is not a common practice, but it is a rational position to hold. For the ministers of the tribunal exercise the bishop's judicial function within the diocese. They do not have the innate competence to represent that judicial function *ad extra*. Conversely, any tribunal may presume that external judicial activity intersecting with a diocese would be under the authority of its bishop moderator, who in law is also the judge of that diocese. Therefore, it is he who is the appropriate authority to approach. If he should wish the ministers of his tribunal to be approached or to approach other tribunals directly, a special mandate should be given to them, especially to the judicial vicar, though perhaps also to other judges.

B. The Competent Forum

1. General Notion and Titles of Competence

15. – Father Gordon defines competence as "the concrete part or portion of jurisdiction legitimately assigned to each judge." Such portions are allotted by the competent authority "in order to make the administration of justice simpler and fairer." Each title or source of competence is ultimately a matter of "a concession of the legislator."[37]

16. – He states that competence is allotted for determined persons, for a certain level of jurisdiction, and for a territory, but he omits mention of the matter of the trial (*materia litis*), or material (in)competence. Rather he "absorb[s] the object of causes in the determination of persons." References to the matter of the trial are made especially in relation to the nature of the trial and to the determination of special procedural norms, but not competence *ratione materiae*.[38] The reservation of causes to the Congregation for the Doctrine of the Faith (CDF) is something in the more immediate consciousness of canonists today, but one

---

36. Cf. *Pars statica*, 187, no. 290, 4º.

37. See ibid., 110–111, 113, nn. 156, 159.

38. Cf. ibid., 111–113, nn. 157–158, quotation from 114, note 7. Likewise, he says it in passing when explaining that competence is given for a tribunal to exercise judgment, among others, "relate ad determinatas personas (et obiecta), in certo iurisdictionis gradu. . ." (ibid., 118, no. 166). But among the "kinds" (*species*) of tribunals in his general treatment he does not include those that handle reserved causes, apart from reservations by reason of the dignity of persons (ibid., 164, no. 256). It is mentioned briefly, though, in the context of his study on administrative tribunals (see "De Tribunalibus administrativis," 638, 652, nn. 43–44, 67).

wonders why he did not draw attention to it even though he mentioned in another context that the CDF "judges delicts against the faith" and "delicts against the sacrament of penance" and that to it certain causes are "reserved, e.g., concerning the worst crime (*de crimine pessimo*)."[39]

17. – Even if a tribunal is competent by law, "it cannot act on its own initiative" but depends upon the initiative of an interested party. On the other hand, if it is competent it is "bound to admit the petition and carry out a regular process"; that is, it is bound to exercise legitimately its judicial function.[40]

18. – There are cases in which a tribunal is incompetent, but its incompetence is sanated by the law itself, which Father Gordon presents as a form of extension (*prorogatio*) of competence. This is implicit in the fact that relative incompetence is not a ground of nullity of the sentence; thus, issuance of the sentence would seem to sanate the nullity of the judge's acts. And in fact, if no exception of relative incompetence is proposed by a party prior to the formulation of the doubt, the judge already then becomes competent by the law itself.[41] This is so on account of the legislator's solicitude for the juridical certitude of judicial decisions. "All of this is true and firm. Nevertheless, it is necessary to keep in mind that the legislator wants relative incompetence to be observed and, as far as possible, access to prorogation [i.e., sanation] of competence to be precluded."[42]

19. – Derogation from the age-old principle *actor sequitur forum rei* in causes of nullity of marriage perhaps does not pose difficulties (cf. *MI* c. 1672, 2º).[43] For some such broadening of the competence for petitions for dissolution of a non-consummated marriage had already been instituted in 1923 and did not seem to give an occasion for abuses (cf. 1983 *CIC* c. 1699 §1 *cum fonte*). And in causes of nullity of marriage, the respondent is often not Catholic or may support the petitioner's *libellus*, or his or her domicile may be unknown.[44]

---

39. See *Pars statica*, 106, no. 152. See also ibid., 169, no. 267, 2º and 281, no. 406.

40. See "Dichiarazione di nullità," 140, §2, 2. Cf. 1983 *CIC* cc. 1457 §1; 1501; 1620, 4º.

41. Cf. 1917 *CIC* c. 1628 §1; 1983 *CIC* c. 1459 §2; *DC* art. 10 §3.

42. See *Pars statica*, 153–155, nn. 237–240, quotation at 155, no. 239.

43. However, in principle, derogation from that principle is "something odious" (see "La renovación de la Signatura Apostólica," 581, no. 34, citing Lega in the context of pontifical commissions).

44. Cf. "De nimia processuum matrimonialium duratione," 682–683, no. 195. On this doctrine, see Thomas J. Green, "Marriage Nullity Processes in the Schema *De Processibus*," *The Jurist* 38 (1978) 322. On the importance of rules of competence for the protection of the rights of the respondent in traditional doctrine and legislation, see *Pars statica*, 118–119, nn. 166–169.

20. – The competent forum is ideally also the one in which the proofs can be most easily collected, since this also reduces delays and expenses. Indeed, such a forum allows the tribunal to proceed without relying on other tribunals, such as when making a rogatorial commission.[45] The forum of proofs (*forum probationum*) was newly introduced by *CM* (IV §1, *c*)) and "is based on the fact that the proofs are really found within the territory of the approached tribunal."[46] This forum is beneficial since it reduces the likelihood of a tribunal's dependence on another for instruction and on the Apostolic Signatura for a prorogation of competence. For these reasons, Father Gordon proposed that the forum of the most proofs be introduced into the revised *CIC* as a title of competence for any kind of cause.[47]

The formulation of this title of competence in *CM* is "far better and safer than that contained in the Norms for the U.S.A." (the APN), in which competence is based on the judgment of a judge about "his Tribunal [being] better able to judge the case than any other Tribunal" (Norm 7). When this forum is approached by the petitioner, the latter must indicate in the *libellus* which are "the proofs and their importance for the instruction of the cause."[48]

2. Conflicts of Competence and the Connection of Causes

21. – A true conflict of competence would require "that tribunals in the same cause admit the *libellus* or prosecution of an appeal, even if there were no contention or even one of them—for example, out of reverence toward the other—

---

45. Cf. "De nimia processuum matrimonialium duratione," 683, no. 196; "Dichiarazione di nullità," 139, §2, 2.

46. See "El M. P. '*Causas matrimoniales*' y las normas americanas," 201, no. 1a. The expression "*depositiones seu probationes*" undoubtedly means "todas las pruebas admitidas en el derecho procesal de la Iglesia."

47. Cf. PCCICR Archives, *vol. 181. XI. De processibus. Series II*: *Sessio I*ʾ*diebus 3–8 aprilis 1978 habita. Relatio*, 18; *Communicationes* 10 (1978) 223–224. It is described in the report as "*titulus competentiae oriens ex probationibus*" and the tribunal "*loci de facto validiores probationes inveniuntur*." The proposal was not accepted, however, because a) while Fr. Gordon argued that it was the principle underlying the titles of competence listed in cc. 1560, 1564–1566 of the 1917 *CIC*, which could thus all be derogated, four consultors argued that each of these titles has its own elements; b) the forum of proofs can be unclear since important proofs may emerge during the trial; and c) the forum of proofs can be controversial, since a respondent can object to it.

48. See *Adnotationes in m.p. "Causas matrimoniales,"* 255–257, §3 at 1, 2a, 4. Still, he found "the number of conditions" in *CM* to be "excessive," especially the hearing of the bishops; he said it would be sufficient to hear the judicial vicar and the respondent (see "El M. P. '*Causas matrimoniales*' y las normas americanas," 201, 1a).

was, as it were, deferential."[49] There indeed may not be any "tension" or "dispute" between them, nor might either of them in fact approach the tribunal competent to resolve a conflict of competence. The conflict might arise simply from a practical decision on the part of both tribunals to assert their own competence.[50] "Once a conflict of competence has arisen, none of the judges holding themselves to be competent can renounce their own competence *pro bono pacis* or out of submission and respect toward the other judges." Rather, the judges must defend their own competence as long as it is defensible: "One of the two judges, who deem themselves competent, is not to omit his own defense for reasons foreign to the merits of the question."[51]

22. – Conflicts of competence are anticipated somewhat by legislator, who provides rules on the connection of causes and the prevention of conflicts (1917 *CIC* cc. 1567–1568; 1983 *CIC* cc. 1414–1415).[52] In virtue of connection, a tribunal is competent over a distinct principal cause when it is competent over a related principal cause (*connexio*, properly speaking),[53] or over a lesser or acces-

---

49. See Ignacio Gordon, *votum* ("De recursu ad hoc Supremum Tribunal propter tribunalium conflictum"), *Separationis*, prot. n. 4530/73 VT, July 7, 1973: in SSAT Archives, 4, no. 3. This principle needed to be stated in this case, because the respondent's advocate was erroneously alleging a conflict of competence when in fact the cause was being treated administratively and only one organ (i.e., an ordinary) had begun treating it. The dispositive part of the July 17, 1973 decision of the Prefect in *Congresso*—declared two days later by the promoter of justice—corresponded with Fr. Gordon's opinion (ibid., document no. 4).

50. Cf. Ignacio Gordon, *votum* ("De recursu contra Congressus decisionem latam in quaestione de iure appellandi"), prot. n. 2120/71 CG, April 3, 1972: in SSAT Archives, 24, nn. 101–102.

51. See ibid., 25, no. 104. This was a case of a conflict of competence between the Roman Rota and an ordinary appellate tribunal. The defender of the bond had appealed an affirmative sentence to the latter, and the respondent to the Roman Rota but outside the peremptory time limit. The ordinary appellate tribunal, which recognized its own competence, freely yielded to the Roman Rota, which initially considered itself incompetent but later asserted its competence. The conflict arose before the Signatura at the instance of one of the parties. In the end, Fr. Gordon would conclude that "a true conflict of competence of tribunals was illegitimately created by the Sacred Roman Rota, since it placed into doubt the certain and exclusive competence of the appellate tribunal [X] in this case" (ibid., 33, no. 142, I.2). Without reference to this particular conflict, many of these principles are imparted in *Pars statica*, 329–330, no. 473a–b. See also "La renovación de la Signatura Apostólica," 582, no. 40.

He argued with another consultor in favor of attributing to the Apostolic Signatura competence to resolve such conflicts whenever the tribunals in conflict were not subject to the same appellate tribunal, thus simplifying c. 1612 of the 1917 *CIC* (cf. PCCICR Archives, *vol. 181. XI. De processibus. Sessio II^-Series II^ diebus 15–19 maii 1978 habita. Relatio*, 46; *Communicationes* 10 [1978] 249). This was received into c. 1416 (2nd part) of the 1983 *CIC*. See *Novus processus nullitatis matrimonii*, 57, note a.

52. Cf. *Pars statica*, 138–152, nn. 204–235.

53. E.g., see *DC* art. 15.

sory cause when such is *contained* (*continentia*)[54] within the principal cause falling within its competence.[55] This entails an extension (*prorogatio*) of competence by the law itself, inasmuch as the tribunal is not independently competent over the lesser, accessory or distinct principal cause but is given such competence on account of its competence over the one principal cause.[56] In all such cases, the commonality between the connected causes is objective, that is, it concerns the object of the cause. Prevention excludes competence from tribunals competent by law once another competent judge has completed the judicial citation.[57]

23. – A conflict of competence, which is always between two tribunals, must be kept distinct from an exception (or objection) of incompetence, which is made by one party against the supposed competence of some tribunal or judge. Such an "exception is optimal for preventing conflicts of competence."[58] For it can lead to an authoritative declaration of competence or incompetence, preventing further contention in the early stages of a trial.

Thus, (*a*) if a tribunal should assume treatment of a cause connected to another already pending but not assumed by that tribunal, one of the parties would object to this by raising an *exceptio connexionis* (an objection of connection of causes). In other words, the party would both object to the handling of the cause by the one tribunal and petition the other tribunal to assume the cause over which it has competence by reason of connection. If this is never done in any way, such that both tribunals proceed to define two distinct causes, both sentences are presumably valid, since the theoretical fact of connection in itself only renders other tribunals relatively incompetent.

---

54. Fr. Gordon explained in *Pars statica* 143, no. 212 that *connexio* and *continentia*, while distinct, are treated as largely synonymous. Thus he proposed that the latter term be omitted from the *CIC*, and this was accepted by all the consultors (cf. PCCICR Archives, *vol. 181. XI. De processibus. Series II*: *Sessio I* *diebus 3–8 aprilis 1978 habita. Relatio*, 22; *Communicationes* 10 [1978] 227).

55. The connection of causes is a material reality, not a merely formal one. Thus, causes may be unconnected "even if they are contained in the same *libellus*," while they may be materially connected "even if they were proposed in different *libelli* and by different petitioners" (see *Pars statica*, 336, no. 480a).

56. This would not occur, however, when the related cause is one over which the tribunal suffers from absolute incompetence, e.g., because judgment of a party is reserved to the Apostolic See, because of a functional defect, or because of the Church's lack of jurisdiction.

57. In *Pars statica* at 147, no. 220, Fr. Gordon asserts that there may be a connection of a penal cause and a contentious cause for damages. This is clear enough in the current c. 1729, but this had no precise precursor in the 1917 *CIC*. Still, Fr. Gordon found it to be implicit in c. 2210 §2 of the 1917 *CIC*.

58. See *Pars statica*, 329, note 4, citing Lega.

Or (*b*) if the competent tribunal has assumed the connected cause but the other tribunal tries to assume treatment of it, a party should raise an *exceptio litispendentiae* or *exceptio praeventionis*. In other words, the party would be objecting to the one tribunal's illegitimate assumption of a cause already pending before a tribunal competent by reason of the connection of causes. If the parties are negligent, it is for the tribunal that is illegitimately handling the cause to declare its own incompetence immediately and, as the case may be, defer the cause to the tribunal competent by reason of the connection of causes. If all are negligent in this matter, the sentence issued by the tribunal deciding only the connected cause would be null due to absolute incompetence.

24. – The connection of causes is distinct from the accumulation (*cumulus/ cumulatio*) of causes and from countersuits (*actiones reconventionales*),[59] wherein there is a subjective connection; that is, not the object but the subjects (the parties) are the same. In the case of the accumulation of causes, the petitioner introduces multiple causes against the same party or parties (cf. 1917 *CIC* c. 1669 §1; 1983 *CIC* c. 1493). In the case of a countersuit, multiple causes are introduced among the same parties, but the respondent holds his position in relation to the principal cause while becoming the petitioner in the cause that he introduces (1917 *CIC* c. 1690 §1; 1983 *CIC* c. 1494 §1).

C. Ministers of Justice

1. Their Preparation[60]

25. – The preparation (*praeparatio*) of future ministers of justice refers to the academic formation in canon law that is obtained in a basic sense, such as in the context of priestly formation, and in a thorough sense in the earning of a degree, especially a doctorate, in canon law.[61] As Father Gordon "authoritatively wrote,"[62] the non-obligatory earning of a canon law degree in the 1917 *CIC* was itself the root of the lack of preparation of ministers of justice, since there is a slippery slope (or *scala descendens*, as he says) "from *truly* expert, to expert, and to non-expert."

---

59. For a pure treatment of the *actio reconventionalis*, see ibid., 375–377, nn. 586–588.

60. For Fr. Gordon's own dedication to the work of preparation of ministers of justice, *vide supra* Chapter II.

61. Cf. "De nimia processuum matrimonialium duratione," 523–524, no. 49.

62. See Piero Antonio Bonnet, "I tribunali nella loro diversità di grado e di specie," in *Il processo matrimoniale canonico. Nuova edizione riveduta e ampliata*, Studi Giuridici 29 (Vatican City: Libreria Editrice Vaticana, 1994) 193.

And one slides quickly down it, "especially if a diocese abounds in pastoral works and suffers from a certain scarcity of priests."[63] It is no wonder, therefore, that "grave complaints were not infrequently heard about the lack of preparation of judges and published in journals."[64] The lack of an obligation to earn a canon law degree as a qualification for a judicial office was characterized by Father Gordon, in harmony with other authors, as a "defect" and a "lacuna" in the law.[65]

26. – Without such preparation, prescinding from substantive implications, the administration of justice suffers inadequacies and disorder.[66]

> Negligence in preparing men who must issue decisions of such great weight and the disregard with which truly ignorant people are entrusted with treating the gravest causes, if considered objectively, carries with it no light responsibility before God, before the Church, and before those members of the faithful whose life has perhaps become irreparably unhappy in this world and whose eternal salvation has possibly also been led to serious peril.[67]

2. The Bishop as Judge and Moderator

27. – "It is highly recommended to the bishop that he abstain from judging." And this recommendation comes not only from the *CIC*[68] but also "implicitly but strongly" by the teaching of the Second Vatican Council. For the Council mentions his judicial power only once, while much teaching is given on his roles of teaching, sanctifying, and governing (i.e., exercising administrative as well as legislative power).[69] There are certain causes that are reserved to him, but "with the mandate of the bishop the *officialis* can also judge causes reserved to him by the law itself."[70]

28. – The bishop's principal relationship with the administration of justice in his particular Church is that of the *dominus tribunalis*[71] or *Episcopus moderator*.[72]

---

63. See "De nimia processuum matrimonialium duratione," 528, no. 56.
64. See *Pars statica*, 182, no. 287a.
65. See "De nimia processuum matrimonialium duratione," 529, no. 57.
66. Cf. ibid., 524–525, nn. 51–52.
67. See ibid., 528, no. 55.
68. See 1917 *CIC* c. 1578; cf. *DC* art. 22 §2.
69. See *Pars statica*, 185–186, no. 290, 1a.
70. See ibid., 193, no. 301, at c, 1).
71. Ibid., 206, no. 316.
72. *Processus nullitatis matrimonii*, 96; *Novus processus nullitatis matrimonii*, 51, no. 202.

This is "an administrative function," since "it does not entail issuing sentences."[73] Rather, it situates him in the supreme local position as governor of the tribunal, by virtue of which he establishes it, provides suitable ministers and resources for it, and exercises vigilance over it.[74] "Even if he should judge through others, the bishop always represents his own tribunal, especially before other ecclesiastical authorities. Therefore, rogatorial letters, letters of delegation, and similar things are sent to him."[75]

3. The Judge

a. The Function of Judging

29. – In addition to academic preparation in canon law, one to be appointed to the office of judge is also to have practical knowledge and the right psychological disposition. Such knowledge is attained "especially through procedural praxis, by the habit of being observant, and by logical deductions." There are also moral qualities that are necessary: "In the judge, there is to be a great sense of what is just and fair, so that he may be as it were 'living justice' (*iustitia animata*), and also certain instincts that may, as it were, guide him in individual cases in applying the law to the facts with security and ease."[76]

30. – The judge is burdened with "a most grave responsibility." For he often has to scrutinize the interior life of man, especially acts of the will, in a way that is not as familiar to the secular judge. And "he must make decisions about the freedom or not of persons, that is, concerning a good which many deeply love and pursue more steadfastly than physical life itself."[77] The judge also has a certain solicitude for the souls of the parties. Indeed, it is for the judge "not only to protect the sanctity of marriage, taking into account also the principle concerning the favor of marriage ([1917 *CIC*] c. 1014), but also to provide for the spiritual good of the respondent in virtue of the law commanding that he supply for the activity of a party."[78]

31. – Essential to the office of judge is the detached investigation and declaration of the truth—that is, what is proven to be true in the trial. Each judge must

---

73. See "Responsio nonnullis quaestionibus," 641, at B.
74. *Vide supra* Chapter V, no. 34.
75. See *Pars statica*, 187, no. 290, 4°.
76. See ibid., 184, no. 287b.
77. Cf. "De nimia processuum matrimonialium duratione," 526–527, no. 54.
78. See "De appellationibus," 315, *sub* no. 2. Here he cites c. 1619 §2 (see 1983 *CIC* c. 1452).

remain free from any other pressure, even from administrative superiors. Thus, for instance, while the judicial vicar constitutes one tribunal with the bishop, he always "decid[es] according to his own conscience and under his own responsibility."[79] Those entrusted with the office of judge, especially the judicial vicar, have a duty to judge the causes introduced before the tribunal. Their refusal to do so (e.g., due to various fears) is a grave injustice against the faithful, whose cause "has been decided *a priori*," as it were.[80]

In addition to his service of the truth, the ecclesiastical judge also carries out a public service that includes attentiveness to the personal good of the parties. In the exercise of his judicial function, this means that he is always to employ two special criteria: the equality of the parties and the maximum brevity of litigation.[81] In other words, both parties should be able to see that their dignity as a person endowed with rights is revered by the tribunal, without any room for favoritism. And they should be able to appreciate that the judge, while detached and officially indifferent to the particular outcome of the trial, is striving to deliver to them a definitive decision in as expeditious a manner as possible.

32. – Those who are appointed judges ought to be given sufficient remuneration. Otherwise they may be forced by necessity to assume other functions, which has the consequences both of delays in the process and of the judges' lack of personal interest and seriousness in judging. Such a disposition would be detected by others and have practical results in the quality of their work, thus leading to the possibility that "the administration of justice would become odious" before the parties and indeed the Church in general.[82]

b. Appellate Judges

33. – In practice, the judges of local appellate tribunals may simply be those that are incardinated or have a domicile in the (arch)diocese in which an appellate tribunal is constituted. Nevertheless, the hierarchy of jurisdiction situates the appellate tribunal in a position superior to that of the first instance tribunal. Its

---

79. See "Dichiarazione di nullità," 139, no. 2. See also *Pars statica*, 170, no. 269.

80. Cf. "De nimia processuum matrimonialium duratione," 503–504, nn. 18–19. This is a graver evil than a tribunal's slow administration of justice, since in the latter case the tribunal at least admits and (eventually) decides causes.

81. Cf. *Pars statica*, 28, no. 40. He states this principle in the context of the interpretation of procedural laws.

82. Cf. "De nimia processuum matrimonialium duratione," 520, no. 44.

decisions are, in a sense, graver, since they can bring to realization the passage of a controversy into a state of being a *res (quasi-)iudicata*. Moreover, there are frequently more complex and technical questions, even of a procedural nature, treated before the appellate tribunal than before the first instance tribunal. Accordingly, appointment to a judicial office in an appellate tribunal suggests special qualifications and experience. One can be seen as qualified to be a judge in an appellate tribunal after he has proved himself by high-quality judging at the first level of jurisdiction. As Father Gordon remarks in passing, "judges can be chosen" for offices in appellate tribunals "who have shown themselves to excel in a tribunal of the first level."[83]

c. The College of Judges and the Single Judge

34. – The collegiality of the exercise of the office of judge is set forth in the 1917 *CIC* as a central principle, even if it found exceptions in mission lands, where an individual priest could judge causes due to a grave scarcity of priests. In *CM*, this collegiality was protected even to the extent of allowing the conference of bishops to permit a layman to complete the college, which was preferential to entrusting causes to a single clerical judge (V §§1–2).[84] One must always hold fast to the "excellence of the collegial tribunal,"[85] for "the collegial tribunal undoubted[ly] surpasses by its nature a tribunal of one judge."[86] Should a single judge be legitimately employed, "the legislator wills that the prescribed collegiality for certain causes, e.g., nullity of marriage, be observed at least in second instance" (1983 *CIC* c. 1441).[87]

35. – If there are some benefits to use of a single judge in causes reserved to a college, each of them is at the same time subject to serious critique. A single judge "1) has a greater sense of responsibility but also a danger of bias"; for there is no authoritative check on his assessment of the persons and goods involved in the trial. "2) He is subject to no one but can more easily yield to public opinion"; for the weight of the decision falls on himself, and not a college of which he is

---

83. See "De Tribunalibus Regionalibus," 591.

84. Cf. *Adnotationes in m.p. "Causas matrimoniales,"* 271–272, at A.1.

85. See "Votum de revisione sententiae," 120, no. 50.

86. See *Adnotationes in m.p. "Causas matrimoniales,"* 274, at B.1.1a.

87. See *Processus nullitatis matrimonii*, 6, a; *Novus processus nullitatis matrimonii*, 3, note 5. Bonnet identifies this, too, as "authoritatively" taught by Fr. Gordon (see his "I tribunali nella loro diversità di grado e di specie," 218, note 158). This hierarchical collegiality remains normative even after the issuance of *MI* (cc. 1673 §5, 1680 §2).

only a member. "3) He has more immediate knowledge but also a danger of delusion"; for, while he has been the one to oversee the instruction, he may be invincibly led astray by a party or witness or by an argument proposed. And "4) he proceeds more easily and quickly, but the serious study of the cause can thereby be easily neglected"; for he may neglect to perceive some lacuna in the proofs or the arguments that another member of the college would have noticed.[88]

36. – A lax acceptance of judgment by a single judge as a standard practice "implies a practical ignorance of the wisdom and liberty that the college of judges gives to the decisions of a tribunal." For it is obvious that a properly functioning college reduces the margin of error and the occasion for pressure, manipulation, and corruption. To this situation can be applied the biblical teaching: "If one might prevail against one man, two may resist him. *And a triple cord is broken with difficulty*" (Eccles. 4:12).[89] For indeed, it is easier to assure a balanced examination of the cause within the discussion and internal psychological dynamics of the college; and public opinion cannot so easily corrupt the whole college as it could an individual who was acting with bad motives, error, or external pressure.[90]

37. – On the other hand, a tribunal obviously may not deem itself competent to judge only when it can act collegially, if a cause may legitimately be treated by a single judge. Nor should a tribunal act collegially when the law itself entrusts the administration of justice to a single judge, such as in a documentary pro-

---

88. See *Pars statica*, 201, no. 310b.

89. Cf. "El M. P. '*Causas matrimoniales*' y las normas americanas," 209, including notes 71–72. He was commenting in particular on the norm of APN 23, I, which envisioned the possibility of a single appellate judge.

90. See *Pars statica*, 201–202, no. 310b. Evidently, these concerns especially pertain to the issuance of decisions, since individual members of the college also frequently act on behalf of the college during the course of the trial (e.g., presiding judge, *ponens*, instructor). For these reasons, Fr. Gordon had suggested that the strong language of the legislation—reading, "the collegial tribunal *must* (*debet*) proceed collegially"—be tempered to read "the collegial tribunal is to act collegially at least in issuing decisions"; but this was rejected (see PCCICR Archives, *vol. 181. XI. De processibus. Series II*: *Sessio I* *diebus 3–8 aprilis 1978 habita. Relatio*, 30; *Communicationes* 10 [1978] 235). Cf. *Processus nullitatis matrimonii*, 14, h; *Novus processus nullitatis matrimonii*, 7, note h.

91. In his examination of a draft decree of erection of regional tribunals, Fr. Gordon observes: "Infelix modus dicendi adhibetur, ex quo sequitur ut dicatur cognoscendas esse a Tribunali trium iudicum, tum causas nullitatis per processum documentalem seu summarium, tum causas separationis quoad mensam et thronum. Sed, ut patet, neutrum admitti posset.... [...] Nec satis intelligitur cur competentia horum Tribunalium restringitur ad causas contentiosas iurium et criminales *quae Tribunali collegiali egent*" (*votum* ["[Y]. Reorganizzazione Tribunali Ecclesiastici"], prot. n. 265/70 VT, May 28, 1971: in SSAT Archives, 1, no. 1 ["*Quoad competentiam*"]).

cess.[91] The legitimate use of a single judge depends upon the diligent observance of the law and attentiveness to the particular situations that may exist in an individual diocese.[92]

d. Non-clerical Judges

38. – Prior to the promulgation of *CM*, Father Gordon had the opportunity to examine the question of non-clerical or lay judges in a free and objective way.[93] For him, the foundational impediment to the conferral of the office of judge on a layman resided in his conviction that the ecclesiastical judge exercises "strictly priestly power" when issuing a definitive sentence in "sacramental causes." The teaching of the Second Vatican Council (e.g., *LG* 21) "united the *munus regendi* with ordination." For those who judge matters in which sacramental grace is in question must be endowed with sacramental power.[94] Historical examples of delegation of judicial power to non-clerics were instances of judgments made in virtue of the "social power" in the Church that is sufficient for treating non-sacramental causes. Such also are exceptional; the general discipline should be in accord with "the more universal praxis in the Church" which "was always to exclude laypeople from any judging role." A layman was therefore to be understood as "absolutely incapable of assuming and exercising" such power.

39. – Certain authors promoting the institution of lay judges—especially in the United States and Germany—seem not to have scrupled about the nature of ecclesiastical power but were motivated perhaps by more pragmatic goals, such as addressing the problem of the lack of priests to take up judicial functions, promoting the involvement of laypeople in governance, and ensuring that the perspective of laypeople is introduced especially in matrimonial causes. Father Gordon reasonably pointed out that offices heretofore held by priests for which laypeople could already be qualified by law, such as notary and advocate (cf. 1917 *CIC* cc. 373 §3, 1585 §2, 1657 §§1–2), could be entrusted to laypeople, thus freeing the priests to judge.

---

92. This is why Fr. Gordon, together with then-Archbishop Sabattani, wanted the expression "in singulis casibus" to remain in the canon treating the exception of a single judge. Cf. "'De processibus.' Relazione della sessione tenutasi dal 5 al 7 marzo 1981," in PCCICR Archives, *vol. 182, XI. De processibus, Parvus coetus (5–7 martii 1981). Relatio,* second folder, 6–7.

93. For the teaching in this number, see "De nimia processuum matrimonialium duratione," 514–518, nn. 38–41.

94. He would elsewhere refer to the "the priestly (or clerical) character of judges" (see "El M. P. 'Causas matrimoniales' y las normas americanas," 206).

40. – Nevertheless, *CM* famously authorized the conference of bishops "to permit, at the first and second level, the constitution of a college of two clerics and one layman" (*vir laicus*)[95] if a college of three clerical judges could not be composed in a diocesan or regional tribunal (V §1). This was "a matter of conferring the function of judge on a layman" (VII), not merely some non-jurisdictional supplemental ministry. Father Gordon declared that, in so doing, "Paul VI solved the controversy." And so "it is necessary that that power has been received not through ordination but by delegation." He did not accept the explanation of some authors according to which the college of two clerics and a layman should be considered somehow equivalent to a single priestly judge, as if the other cleric and the layman were mere assessors. Others, though, characterize the definitive sentence as some mere declaration of fact and not as a jurisdictional act. Father Gordon observed that the latter do not see "any difficulty from a theological perspective"; presumably, though, he himself thought that difficulty remained, even if he did not want to emphasize it after the supreme legislator had made his choice.[96]

He would hold to the general principle that, outside the exceptional circumstances defined in law, "judges must be at least clerics and indeed"—citing a document of the Signatura—"'ordinarily endowed with priestly dignity,'" but the office could be entrusted to a layman "exceptionally" in order to constitute a college.[97] Nevertheless, he was in agreement with the decision to admit the norm of *CM* into the *CIC* of 1983.[98] And, no doubt for the sake of simplicity and stability, he proposed with another consultor that it be a matter not merely of authorization for a single case but a real office.[99]

---

95. In 1979, some were suggesting that women, too, should be included. He rightly observed that this was expressly excluded by *CM*, both by the use of *vir* in no. V §1 and in view of no. VI, which deliberately mentions both *viri* and *mulieres* as possible candidates for the office of notary. Also, he observed—in a time of such rapid change and the growing tendency in western culture to eliminate any sexual distinctiveness—that "it would be too much for the legislator to open up a function reserved until now to priests not only to deacons and laymen but also to women." He did not exclude the possibility that that could be studied, but he seemed not to approve of efforts made by some to stir up the question, since that provoked "bitterness and lack of consideration" (see *Adnotationes in m.p. "Causas matrimoniales,"* 275, at B.1.2a).

96. See ibid., 273–274, at A.3.

97. See *Pars statica*, 181, no. 287.

98. "1) Riguarda un problema più generale, quello della Potestà sacra, meglio lasciare com'è. Concordano tutti. 2) I Consultori unanimemente pensano che il prescritto M.P. 'Causas Matrimoniales' inserito nel Canone [1373], circa l'ammissione dei laici nel Collegio dei giudici debba rimanere" (see "'De processibus.' Relazione della sessione tenutasi dal 5 al 7 marzo 1981," in PCCICR Archives, vol. 182, XI. *De processibus, Parvus coetus [5–7 martii 1981]. Relatio,* second folder, 4).

99. Cf. PCCICR Archives, vol. 181. XI. *De processibus. Series II*: *Sessio I* diebus 3–8 aprilis 1978 habita. Relatio,* 26; *Communicationes* 10 (1978) 231. The proposal was accepted.

4. The Assessor

41. – When a single judge is legitimately used, he is to employ two assessors. The assessor assists the judge "in iudicio," in the sense not of the very judgment he is making strictly, but broadly "in the trial": thus in the whole first instance. The assessor thus "gives his counsel whenever he is asked by the judge." And this surely includes the deliberation to be made prior to the issuance of the sentence.[100] The reason for this encouragement of the legislator to employ assistants, especially an assessor, is "the gravity of a cause of nullity, which is so great that the Church does not want a sentence to be issued about it without the collaboration of several persons."[101]

Nothing prohibits the functions of auditor and assessor from being entrusted to the same person. An auditor could even be a second assessor.[102]

5. The Defender of the Bond

42. – In regard to procedural law, the principal way the supreme legislator expresses the *favor matrimonii* is the office of defender of the bond.[103] He has traditionally had the position of "a public person and a privileged party."[104] With the revision of the 1917 code, however, "the rights of the advocate and those of the defender of the bond have been equalized," especially as regards awareness of the state of the proofs throughout the course of the trial.[105]

---

100. See *Adnotationes in m.p. "Causas matrimoniales,"* 279, at g.

101. See ibid., 279, at f.

102. Cf. ibid., 278, at 6a, c.

103. Ignacio Gordon, *votum* ("De recursu contra Congressus decisionem latam in quaestione de iure appellandi"), prot. n. 2120/71 CG, April 3, 1973: in SSAT Archives, 17–18, no. 73: "Revera omnes causae de statu personarum, propter earum naturam publicam, gaudent favore iuris, qui praesertim obtinet in causis de vinculo matrimonii, prout solemniter enuntiatur in can. 1014: 'Matrimonium gaudet favore iuris'. Attamen hic favor non est principium quoddam genericum, cuius applicatio relinquitur liberae Iudicum aut Administratorum inspirationi; sed e converso, ipse Legislator curavit in ipsa lege determinare modos concretos, quibus hic favor intelligendus est in iure substantivo sive in iure processuali. Iam vero, quoad ius processuale attinet, praecipua instituta ac praescripta favorem matrimonii exprimentia haec sunt: 1º Institutum Defensoris vinculi (can. 1586-1590) eiusque privilegia (can. 1968-1969), 2º prima necessaria appellatio, etiamsi fatalia ob negligentiam ipsius Defensoris vinculi transacta fuerint (can. 1986), 3º possibilitas alterius appellationis ex conscientia (can. 1987), 4º possibilitas propriam appellationem transferendi (art. 216, § 3), etc., praesertim vero beneficium novae propositionis causae ad normam can. 1903 et 1989."

104. See ibid., 9 and 16–17, nn. 32 and 68.

105. See "Elementi innovativi nei processi," 8, citing c. 1678 (cf. *MI* c. 1677 §1).

The defender of the bond ought to be a full time official, so that he may carry out his function in a timely manner.[106] Only by continuous dedication to this function may he really know about a cause from its beginning.[107]

43. – It would be an "extreme" view to assert that the defender of the bond proposes observations *pro rei veritate*. For he is always to carry out his "traditional and specific function" of acting *pro vinculo*. If no reasonable argument can be proposed in favor of the bond, then he is to "be quiet; but [he is] never to act against the bond."[108] In such a case, "it is his duty to communicate to the judge that he has nothing to propose in defense of the matrimonial bond."[109]

44. – In the era of the facultative appeal of the defender of the bond, some may be given to draw objective conclusions from the defender's decision not to appeal an affirmative sentence. However, "omission of an appeal on the part of the defender of the bond does not carry with it a presumption of the objective value of the sentence. And how much less if, in the function of his associates, experience teaches him that by appealing he will be met with murmuring, bitterness, and perhaps removal from his function."[110]

D. The Parties

45. – When a cause is introduced, those involved mutually assume a procedural relationship by becoming parties. Prior to the trial, the physical persons who are the parties are in some substantive relationship. Father Gordon uses the

---

106. Cf. "De nimia processuum matrimonialium duratione," 535, no. 68.

107. Cf. ibid., no. 67.

108. See "De appellationibus," 314, note 41. This affirmation was made in the context of discussing the role of the defender of the bond during the abbreviated appellate process instituted by Paul VI in *CM*. Since the respondent could not appeal an affirmative sentence and might not even be heard before the possible confirmation of the sentence, it was for the defender of the bond to protect the respondent's rights, even if he certainly was not "to act after the manner of a Procurator-Advocate." Should the defender abuse his office by acting *pro nullitate* or merely *pro rei veritate*, the judge should take some measure to supply the protection of the respondent opposed to the alleged nullity of marriage (ibid., 315, *sub* no. 2). See also *Adnotationes in m.p. "Causas matrimoniales,"* 9–10, no. 2a. Fr. Gordon hereby "correct[ed] the interpretation made by some commentators on the MP *CM* on the *munus* of the defender of the bond" (see Bassiano Uggé, *La fase preliminare/abbreviata del processo di nullità del matrimonio in secondo grado di giudizio a norma del can. 1682 §2*, Tesi Gregoriana – Serie Diritto Canonico 60 [Rome: Editrice Pontificia Università Gregoriana, 2003] 105, note 25 *in fine*).

109. See "Dichiarazione di nullità," 141, note 6.

110. See "Votum de revisione sententiae," 117, no. 32. On the defender of the bond's duty to appeal, *vide infra* Chapter VII, nn. 46–50.

example of the sale of a watch. Titius buys a watch from Caius by paying him the price he named. Prior to the trial, the object (*obiectum*) of their substantive relationship is the watch; its foundation (*fundamentum*) is the right of ownership; and its terms (*termini*) are the physical persons involved. When Caius accepts the money but refuses to hand over the watch, Titius sues Caius, and the terms of the relationship become litigious in nature. Titius and Caius thus enter a procedural relationship as parties in the cause: the petitioner (*actor*) and the defendant (*reus*) standing before the judge.[111] They are those "who contend among themselves so that one may obtain victory over the other" after the trial has been initiated by the one who effectively exercises the action and the other has been cited by the judge.[112] Thus, if the party being accused "does not wish to contradict and litigate, there is no place for a trial."[113]

46. – Partially in order not to burden the parties, it is sufficient that, when they need to place a procedural act (such as appear to be heard by the judge before he places an act), they do so not themselves but through their procurator.[114] At the same time, petitioners are to be diligent in communicating the correct contact information of the witnesses they introduce and in informing the tribunal of their own unavailability during the course of the trial, such as can occur when a party takes an international trip of some length.[115]

47. – Canonical procedural law operates out of the principle of the "equality of procedural rights that both parties enjoy under the same conditions." Accordingly, "if either party requests something that can affect the right of the other, it is necessary that this other party also be heard."[116]

E. Advocates

48. – The "greatest praise" given to advocates is their designation in Roman law as priests of the law (*iuris sacerdotes* [cf. D.1.1]). They are held "in honor" by the Church and are encouraged in the "exercise of the virtues and the study of

---

111. Cf. *Pars statica*, 35, no. 52, 2º.

112. See ibid., 37–38, nn. 57–58.

113. See ibid., 39, no. 62, 3º.

114. Cf. "De nimia processuum matrimonialium duratione," 686, note 4, where this is applied to the derogated norm of 1917 *CIC* c. 1727 on the parties' obligation to appear at the tribunal for the *concordantia dubiorum*.

115. Cf. "De nimia processuum matrimonialium duratione," 532, no. 61.

116. See *Adnotationes in m.p.* "*Causas matrimoniales*," 259, "*4a conditio*." The context concerned the hearing of the respondent prior to admitting a cause in the forum of the majority of the proofs.

juridical science."[117] Advocates are in particular to be taught to cultivate "veneration for truth, justice, and that form of poverty that consists in the free acceptance of a non-excessive stipend."[118]

However, some advocates need to be corrected when they find it sufficient in their work "to transcribe several canons and interpret them in a civil law manner without perceiving their genuine meaning and connection with the whole system of the Code of Canon Law."[119] And those advocates inflict "grave damage" who fabricate causes by instructing their clients falsely and bribe or cunningly direct witnesses. Such behaviors are destructive, by "uselessly occupying the labor of the tribunal and provoking unjust delays of the processes in it."[120]

49. – It can be difficult to ensure a stable body of advocates, so this may need to be done with greater deliberation in some tribunals. A solution proposed by others that Father Gordon commends is the institution of a college of advocates proper to the tribunal (cf. *DC* art. 112 §1). The existence of such a college would ensure that there be a body of chosen advocates, provide for the advocates to be paid a suitable stipend even in cases of gratuitous representation, and allow for the selection of an advocate to assume the cause of individual parties. This may not be possible everywhere but could be offered as the ideal solution.[121]

F. Judicial Expenses

50. – The matter of judicial expenses is somewhat complicated because of the various factors that necessarily bring financial demands with them. These including the operating expenses of the tribunals themselves, the payment of advocates, and the cost of hiring an expert in a cause of impotence or mental illness.[122] It is therefore not surprising to find among dioceses a diversity of practice. In some, "the administration of ecclesiastical justice is totally gratuitous." In others, the general rule is that the diocese pays part and the parties pay the other part of the expenses. In still others, the diocese has the parties pay all the expenses, even while making room for a partial or total reduction of them.[123]

---

117. See "De nimia processuum matrimonialium duratione," 539–540, no. 76. In note 2, he quotes at length a kind of "Decalogue of advocates" formulated by St. Alphonse Liguori.

118. See ibid., 551, no. 92.

119. See ibid., 545–546, no. 84.

120. See ibid., 547, no. 85.

121. Cf. ibid., 549–551, nn. 89–92. On advocates acting before the Signatura, see "Normae speciales," 93, no. 39.

122. Cf. "Dichiarazione di nullità," 145, §4,2.

123. See *Novus processus nullitatis matrimonii*, 51, no. 202.

CHAPTER VII

The *Pars dynamica*

SUMMARY — Introductory Remark (no. 1). ▪ A. STAGES OF
THE ORDINARY CONTENTIOUS TRIAL (nn. 2–4). ▪ B. THE
INTRODUCTION OF THE TRIAL: 1. Submission of the *Libellus* (nn. 5–7).
2. Admission of the *Libellus* (nn. 8–9). 3. Citation (nn. 10–12).
4. Formulation of the Doubt (nn. 13–15). 5. Declaration of
Absence (no. 16). ▪ C. THE INSTRUCTION OF THE CAUSE: 1. Judicial
Instruction and Proofs in General (nn. 17–21). 2. Declaration of
Parties (nn. 22–24). 3. Testimony (nn. 25–26). 4. Experts (nn. 27–28).
5. Publication of the Acts (no. 29). ▪ D. THE DISCUSSION OF
THE CAUSE (no. 30). ▪ E. THE DECISION: 1. Deliberation of the
College of Judges (nn. 31–33). 2. Moral Certitude (nn. 34–39).
3. *Res iudicata* (no. 40). 4. Execution of the Sentence (no. 41). ▪ F.
THE CHALLENGE OF THE SENTENCE: 1. Challenges in General (no. 42).
2. The Appeal: a. Peremptory Time Limits for Appealing (nn. 43–45).
b. Appeal of the Defender of the Bond (nn. 46–50).
c. Double Conformity of Sentences (nn. 51–54). 3. The Complaint of
Nullity (nn. 55–56).

1. – As was explained above,[1] the *pars dynamica* is that dimension of the judicial process in which the protagonists in the trial are set in motion and procedural relationships are constituted by the placing of procedural acts. In other words, it is the practical evolution of the trial. Father Gordon explained the general legislation on the whole *pars dynamica* and the complementary norms (*PME*), especially in his *dispense* on the *pars dynamica* and on the revised marriage nullity process, as well as in his "Discorso generale." In these, one finds a detailed and methodical commentary on the norms. The goal of this chapter is to draw attention to his particular insights and to areas of the discipline that captured his special attention. Naturally, the form of trial that is the object of concentration in this chapter is the ordinary contentious trial, which is the "normal" form in the canonical system.[2]

---

1. *Vide supra* Chapter IV, nn. 23 and 25.
2. On this point, *vide supra* Chapter V, no. 25.

111

A. Stages of the Ordinary Contentious Trial

2. – There are four essential stages to the ordinary contentious trial; Father Gordon first identified these as three in number following the introduction of the cause, which thus seemed to be for him an essential preparatory stage. The three he had in mind are the probatory or instructional period (*periodus probatoria seu instructoria*), the discussion period (*periodus discussoria*), and the decision period (*periodus decisoria*).[3] Following these there may be challenges against the sentence. Later in his reflections, he would accordingly explain that the process has "five fundamental parts: 1) introduction, 2) instruction, 3) discussion, 4) sentence, and 5) challenge of the sentence."[4]

3. – Presupposing the introduction, he explains the interrelation between the three principal periods: "It is customarily said that the sentence is the *conclusion* of a syllogism, whose *major* premise is the law which governs the disputed matter, and whose *minor* premise is the disputed matter itself, or the facts. In the instructional period, the facts were clarified. But the discussion period is wholly about determining the law that is to be considered in this case and the relationship of the facts to it."[5]

Elsewhere, commenting on the expression "medium iudicium" (the middle [part of the] trial) used by Michele Cardinal Lega, he speaks of three stages of the trial: the beginning, the middle, and the end (*initium-medium-finis*). The beginning is the introduction of the cause and the *contestatio litis*. The middle is "the instruction of the process, or the collection of proofs (Titles IX–XI), and the preparation of the cause for the sentence (Title XII)"—in other words, the instruction and the discussion. And the end is the definitive sentence itself.[6]

4. – The trial consists in the multiplicity of procedural acts—that is, "the juridical acts by which the process is constituted, evolves, and is completed." This triad further expresses the various stages of the trial: the beginning or constitution of the trial, the evolution of the trial during which proofs are introduced, obtained, and interpreted, and the completion of the trial, when the controversy

---

3. Cf. "Dichiarazione di nullità," 142–143; *Pars statica*, 39–42, nn. 61–67.

4. See "Discorso generale," 63.

5. See *Pars dynamica*, 93, no. 402.

6. Cf. *Pars statica*, 218, note 3. See also ibid., 221, where he teaches that "in brief, it can be said that it is appropriate to entrust the middle part of the cause (*medium causae*) to [an auditor]— that is, from the completion of the *litis contestatio* to the publication of the process, inclusive."

is definitively resolved. These acts "proceed from those who participate in the procedural relationship," and "they have a juridical and immediate influence on the process itself."[7] For the acts of the parties and especially of the judge give impulse to the evolution of the trial, from its beginning to its completion.

B. The Introduction of the Trial

1. Submission of the *Libellus*

5. – As is suggested also in the most recent reform of the norms of the marriage nullity process by Pope Francis,[8] the preparation of a *libellus* is a technical matter for which a member of the faithful who is not a canonist usually needs personal and technical assistance. This is typically a service best offered by an advocate. Whoever it is, the one consulted by a member of the faithful to inquire about the process may justly try to dissuade him from introducing it when there are clear reasons not to accuse his marriage of nullity.[9] For while one may have the generic right to introduce a cause, he may not have a firm basis in law and in the facts of his claim.

6. – While the *libellus* has essential elements prescribed by law (1917 *CIC* c. 1708), it is an act or declaration not of the judge but of the party.[10] It is an act that is to be founded on a right protected by the law. "The author of the *libellus* must have knowledge of both substantive and procedural canon law in general; and if it concerns a matrimonial cause, he must have clear knowledge of the impediments, of Rotal jurisprudence, and of the patterns according to which proof of nullity is to be constructed for each of the grounds." As regards the facts, this person, who is usually the procurator and/or advocate, "at the beginning receives from the petitioner his, as it were, biography" and helps identify appropriate and useful witnesses and documents.[11]

---

7. See ibid., 336i, no. 489. These procedural acts (*actus processuales*) are placed at distinct moments in time during the process, and they are reported in the judicial acts (*acta iudicialia*). "Procedural acts are therefore the real matter of the trial, but the written acts are, as it were, the reproduction or recording of the real matter"—"matter of the trial" here being distinct from the object of the trial, or the controversy itself (ibid., 336j, no. 489, including note 3).

8. Cf. *MI, Ratio procedendi in causis ad matrimonii nullitatem declarandam*, artt. 1–6.

9. Cf. *Pars dynamica*, 4, no. 6, at 2c.

10. Cf. "De procedura sequenda," 590, note 50. To the *libellus* can be contrasted the *monitorium*, which was an act of the judge at the outset of the trial.

11. See *Pars dynamica*, 4, no. 5, at 2b.

The *libellus* itself is to avoid excessive brevity and length: "It is not to be so briefly explained that the *fumus boni iuris* is not apparent, nor so long and drawn out that it obscures the facts and seems to anticipate the probatory and discussion periods."[12] In other words, the *libellus* does not attempt to prove or conclusively argue the claim but only to introduce the claim before the judges, whose public service is requested.

7. – The liminal assistance of an advocate has great importance both for the protection of the party's rights and for the submission of an appropriate, focused *libellus* that respects also the rights of the other parties and the integrity of the process. The praxis is altogether to be avoided whereby a petitioner writes up a lengthy biographical report explaining the whole history of the marriage, which is then submitted to the tribunal as one of the acts of the cause. Such reports may be more useful to the advocate deputed for writing or refining the *libellus* proper. But they often also contain inflammatory information against the other spouse that "not rarely contributes little or nothing to the cause." And so if they are used for the benefit of the advocate, they should either be destroyed or at least not submitted for inclusion in the acts. "For the first document of the cause is the *libellus*."[13]

2. Admission of the Libellus

8. – The decree of admission of the *libellus* is an immediate, authoritative, favorable response to the submission of a *libellus*, and so it would not normally be thought to cause any injury to the petitioner. However, at this preliminary moment of the judicial process, the petitioner might in fact suffer an as-yet-unperceived injury if the *libellus* is being admitted without serious consideration. For, despite the initial experience of favor, the decree of admission could in effect con-

---

12. See ibid., 5, no. 8. At ibid., he cites the following as the "golden rule": "It is not necessary, nor is it expedient, that a detailed and long explanation of the arguments be written up, for these pertain to the periods of proof and defense; it is sufficient to make it apparent that the petition was not presented rashly" (*PME* art. 57, 3°).

13. See *Novus processus nullitatis matrimonii*, 13–14, no. 51. This teaching is identified by one author as stated by "authoritative doctrine" (see Joaquín Llobell, "La pubblicazione degli atti, la 'conclusio in causa' e la discussione della causa [artt. 229–245]," in *Il giudizio di nullità matrimoniale dopo l'Istruzione "Dignitas connubii." Parte Terza: La parte dinamica del processo*, Studi Giuridici 77, ed. Piero Antonio Bonnet and Carlo Gullo [Vatican City: Libreria Editrice Vaticana, 2008] 555, note 127). See also Michael P. Hilbert, "De publicatione actorum," *Periodica* 81 (1992) 526–527, 531–532; Pio Vito Pinto, *I processi nel Codice di diritto canonico: Commento sistematico al Lib. VII* (Vatican City: Pontificia Università Urbaniana, Libreria Editrice Vaticana, 1993) 227, note 319.

stitute the passage into a process that will be juridically useless to the petitioner and ultimately cause him to incur both moral and material expenses.[14]

9. – When a *libellus* is rejected, the petitioner enjoys the ordinary right to make recourse against the decree of rejection. Such a recourse is not in itself a question of the nullity of the decree of rejection. "For it is clear that a decree rejecting a *libellus* can be entirely valid according to the norm of canons 1892 and 1894 [of the 1917 *CIC*] and nevertheless be unjust; and also, if some such decree should be overturned by the superior tribunal, it is not therefore declared to have been null. Consequently, when a decree of rejection of a *libellus* has been overturned, the cause must in itself be judged before the tribunal that rejected the *libellus*."[15]

3. Citation

10. – The communication of the citation is the "authoritative leaving of it in the hands of the accused [or respondent]," which marks the completion of the citation.[16] The respondent's reaction to the citation is a question of obedience to the command of the judge; he is declared contumacious or absent when he disobeys that command.[17]

In virtue of canon 1507 §1 of the 1983 *CIC*, it is within the discretion of the judge to decree whether the respondent is to appear personally before the judge or is to respond to the citation in writing. In the first case, Father Gordon taught that the citation sheet (*scheda citatoria*) could include the elements listed in canon 1715 §1 of the 1917 *CIC*: "a precept of the judge made to the respondent to appear. . . , that is, by which judge, for which cause indicated in at least general terms, with which petitioner," the full name of the respondent, the place, and the date and time. This would naturally be different in some ways when the response to the citation is to be given in writing.[18]

11. – A most important effect vis-à-vis the object of the controversy is that of the pendency of the litigation (*litis pendentia*) and thus the beginning of the

---

14. Cf. "De nimia processuum matrimonialium duratione," 683–684, note 2.

15. See Ignacio Gordon, *votum* ("De recursu ad S.Tribunal Signaturae Apostolicae contra decretum Decani S.R.Rotae dierum 21–25 octobris in una [X]"), prot. n. 715/68 CG, July 7, 1969: in SSAT Archives, 10, no. 33.

16. See *Pars dynamica*, 9, no. 28 and 11, no. 37.

17. Cf. *Pars statica*, 39, no. 62.

18. Cf. *Novus processus nullitatis matrimonii*, 17, note 10; *Processus nullitatis matrimonii*, 26, no. 10.

judicial instance. This principle was stated clearly in canon 1725, 5º: "Once the citation has been legitimately completed or the parties have come to trial spontaneously: [...] litigation begins to be pending (*lis pendere incipit*)." Father Gordon stressed this principle, because it was undermined a few canons later, where one reads, in part: "The beginning of the instance occurs by the *litis contestatio*" (c. 1732). This he deemed to be "a remnant of pre-code law, which mistakenly remained in the 1917 code."[19] He was thus satisfied when this was resolved by canon 1517 of the 1983 code.[20]

Clarity about the beginning of the instance is necessary for attaining certitude about the jurisdiction of the tribunal. This effect impedes the parties from introducing the same cause before another tribunal "lest litigation remain unresolved," being given one treatment before one tribunal and another before another, "to the great detriment of justice and social order."[21]

12. – When it was suggested that the law of the 1983 *CIC* not require that the *libellus* be attached to the citation, some consultors agreed. Father Gordon was among those who did not think that it needed to be attached in causes of nullity of marriage.[22] In harmony with Sabattani and Pinto, though, he held that the "substance" of the *libellus* had to be communicated, while conceding that the whole *libellus* did not have to be communicated, "since the party, learning all the particulars, could be led to distort his deposition."[23]

4. Formulation of the Doubt

13. – In the 1917 *CIC* the *contestatio litis* was understood to be the manner in which the matter of the trial was determined. The formulation of the doubt was, in effect, the result of the *contestatio litis*. Its result ordinarily comes about by hearing both parties who, in a way, define the terms of the controversy by their responses, though this is always accomplished "with the assistance and approval

---

19. See "Discorso generale," 64. See also *Pars dynamica*, 10, 22, nn. 31, 87.

20. Cf. *Processus nullitatis matrimonii*, 30, I; *Novus processus nullitatis matrimonii*, 19, note i.

21. See *Pars statica*, 150–151, no. 229.

22. Cf. PCCICR Archives, *vol. 181. XI. De processibus. Sessio VI ÷ Series II ˆ diebus 26–31 martii 1979 habita. Relatio*, 183; *Communicationes* 11 (1979) 261: at "Fit brevis discussio," Fr. Gordon was among the "quattuor Consultores" mentioned there.

23. See "'De processibus.' Relazione della sessione tenutasi dal 5 al 7 marzo 1981," in PCCICR Archives, *vol. 182, XI. De processibus, Parvus coetus (5–7 martii 1981). Relatio*, second folder, 12. See also ibid., *vol. 181. XI. De processibus. Sessio III ÷ Series II ˆ diebus 23–28 octobris 1978 habita. Relatio*, 91; *Communicationes* 11 (1979) 90.

of the judge."[24] In the 1983 *CIC*, it came to have a "new nature," being now identifiable with the establishment of the matter of the trial.[25]

14. – The formulation of the doubt is included in the "outline of the whole process," being both a "step standing by itself and one incorporated into each and every other step."[26] Its essence is the determination of the object of the judicial controversy, and this must be done clearly "lest the whole instruction become otherwise uncertain or the sentence be pronounced in vain."[27] For what is defined in it "must be clarified over the course of the instruction, defended or challenged in the discussion, and finally defined by the sentence of the judge."[28] If the formulation of the doubt is omitted, "the whole instruction becomes unstable and uncertain, nor will it be just to respond in the sentence to ill-defined doubts."[29] It must be clear, lest there be "continual confusion throughout the whole process."[30]

15. – The formulation of the doubt poses the questions to be answered by the definitive sentence, and an eventual appeal would challenge the definitive answer to one or more of those questions. Nevertheless, in causes of nullity of marriage, a new ground of nullity can be added during the appellate level of the process, whether the tribunal is also a first instance tribunal or only an appellate tribunal.[31]

---

24. See *Pars dynamica*, 15, no. 55. This is the "normal way." The "subsidiary way" is necessary when the respondent is absent, so that the judge has to determine the object of the controversy according to what the petitioner alone has said (ibid.). Fr. Gordon supported a certain legal flexibility in the manner of stating the terms of the controversy, especially in relation to the citation; but preservation of the *contestatio litis* as an essential stage prevailed. See PCCICR Archives, *vol. 181. XI. De processibus. Sessio III ̇ Series II ̇ diebus 23–28 octobris 1978 habita. Relatio*, 93; *Communicationes* 11 (1979) 92–93. Probably because of its history in Roman judicial activity, he thought the expression *contestatio litis* should be reserved for more difficult causes in which the parties are convoked by the judge, as described in the second part of c. 1513 §2 of the 1983 *CIC* (cf. ibid., 94, 93, respectively). He also thought it should be clear that the judge has "the faculty to establish the doubt(s) *ex officio*" (see ibid., 95, 94, respectively).

25. See *Processus nullitatis matrimonii*, 32, a; *Novus processus nullitatis matrimonii*, 20, no. 72.

26. See "De nimia processuum matrimonialium duratione," 685, no. 201.

27. See *Pars dynamica*, 15, no. 54.

28. See "Discorso generale," 64.

29. See "De nimia processuum matrimonialium duratione," 685, no. 200.

30. See ibid., 524, no. 51a.

31. Cf. Ignacio Gordon, *votum*, prot. n. 20582/88 VT, March 17, 1989: in SSAT Archives, *Libro cassa (1981–1989)* 2–3, at III. Cf. *MI* c. 1680 §4.

5. Declaration of Absence

16. – The declaration that a party or witness is contumacious and the imposition of penalties upon them (cf. 1917 *CIC* cc. 1845, 1851) has been a legitimate element of procedural law for ages. However, "it seems more opportune to refrain from such remedies today." Rather, retaining communication with the party may be more effective.[32] "Care is to be taken that justice thus be given to the party that is innocent or acting properly; however, the dignity and rights of the party presumed disobedient or negligent are not to the put in jeopardy."[33] When the respondent refuses to reply to citations, "it is more important that the petitioner, as far as possible, not suffer irreparable damage in the prosecution of his right due to the absence of the other party or of the witnesses."[34]

C. The Instruction of the Cause

1. Judicial Instruction and Proofs in General

17. – The instruction of the cause is completed by means of "jurisdictional" acts, "since they constitute part of the trial, which wholly proceeds from the power of jurisdiction."[35] This is partly why the one questioned is bound to respond to questions posed by the judge or auditor.[36] And in virtue of the character of this power, the judge must be able to exercise real dominion over the instruction of the cause, avoiding the repeated admission of proofs after the conclusion in the cause and the feeble admission of dilatory incidental causes.[37]

Because instruction is jurisdictional in character, even its particular elements are under the authority of the judge. Thus, for example, while the defender of the bond has the right to propose matters about which the parties and witnesses are to be questioned, it is fitting that the judge be the primary agent in preparing the elements for interrogations. For "the questions to be posed pertain to the discovery of the truth rather than to the protection of the bond, and the former is the duty most proper to the judge."[38]

---

32. See "De nimia processuum matrimonialium duratione," 533, no. 63; *Pars dynamica*, 88, no. 378.

33. See *Pars dynamica*, 87, no. 374.

34. See "De nimia processuum matrimonialium duratione," 533, no. 63.

35. See *Pars statica*, 223, no. 340, *sub* "1a Quaestio."

36. Cf. *Pars dynamica*, 31, no. 131.

37. Cf. "De nimia processuum matrimonialium duratione," 525, no. 51e.

38. See ibid., 535, no. 67.

18. – Each act of instruction is best carried out "by the judge instructor of the whole process . . . [rather] than by another judge, even if highly expert."[39] In other words, the singularity of the work of judicial instruction best promotes the completeness and depth of the instruction. As far as determining who should be the instructor, while it is certainly legitimate to employ an auditor *extra collegium*, it is not necessarily recommended or better than instruction carried out by a member of the college. Nor should one sustain grave fears of some partiality of a judge who carried out the instruction, for "even if it can happen, it cannot however be considered a practically necessary effect" that "the hearing of parties and witnesses will weaken . . . the judgment of the instructor." If one were to insist that this were necessary, "it should be necessary likewise to distrust the instruction carried out by him." In fact, it would be better for a judge who will participate in deciding the cause to be the one that instructs the cause.[40]

19. – Obviously the instruction of the cause cannot be carried out by one person acting as both judge and notary.[41] For the judge is the one exercising jurisdictional instructional authority. In turn, the notary independently guarantees the authenticity of the acts emanating from that authority: "Without his presence and without his signature, the records are null."[42]

This is to be borne in mind also when a cause is being handled by a regional tribunal and its instruction is carried out locally, far from the seat of the tribunal. One person is not sufficient for completing acts of instruction even in such circumstances. There must be both an instructor and always a notary. The public ministers intervening in the cause are also to be represented on the local level.[43]

It may be most efficient in the collection of proofs for the judge-instructor to travel with a notary and defender of the bond to a central place closer to witnesses. This may naturally occur in the case of a regional tribunal, which has a larger territory. Or a judge could be admitted into an extern territory and employ one of the local tribunal's notaries for the instruction.[44]

---

39. See ibid., 539, no. 74.

40. See *Pars statica*, 227, nn. 343–343a, including note 38.

41. Cf. "De nimia processuum matrimonialium duratione," 525, no. 51c.

42. See "Dichiarazione di nullità," 140–141, note 5; 142.

43. Ignacio Gordon, *votum* ("Tribunalia Regionialia in [X] erigenda"), prot. n. 437/70 VT, September 8, 1971: in SSAT Archives, 2, no. 3, 5º, b): "Valde notandum quod illud membrum Tribunalis in dioecesi singulariter residens nequit se solo, v.g., testes interrogare; sed ad normam Iuris oportet ut adsit semper Notarius (can. 1585, §1), necnon, si casus fert, citari etiam debet Defensor Vinculi aut Promotor Iustitiae (can. 1587)."

44. Cf. "De nimia processuum matrimonialium duratione," 538, no. 74.

20. – As regards the qualities of the instructor, he is to have the canonical knowledge necessary for understanding "what is required for the sentence in the particular case and the pattern of proofs." Thus, for example, in a cause of simulation of matrimonial consent, the instructor is to try to obtain from a party a direct declaration about the commission of simulation (i.e., a judicial confession or not), statements about the motive for simulating and the motive for celebrating marriage, and explanations about all the circumstances. In order to accomplish this, he needs to have mastered "the art of directing the instruction (…), of questioning, and of summarizing (*verbalizandi*)." These presuppose the ability "to perceive correctly [and] to synthesize clearly and precisely," while "faithfully retaining the ideas, character, and style of the questioned person."[45]

The good preparation of the instructor also better fosters the thoroughness of the instruction. This is a critical service to the correct and expeditious administration of justice. For defects in the instruction not only negatively affect the deliberations of the judges but can also cause delays at further levels of jurisdiction. At the level of appeal, it should be able to be presumed that "the cause is usually already sufficiently instructed."[46] When it truly is, the examination of the cause by superior tribunals can be focused on issuing a just decision without being delayed or distracted by supplementary instruction.

21. – "Natural law demands that the source of proof both have and express the truth with moral certitude."[47] Thus, proofs that are doubtful do not readily give rise to moral certitude.

Proof of nullity of marriage is something marked with "inherent difficulty." It requires good knowledge of canon law, practical experience, and shrewdness in evaluating and weighing proofs. This difficulty demands that a cause be examined by a college of judges (not only one judge), that a party trying to prove his cause be aided by an advocate, and that in fact not only one college but two reach the same moral certitude before a marriage be considered definitively null.[48]

---

45. See *Pars dynamica*, 29, no. 122.

46. See *Pars statica*, 258, no. 381, at b. In the context, his point was that an auditor would therefore not be necessary in the appellate tribunal.

47. See "De nimia processuum matrimonialium duratione," 688, no. 208.

48. See "Dichiarazione di nullità," 141, §3,2. The firmness of these principles suggests the *gravitas legis* reserving certain kinds of causes to a college of judges (cf. 1983 *CIC* c. 1425 §1; *MI* c. 1673 §3).

2. Declaration of Parties

22. – The interrogation of parties is to be done at the beginning of the instruction period, since it is meant to "shed light on the disputed facts" and "direct the [rest of the] instruction."[49] Naturally, then, does the judge examine the parties before examining the witnesses.

23. – Apart from the judicial citation of the respondent, which can also take written form, during the instruction of the cause "the citation, for example, of parties (c. 1530), witnesses (c. 1556), and others always decrees the personal appearance before the judge."[50] This is necessary in order that the judge may personally examine the one summoned. A judicial examination is illegitimate if it is done "without a preceding citation, without the presence of a notary, outside the place of the tribunal, concerning facts which do not pertain to the cause or which fall under committed or professional secrecy."[51]

While the judicial examination is a grave moment, it should be carried in a "climate [that] is serene, free of haste, and secure." It should be one in which the judge can accomplish "a good and pastoral conversation with other brothers" or "members of the faithful." It should thus have also a "priestly" character.[52]

24. – The confession of either or both spouses can be admitted and even have the force of full proof under certain conditions. These conditions are the following: there is a defect of contrary arguments, the credibility of the one confessing is established, especially with the aid of witnesses, and it is confirmed by indications and presumptions.[53] "This 'subsidiary proof' is therefore a means wisely

---

49. See *Pars dynamica*, 29, no. 124, 2º.

50. See *Novus processus nullitatis matrimonii*, 16–17, no. 59.

51. See *Pars dynamica*, 31, no. 130.

52. See "Dichiarazione di nullità," 143, quoting Pope Paul VI in the second quotation, which seems to be from spontaneous comments spoken by the pope "from the abundance of his heart" at the general audience of December 4, 1974 (cf. "Paulus PP. VI alloquitur," 7, no. 2). See also "Discorso generale," 65.

53. Cf. "De nimia processuum matrimonialium duratione," 693–694, nn. 220–222; *Pars dynamica*, 49, no. 211. This complex of elements could be conceived of as a distinct form of proof that could be called "the moral argument" (see "Discorso generale," 66–67, no. 3; "Elementi innovativi nei processi," 8), as distinct from "the physical argument" based on bodily inspection (*Processus nullitatis matrimonii*, 58, 26; *Novus processus nullitatis matrimonii*, 33, note r). This terminology is attributed to Fr. Gordon in the following: Antoni Stankiewicz, "Le caratteristiche del sistema probatorio canonico," in *Il processo matrimoniale canonico. Nuova edizione riveduta e ampliata*, Studi Giuridici 29 (Vatican City: Libreria Editrice Vaticana, 1994) 583.

offered by the legislator so that he may offer a solution in the judicial forum for so-called 'internal forum cases'—which they truly are."[54]

The question of the force of proofs, such as whether the declaration of a party may have the force of full proof, is a matter of procedure.[55] For it is an element that directs the judge's instruction of the cause and aids his judgment about whether the cause has been sufficiently instructed.

3. Testimony

25. – The judge is to strive for efficiency and ease in the collection of testimonies, without violating the law governing the manner of collecting them. Father Gordon agreed with a suggestion that the use of tape recorders be given general, positive regulation in the law. In particular, he suggested that a draft norm from the summary or oral process be transferred so as to apply to all processes. This was accepted, at least with regard to the parties and witnesses.[56]

In the canon treating the place in which witnesses are to be questioned (see 1983 *CIC* c. 1558), he proposed that a norm be included that permitted the receiving of a judicial deposition by telephone. This was—in this author's view— justly rejected. It is notable, though, that even in making this proposal, Father Gordon was in search of an exception ("for a grave cause") that was subject to the condition that "the judge or notary attest to the authenticity of the deposition."[57] For proofs lacking authenticity are for the most part useless.

26. – The 1917 *CIC* had said that priests were incapable of testifying to what they knew from hearing confessions "even if they have been released from the bond of the seal" (c. 1757 §3, 2°). However, Father Gordon observed that "no one, in the common view of theologians, can be released from the bond of the sacramental seal of confession." He therefore proposed that the quoted phrase be changed to "even if the penitent has requested their manifestation," and this was agreeable to all.[58]

---

54. See *Novus processus nullitatis matrimonii*, 33, note r.

55. Cf. "De nimia processuum matrimonialium duratione," 533 and 688, nn. 63 and 207.

56. Cf. PCCICR Archives, *vol. 181. XI. De processibus. Sessio II^-Series II^ diebus 15–19 maii 1978 habita. Relatio,* 37; *Communicationes* 10 (1978) 240. The draft canon (326 §2) read (in translation): "The use of a recording machine can be admitted, provided that the responses then be put to writing and signed by the deponents"; it found expression in c. 1567 §2 of the 1983 *CIC.*

57. See PCCICR Archives, *vol. 181. XI. De processibus. Sessio IV ÷ Series II^ diebus 20–25 novembris 1978 habita. Relatio,* 114; *Communicationes* 11 (1979) 114.

58. See ibid., 111 and 110, respectively.

4. Experts

27. – While a witness may be thought of as a "long-range eye" of the judge (*longus oculus*), the expert is his "long-range intellect" (*longus intellectus*).[59] The witness extends the judge's sight to events from which he stands at a social and/or temporal distance. The expert, though, extends the judge's range of knowledge, such that he enables the judge to understand what is outside his own expertise *qua* judge. At the same time, "the judge is not bound to follow the opinion of the experts, even if they are in agreement. For he in fact also possess other sources of truth as well."[60] He is the *peritus peritorum* in matters of justice.

The expert's assistance (*opera*) to the tribunal includes "either a visit between persons or a reading of the acts, or perhaps both."[61] For these means allow for a deeper examination of the person by the expert.

28. – In the law prior to 1983, two experts were required for cases of impotence and non-consummation (*CIC* 1917 c. 1979 §§1–2), while two could be required for more serious cases of psychological incapacity (cf. *PME* art. 151). In fact, while multiple experts may be illuminating, a single expert may be sufficient. Nor is it presumed to be necessary for him to come to the tribunal to be questioned.[62] Acceptance of these principles is helpful for the administration of justice, since it can be difficult to find an expert qualified to intervene in ecclesial-judicial questions. Paying them is also challenging: a competitive rate makes the judicial expenses excessive, while a modest rate results in the slow submission of expert reports.[63]

5. Publication of the Acts

29. – There had been a late proposal to omit the possibility of the parties examining the judicial acts. However, Father Gordon—obviously opposed to the suggestion—observed that the proposed law was already exercising caution by permitting not the parties but only the advocates to request a copy of the acts.[64] These rights of the advocates and parties are enshrined in canon 1598 §1 of the 1983 *CIC*.

---

59. *Pars dynamica*, 66, no. 286; "Discorso generale," 65, citing Wirth.

60. See *Processus nullitatis matrimonii*, 46, 12; *Novus processus nullitatis matrimonii*, 27, note 13.

61. See ibid., 44, e and 26, note f, respectively.

62. Cf. "De nimia processuum matrimonialium duratione," 537, no. 71.

63. Cf. ibid., 536, no. 70.

64. Cf. "'De processibus.' Relazione della sessione tenutasi dal 5 al 7 marzo 1981," in PCCICR Archives, *vol. 182, XI. De processibus, Parvus coetus (5–7 martii 1981). Relatio*, second folder, 17.

D. The Discussion of the Cause

30. – Father Gordon's various explanations of the discussion of the cause—that is, the period designated for the parties to submit argumentation—are brief and usually repeat what was stated in the norms in force. However, he uniquely questions the prohibition against advocates giving so-called "oral information" to the judge, which remains outside the acts but informs his assessment of a cause (1917 *CIC* c. 1866 §1; cf. 1983 *CIC* c. 1604 §1). Even the meaning of such oral information "certainly escaped me"—he writes—"until I began to work on these questions concerning the Signatura of Justice."[65]

He comments: "I have always been confused about this prohibition and its purpose. I have not been able to be convinced that there would be an advocate who would claim to become the judge's teacher." And he highlights how in the praxis of the Signatura of Justice in the seventeenth century and later, it was *expected* that advocates and parties would hold private meetings with those charged with making or influencing the decision in order to relate information privately. The sequence of events were these: the parties would exchange written information among themselves and submit it to the Prefect and the *votantes*; the next day, oral information would be shared in a private, familiar meeting, and the parties would have a chance to try to refute their adversary's arguments and respond to difficulties the referendary or *votans* was having with the decision to be made, even indicating the decision he was inclined to advise; then, written responses would be submitted; finally, after a day of study, the Signatura would convene and decide the matter.[66]

Nevertheless, Father Gordon admits, "taking the human condition into account, the disadvantages that followed from" the presentation of oral information "far outweighed the benefits."[67] "The practice, which is theoretically good, undoubtedly lent itself to abuses"; and so it was suppressed in the procedural legislation of the twentieth century.[68]

---

65. See "De procedura sequenda," 599, note 79.

66. The time limits would be expanded somewhat by Pius VII's reform. There was an intervening day between submission of written arguments and submission of oral arguments, as well as between the latter and the submission of written responses (cf. "Codificationes legum," 91, no. 4). On the evolution of time limits between the seventeenth and eighteenth centuries, see "De procedura sequenda," 583–586.

67. See "De procedura sequenda," 597–599, at 598.

68. See "Discorso generale," 71–72, 3.2. See also *Novus processus nullitatis matrimonii*, 37, note f.

E. The Decision

1. Deliberation of the College of Judges

31. – The decisional stage of the judicial process, in which the decision is reserved by law or entrusted by the bishop moderator to a college of judges, obviously demands that the individual judges have an opportunity for a solitary examination of the acts of the cause. "A suitable period of time" should be allotted the judges for their individual study of the cause, "proportionate to the difficulty of the cause and the size of the acts."[69] This is directed toward each judge's individual determination about whether or not he is morally certain of the allegations introduced in the cause.

32. – The secrecy of the discussion and conclusions of the members of the college of judges is protected by virtue of the fact that no one else is present at the meeting of the college. This is necessary "in order to protect the freedom of the judges in issuing the sentence, and therefore the public good."[70]

33. – Father Gordon had some concerns about the right of a judge voting in the minority to have his *votum* transmitted to the appellate tribunal in the case of an appeal. For "secrecy . . . in the judicial procedure is something so sacred that the opinions of each judge in the discussion of the college are kept in a sealed envelope." However, he could ultimately agree that it had merit.[71]

Once the code was promulgated, he offered some teaching on the matter, which he called the judge's *ius exigendi*. Finding support in art. 198 §4 of *PME*,[72] he held that the dissenting judge was to make his act of dissent within the discussion itself. This would "strengthen the opinion of the judge not assenting to the decision of the others" and "can invite the judges to further reflection before they finally come to their vote." Practically speaking, the judicial vicar would take note of the dissent so that, in the event of an appeal, he could prompt the presiding judge to arrange for transmission of the dissenting conclusions to the appellate

---

69. See "Dichiarazione di nullità," 143.

70. See "Responsio nonnullis quaestionibus," 642, no. 4.

71. See "'De processibus.' Relazione della sessione tenutasi dal 5 al 7 marzo 1981," in PCCICR Archives, *vol. 182, XI. De processibus, Parvus coetus (5–7 martii 1981). Relatio,* second folder, 18.

72. "However, in the discussion, each has the right to withdraw from his previous conclusion, but the reasons are to be briefly indicated in the written *votum* itself."

tribunal, enclosed in a separate envelope. It was to be read solely by the judges of the superior tribunal, not the defender of the bond or the advocates or procurators. It is not to be transmitted to instances beyond the one to which it was initially sent, since the appellate definitive sentence will have rendered this superfluous in one way or another.[73]

2. Moral Certitude

34. – Moral certitude is reached either on the basis of some truly conclusive proof or from a collection of probative indications. In either case, it is attained "whenever no other sufficient reason can be given except the existence of the disputed facts"—that is, what is claimed by the one asserting it. "From this it follows that moral certitude is not merely subjective but that it is also heavily objective."[74]

In addition to citing the classic formulations from Pope Pius XII's 1942 discourse to the Sacred Roman Rota, Father Gordon defines moral certitude as exclusion of "any probability of the opposite." The tribunal is thus not morally certain even when "one out of a hundred probabilities" contrary to what is alleged is sustained; this truly prescinds from the number of probabilities, whether it is a matter of "one or many or all." In order for the tribunal to be morally certain, "it must persuade itself that no probability at all" exists to the contrary of what is being alleged.[75]

35. – The object of moral certitude (or its absence) is necessarily specific to the individual doubts at issue in the trial. It is a question of moral certitude about each question, in response to each of which a sentence is to be issued. Here "sentence" is understood in a material sense (concrete disposition of the judge), not a merely formal sense (decision-document issued by the judge). "The majority [of the votes] is to be considered, not in relation to the generic question but the specific questions: 'there are as many sentences as there are grounds'!"[76]

36. – The universality of the standard of moral certitude, while promoting legislative simplicity, is "perhaps excessive," since it does not take into account the gravity of diverse species of judicial causes. This equitable consideration of the diverse gravity of causes is what informs the canonical tradition, as a result of

---

73. See "Responsio nonnullis quaestionibus," 643–645.
74. See *Pars dynamica*, 100, no. 433.
75. Cf. "De diverso regimine appellationum," 714–715, no. 1a–b.
76. See *Pars dynamica*, 101, no. 440 (*quot capita, tot sententiae*).

which penal causes and more serious contentious causes, especially concerning marriage, demanded moral certitude (*rectius*: full proof), while the standard of probability was sufficient for contentious causes of lesser importance.[77] This was not a concession on Father Gordon's part to radical proposals in favor of the elimination of moral certitude[78] but a rational recognition that judicial causes are not homogenous.

37. – The meaning of the definitive sentence, which is the act of the judges that can absolve, condemn, declare, and so on,[79] is properly understood in relation to the objective truth. An affirmative sentence—presuming it is the correct decision—declares the objective truth ("coniunctissimam cum veritate"): what is provable and proven by means of the process is in conformity with reality. A negative sentence, however, does not univocally declare the objective truth but only what is (not) proven. Thus a negative sentence does not necessarily mean that objective reality is the opposite of what has been alleged by the *libellus*; this may be so, but it is just as likely that the negative decision is merely stating that what is alleged is not proven.

Therefore, in a cause of nullity of marriage, the affirmative sentence is declaring that the marriage is in reality null and that this has been proven. However, a negative sentence cannot precisely be termed "pro vinculo" in the sense that the bond is declared to exist. The bond may exist, but it also may not exist, while this is merely unproven.[80] The same is true in any kind of cause. For example, in a cause of rights a hospital might claim that a church belongs to it, against a religious institute that claims ownership. An affirmative sentence establishes that the church indeed belongs to the hospital; a negative sentence, though, does not necessarily mean that the church, in truth, belongs to the institute but perhaps only that it is not proven to the exclusion of any contrary probability that it belongs to the hospital.[81]

38. – Father Gordon deems this close connection of the affirmative sentence with the truth to be a secure one, even one that can be presumed, in part "on

---

77. See "De nimia processuum matrimonialium duratione," 722, no. 284, together with 717–720, nn. 273–277.

78. On the contrary, *vide supra* Chapter III, nn. 17–18.

79. *Pars statica*, 41, no. 67b: "tribunal…ad conclusionem quamdam pervenit, sive absolutoriam, sive condemnatoriam, sive declaratoriam, etc."

80. Cf. "De diverso regimine appellationum," 715–716, no. 1c. On this argument, see also *Adnotationes in m.p. "Causas matrimoniales,"* 4–5.

81. Cf. "Dichiarazione di nullità," 143–144.

account of the danger of violating the divine law fixed in the sacrament [of marriage]."[82] This may be a relevant factor to weigh, but the deontology of the ministers of justice may compromise its force in a particular case.

39. – The Church has established within her structures a hierarchy of tribunals, related by reason of appeal, on account of "the fallibility of human judgment. Judges, notwithstanding their preparation and honesty, can err." Accordingly, when a superior college of judges confirms the judgment of an inferior college, "the conformity obtained becomes … a strong safeguard of the truth." How much more important is this dynamic in "grave and difficult cases," such as those concerning nullity of marriage.[83]

3. *Res iudicata*

40. – In the broad sense, a *res iudicata* is what arises in any cause definitively decided by a sentence. In the "strict and specific sense," though, it arises from a sentence "which obtains particular firmness (*firmitas*) from the fact that it can no longer be attacked by means of the appeal."[84] It is not an act of the judge but "the greater firmness which, by the law itself, comes upon some sentence," such that "it cannot be challenged by the ordinary remedy of the appeal."[85]

4. Execution of the Sentence

41. – While there are some divergent opinions and different approaches in the judicial tradition, in the current discipline of the Church, the execution of the definitive sentence is entrusted to the administrative authority. It therefore does not pertain to judicial power. For the execution is outside the judicial activity of the trial itself; it is more expeditious for the administrative authority to attend to it; and it allows judges to limit their attention to more arduous functions.[86]

In causes of nullity of marriage, there is, in a sense, no execution of the definitive sentence, even one that is *pro nullitate*. "It alone is 'executive,' since it declares

---

82. See "De diverso regimine appellationum," 715, no. 1c.

83. See "Dichiarazione di nullità," 141–142, §3,2.

84. See *Pars statica*, 43, no. 70. See also *Processus nullitatis matrimonii*, 86, 15; *Novus processus nullitatis matrimonii*, 48, note 18.

85. See "De obiecto primario competentiae," 526, note 37.

86. Cf. *Pars statica*, 63–64, no. 98. On the suspension of execution of the sentence particular to the Signatura of Justice (viz., the *supersessoria*), see "De procedura sequenda," 586–590.

that the parties had never been true spouses but only putative ones."[87] In other words, its juridical consequences are immediate and do not require integration into the lives of the parties.

F. The Challenge of the Sentence

1. Challenges in General

42. – The public good of the Church stands in a certain state of tension when it comes to the right to challenge the sentence: "On the one hand, it pertains to the common and public good that there be remedies of law, and even for a long period of time, in order to heal possible defects and the like." For it harms society to allow unjust judicial activity to be tolerated and immune from confrontation. "Nevertheless, on the other hand it also pertains to the public good that the execution of a sentence not be too protracted, since rights would otherwise remain uncertain and the usefulness of the sentence would disappear."[88] For what good would judicial activity be at all if its sentences were never able to be brought to effect in the real life of the parties and of society?

2. The Appeal

a. Peremptory Time Limits for Appealing

43. – It is of great importance to recall that the foundation of time limits rests on the necessity of acquiring certitude about rights (*iurium certitudo*), especially in regard to the one who does not appeal or who has first appealed and has freely chosen, e.g., the local appellate tribunal in place of the Sacred Roman Rota, or in regard to the spouses who after two conforming sentences decide to enter marriage. In order to remove all incertitude in such grave matters as far as possible, and in order to urge appropriate diligence in them, the legislator establishes peremptory time limits.[89] This is a theme that occupied some of Father Gordon's technical forensic attention.

---

87. See *Novus processus nullitatis matrimonii*, 49, no. 198. In the 1981 version of this booklet, he did not make this statement but rather presented the norms with some commentary on the execution of the sentence (*Processus nullitatis matrimonii*, 89–92).

88. See *Pars dynamica*, 106, no. 471. Pertinent here, too, is his later quotation of Cicero: "Salus et felicitas reipublicae rebus iudicatis maxime continetur, cum publice magis expediat quod res iudicatae firmae, quam ut semper iustae sint" (ibid., 119, no. 536).

89. See Ignacio Gordon, *votum* ("De recursu contra Congressus decisionem latam in quaestione de iure appellandi"), prot. n. 2120/71 CG, April 3, 1972: in SSAT Archives, 18–19, no. 76.

44. – In one cause of nullity of marriage, after an affirmative sentence was issued, the defender of the bond appealed to the local appellate tribunal, and the respondent introduced his appeal to the Roman Rota (*interpositio*), but failed to prosecute the cause (*prosecutio*) before the Rota until thirty days had passed after the expiration of the peremptory time limit. Nevertheless, the Roman Rota admitted the appeal of the respondent, which prompted the petitioner to make recourse to the Apostolic Signatura. Father Gordon recommended that the Signatura overturn the Rota's decree and declare that the cause was to be assumed by the local appellate tribunal.[90] The Signatura acted in accord with his *votum* in the case.[91]

45. – In another cause having a similar fact pattern,[92] Father Gordon offered extensive teaching on the institute of the judicial appeal in relation to the expiration of time limits. It was a cause of nullity of marriage, in which the local tribunal declared the nullity of marriage, and the defender of the bond introduced an appeal to the local appellate tribunal within the peremptory time limit of (at that time) ten days (1917 *CIC* c. 1881)—now extended to fifteen days (1983 *CIC* c. 1630 §1). After the expiration of the time limit, the respondent decided to appeal to the Roman Rota, which claimed competence for the cause. The petitioner's recourse to the Apostolic Signatura against this Rotal decree was the occasion for Father Gordon's *votum*.[93] He explained that, while the "decendium" for introducing an appeal is "entirely absolute" in itself (no. 13), there are some rules of appeal that could seem to legitimate the respondent's late appeal to the Roman Rota.

Here and in other contexts (e.g., "De iustitia administrativa ecclesiastica," 298, no. 74), he would draw somewhat displeased attention to the flexibility in Rotal jurisprudence in regard to the peremptory time limit to appeal.

90. Cf. Ignacio Gordon, *votum* ("De Tribunalium conflictu"), prot. n. 2695/72 CG, April 30, 1972: in SSAT Archives, document no. 7.

91. See Supreme Tribunal of the Apostolic Signatura, decree of the Secretary, *Nullitatis matrimonii*, prot. n. 2695/72 CG, April 26, 1972: in SSAT Archives, document no. 8. This decree declared the decree of the Prefect in *Congresso*.

92. He would note in his *dispensa*, "since a conflict of competence has frequently arisen between some inferior appellate tribunal and the Sacred Roman Rota due to [non-observance of the time limits for appealing], the Apostolic Signatura has decreed that the time limits for appeal stand" (see *Pars statica*, 336e–336f, no. 485).

93. Ignacio Gordon, *votum* ("De recursu contra Congressus decisionem latam in quaestione de iure appellandi"), prot. n. 2120/71 CG, April 3, 1972: in SSAT Archives. The numbers cited in this section are from this *votum*.

(*a*) An "incidental appeal" allows a party who does not initially appeal to appeal after another party has introduced the principal appeal.[94] Since such an appeal "follows the principal one," it is clear that "it is to be treated at the same seat, not before another tribunal, whatever dignity it may have" (no. 16).

(*b*) The apostolic dignity of the Roman Rota gives it precedence over other tribunals (*PME* art. 216 §§1–2; cf. 1983 *CIC* c. 1632 §2). However, apart from an *avocatio causae*, appeal to it must be made within the peremptory time limit for introducing an appeal (cf. nn. 20–21).

(*c*)[95] Appeal "by adhesion" (nn. 22–47)[96] occurs either *presumably*, when one of multiple co-litigants appeals what would also aggrieve the others (the same cause or object of defense) and those others remain silent but automatically benefit from it, or *expressly*, when they express their support of it within the time limit for introducing an appeal. In either case, the adhesion takes effect before the appellate tribunal selected by the active appellant, before which the adhering parties can present proofs and arguments. A separate act of direct appeal, however, does not constitute appeal by adhesion, since it is a distinct act that only happens to have a goal corresponding to the other appeal.

For these reasons, Father Gordon argued in his *votum* in favor of the competence of the local appellate tribunal and the loss of the right of appeal of the respondent. This in fact is what the *Congresso* of the Apostolic Signatura had decreed before it requested Father Gordon's *votum*. His *votum* was requested and submitted after the respondent, who wanted the Rota to judge the cause, made recourse against the decree of the *Congresso* to the College of Judges. Probably the College would have confirmed the decree of the *Congresso* on its merits; but, in any case, the *Congresso* would reject the recourse, since its decree was not subject to recourse, inasmuch as it had to be issued *expeditissime* (cf. *NS* art. 70; 1917 *CIC* c. 1880, 7º [1983 *CIC* c. 1629, 5º]).[97]

---

94. In the 1917 *CIC*, this could be done "even if the time limits for the appeal have passed" (c. 1887 §2). In the current *CIC*, there is a kind of "resetting" of the peremptory time limit: even if the time limits have passed, the incidental appeal may be made "within the peremptory time limit of fifteen days from the day on which the principal appeal was communicated to [the appealed party]" (c. 1637 §3).

95. Another he treats (in nn. 48–53) is the right to request a transfer of one's appeal to the Roman Rota after an appeal is made to the ordinary appellate tribunal (*PME* art. 216 §3) which, however, has not been received into the *CIC* of 1983 or *DC*. He stressed that this right exists only with regard to one's own appeal, not the appeal of another.

96. The current legislation regulates appeal by presumed adhesion in c. 1637 §2 (1917 *CIC* c. 1888).

97. Cf. Supreme Tribunal of the Apostolic Signatura, decree of the *Congresso*, *Incidentis: De jure appellandi*, prot. n. 2120/71 CG, April 26, 1972: SSAT Archives.

b. Appeal of the Defender of the Bond

46. – In 1969, Father Gordon expressed surprise at proposals that the defender of the bond be considered to have merely a right and not a duty to appeal a sentence issued *pro nullitate*, as if he were just another party.[98] The suggestion that there would be no necessary examination of a single declaration of nullity, which could be executed immediately, was deemed by him in the early 1970s to be a "radical opinion."[99] He indeed had serious concern about leaving the choice to appeal to the discretion of the defender of the bond, since such a "solution would provide for brevity indeed, but it forsakes the protection of the bond." This would only be exacerbated by the practice in some places of appointing as defenders of the bond persons "who are of meeker (= laxer) disposition."[100]

"We know that any judges are truly *fallible*. [...] Consequently, if the indissolubility of marriage, called to trial, merits some *serious* caution..., it is not sufficient that there be a defender of the bond in matrimonial causes, but it is also required that the first sentence issued in favor of nullity be subjected to an obligatory *examination*."[101] That examination is necessary in view of "the obligation of the legislator to protect, apart from the rights of the parties, also the indissolubility of marriage; and this protection in practice is a gamble unless it is made *necessary* by the law itself, in one way or another. [...] Were this defense omitted, the pathway to abuses would be opened, as came about at the time of Benedict XIV and even in our time."[102] Such a proposal thus "offers no true protection for

---

98. "De nimia processuum matrimonialium duratione," 707, no. 15: "Habet igitur [secundum Kelleher] Defensor vinculi, post primam sententiam contra vinculum, *ius* (non *officium!*) appellandi, omnino sicut partes" (emphasis in original). This had even been proposed by some fathers of the Second Vatican Ecumenical Council, such as the Archbishop of Izmir and the Bishop of Roermond. Cf. *Acta synodalia Sacrosancti Concilii Oecumenici Vaticani II. Pars VIII: Congregationes generales CXXIII–CXXVII. Sessio publica V* (Vatican City: Typis Polyglottis Vaticanis, 1976) III/8:664–665, 1165 (II).

99. See "De diverso regimine appellationum," 718, no. 3 (above section no. 3 "*Obiectionibus respondetur*"). Msgr. Gianpaolo Montini teaches that, in this era, the relaxation of the obligation of the defender of the bond to appeal an affirmative sentence was in fact a secondary factor of the crisis in the judicial protection of marriage following the Second Vatican Ecumenical Council. The primary factor was the suppression of the requirement of a double conformity of sentences. In his assessment, Fr. Gordon may not have sufficiently appreciated this primary factor, especially when addressing the plenary gathering of the code commission in 1981 (cf. Gianpaolo Montini, "Il difensore del vincolo e l'obbligo dell'appello," *Periodica* 106 [2017] 306–307).

100. See "De nimia processuum matrimonialium duratione," 726, no. 289.

101. See "Votum de revisione sententiae," 117, nn. 33–34, emphasis in original.

102. See ibid., 121, nn. 54–55.

the marriage of the faithful and its indissolubility"; rather, "true divorces are concealed under the name of a declaration of nullity."[103]

47. – These concerns voiced by Father Gordon were either not heard or were dismissed in the most recent reform of the marriage nullity process by means of the motu proprios of 2015—*Mitis Iudex* and its counterpart for the Eastern Catholic Churches, *Mitis et misericors Iesus*. How urgent it therefore is to heed Father Gordon's observation about how the defender of the bond ought ordinarily to be disposed to appeal an affirmative sentence issued in a cause in which he is intervening. "There cannot be many cases in which the appeal is presented as 'clearly superfluous'" from the perspective of the defender of the bond.[104]

48. – Just prior to the coming-into-effect of the APN, an American tribunal sent the Apostolic Signatura a petition for a dispensation from the obligation to appeal two of its affirmative sentences or, in other words, from the necessity of obtaining a double conformity of sentences in two causes. This was something already being proposed by American canonists, and Father Gordon was clearly opposed to it, as discussed above. However, he perceived at that time that the code commission would admit the solution of the *processus brevior*, or the simplified examination of a cause by the appellate tribunal already decided with an affirmative sentence—which in fact would be admitted into the general legislation even earlier (viz., in *CM*). Thus, seeing that the latter "mechanism" was already likely to be received into the Church's general legislation, he advised that the request was not to be granted but that the petitioning tribunal—and perhaps all the tribunals of the U.S.—be given the faculty to use the anticipated *processus brevior*.

This anticipatory concession for the dioceses of the U.S. was suggested by Father Gordon, so that "other truly dangerous solutions would be impeded" (2º, d and 3º) especially that according to which "the obligation of appealing would be left entirely to the prudence of the defender of the bond of the . . . first instance tribunal." He was aware that this approach had "already [been] requested by the conference [of bishops] itself, under the persuasion of American canonists, especially Kelleher, whose theories, even though completely devoid of foundation, are

---

103. See ibid., 127, no. 92. The converse is thus that the safeguard of the hierarchical examination "offers the appropriate remedy against hidden divorces" (ibid., no. 94).

104. See "El M. P. '*Causas matrimoniales*' y las normas americanas," 213.

daily acquiring greater diffusion and authority."[105] But alas, the particular concession to the American tribunals would come into effect not three months later.[106]

This petition directed to the Signatura was also seen by Father Gordon to be unsuitable in regard to its motives. It was presented, as he says, "as if it were the only means for avoiding in both cases a civil marriage, since neither can the tribunal of appeal *quickly* give a second sentence, nor can the interested parties [wait to] celebrate a wedding *later*!"[107]

49. – He was deeply concerned about the praxis in the U.S. under the regime of the APN, which prescribed the obligation of the defender of the bond to appeal an affirmative sentence while permitting a dispensation from this obligation as an exception. One Cardinal Father of the code commission asked in the name of his conference that this be "retained" in the law. Father Gordon observed: "What is really requested, just as it is now requested, had never been granted as a norm but only as an exception (…) which, by means of abuse, became the norm. Therefore, unless I am mistaken, the word *retain* is used in a certain equivocal sense."[108] When it was rather boldly proposed that the U.S. should be given an exceptional norm in this area of procedural law, Father Gordon rightly expressed caution: implicitly and primarily because of the importance of the uniformity of procedural law, but also because "abuses especially come out of that territory."[109]

---

105. See Ignacio Gordon, *votum*, prot. n. 80/70, February 4, 1970: in SSAT Archives: "Impedirentur, per concessionem factam, aliae solutiones vere periculosae (cf. n. 287, 1–3 ["De nimia processuum matrimonialium duratione"] in *Appendice I*), praesertim illa tertia, iam petita ab ipsa Conferentia, suadentibus canonistis americanis, praesertim Kelleher, cuius theoriae, etsi fundamento destitutae ut plurimum, maiorem diffusionem et auctoritatem in dies obtinent (cf. Appendicem II)" (3, d, 3º).

106. The imminence of the APN may have influenced the decision of the *Congresso*—contrary to Fr. Gordon's *votum* and that of the Signatura's defender of the bond, but with the support of the *votum* of another referendary—to approach the Roman Pontiff, advising him to grant the dispensation. In the audience granted to the Prefect on March 12, 1970, the Holy Father indeed granted the dispensation, entrusting the execution of the favor to the bishop moderator of the tribunal "pro sua prudentia et conscientia," but the Signatura declared that the tribunal in all other causes had to proceed according to the norm of law, according to which the defender of the bond was bound to appeal every affirmative sentence. Cf. Supreme Tribunal of the Apostolic Signatura, minutes (*verbale*) from the *Congresso, Nullitatis matrimonii*, prot. n. 80–81/70 VT, March 11, 1970 and letter, March 17, 1970: in SSAT Archives.

107. "Est praeterea alius quod mihi non placet in petitione [X], sc., modus premendi seu instandi pro concessione, quasi esset omnino unicum medium ad vitandum in utroque casu matrimonium civile, quia nec Tribunal appellationis *citius* alteram sententiam dare, nec partes, quarum interest, nuptias *tardius* celebrare possunt!" (Gordon, *votum*, prot. n. 80/70, February 4, 1970: ibid., 1, 1º).

108. See "Votum de revisione sententiae," 115, note 16.

109. See ibid., 119, no. 45.

50. – A critical element of the requirement of the double conformity of affirmative sentences for the definitive nullity of marriage is the collegiality of the tribunal, at least of the appellate tribunal. This, however, was compromised by the APN, which (in no. 23.I, taken together with no. 3) envisioned the possibility not only of a sole judge at the first level of jurisdiction but also—if a defender of the bond should happen to fulfill his obligation to appeal—at the second level, or the level of appeal. Declaring how lacking in wisdom that norm was, he comments that

> the double conformity [of sentences]—and consequently the just defense of the bond—loses 50% of its efficacy when neither of the two tribunals offers the safeguards of wisdom and freedom typical of collegiality. And then we run the risk of returning to the chaotic matrimonial situation which Benedict XIV encountered when he felt obliged to create the figure of the defender of the bond and the safeguard of the two conforming sentences.[110]

c. Double Conformity of Sentences[111]

51. – Even though it might introduce a formal inequality between the parties,[112] Father Gordon could already in 1969 support the institution of an abbreviated appellate process (eventually established in 1971 by Paul VI),[113] wherein there would be no ordinary contentious trial (at least initially) but only a prejudicial decision by the superior college of judges about whether or not to confirm the affirmative sentence. For that solution "happily balances" the goods at stake— "namely, the protection of the bond with a suitable abbreviation of the process."[114] Prior to the institution of that process, "the expenses and time of the longer process of appeal were uselessly spent in order to obtain a conforming sentence which may

---

110. See "El M. P. '*Causas matrimoniales*' y las normas americanas," 209.

111. The remarks made in the following paragraphs apply, *mutatis mutandis*, to the abbreviated appellate process prescribed in c. 1680 §2 of *MI*, since it is the successor institute to that being described by Fr. Gordon. The principal difference between them concerns the mode of transmission of the cause to the superior tribunal: in *CM* and the original c. 1682 of the 1983 *CIC*, the law itself prescribed this transmission; in *MI*, this transmission depends upon the interposition and prosecution of an appeal.

112. Cf. "De diverso regimine appellationum," 719, at 2).

113. Notwithstanding that support, he described the section of *CM* on appeals as the one that "brings with it greater novelty and many difficulties." See *Adnotationes in m.p. "Causas matrimoniales*," 2.

114. See "De nimia processuum matrimonialium duratione," 726, no. 290. He defended it also ten years later within the *Coetus de processibus*: PCCICR Archives, *vol. 181. XI. De processibus. Sessio VI· Series II·diebus 26–31 martii 1979 habita. Relatio*, 190; *Communicationes* 11 (1979) 266.

be equally obtained more quickly and without monetary expense through the new and briefer process."[115] For he detected a high statistical likelihood that affirmative sentences would be confirmed. Thanks to the *processus brevior* instituted by Paul VI (as that process was called in doctrine and jurisprudence), affirmative sentences "might, on the one hand, receive the usual confirmation more easily and quickly; and, on the other hand, protection would be given to the sanctity of the matrimonial bond and to the rights of the respondent."[116]

52. – The *processus brevior* was brought about by a particular "mechanism" in the law according to which the judge would see to the transmission of the acts to the appellate tribunal—a mechanism that "greatly differs from an appeal" introduced by a party. This was, in a manner of speaking, an "appeal" made by the legislator himself, "who is competent by the divine law for the protection of marriage and its indissolubility." And so in that (now derogated) norm, the legislator "*enjoins* the tribunal, not to appeal, but simply to transmit the acts and the appeals, if any were introduced by the spouses, to the tribunal of appeal."[117] Technically speaking, though, "the legislator deliberately omits the word 'appeal,' because he in fact imposes a duty to appeal on no one." Thus, the tribunal's transmission of the cause *ex officio* was not an appeal.[118]

53. – Prior to making the decision about the confirmation of the affirmative sentence, both the defender of the bond and the college of judges had "the duty . . . diligently to examine the acts." If they do not do so, "the defender cannot become informed about whether or not the bond was injured; moreover, the judge cannot make a decision about the objectivity of the sentence."[119] It is a matter of "a study of the sentence in light of the acts, by each of the judges."[120] Indeed, "an examination of the sentence cannot be done unless the complete acts are had before one's eyes; from these the examiner may judge whether some facts or proofs demanding a contrary decision were neglected in the sentence or, on

---

115. See "De diverso regimine appellationum," 719, at 2).

116. See "De appellationibus," 312.

117. See "Votum de revisione sententiae," 125, no. 83 (emphasis omitted for the sake of simplicity) and 126, no. 88.

118. See *Processus nullitatis matrimonii*, 84, l; *Novus processus nullitatis matrimonii*, 47, note k.

119. See *Adnotationes in m.p. "Causas matrimoniales,"* 10, no. 2b.

120. *Processus nullitatis matrimonii*, 86, m; *Novus processus nullitatis matrimonii*, 47, note l. Citing this doctrine are, e.g., Zenon Grocholewski ("L'appello nelle cause di nullità matrimoniale," *Forum* 4 [1993/2] 56, note 83) and Gianpaolo Montini ("L'appello in una causa di nullità matrimoniale," *Quaderni di diritto ecclesiale* 22 [2009] 328).

the other hand, whether the decision is founded on facts which are not sufficiently established in the acts."[121]

54. – The decision of the college of judges in the *processus brevior* (i.e., whether or not to confirm the affirmative sentence) was made with "discretionary power" in the sense that it was not constricted by the arguments of the defender of the bond or, if admitted, of either of the spouses. Thus "it is not 'arbitrary' but is founded on an examination of all the acts; it is governed by the law of nature and has as its scope that provision be more quickly and better made for truth and justice."[122] In other words, "the principle of moral certitude is in force, which the judge must have about the matter to be decided." And so "if the college should not obtain that certitude, it is to decree that the cause is to be admitted to an ordinary examination."[123] The decree of confirmation is indeed a judicial decree of a decisive nature; it is an act "ad instar sententiae," since it definitively decides a controversy,[124] "closes the instance of the principal cause,"[125] and, as such, is "irreformable (in an explicit sense)."[126]

3. The Complaint of Nullity[126]

55. – Together with the appeal, the complaint of nullity (*querela nullitatis*) is a main, ordinary remedy of law against the sentence.[128] The nullity of a sentence is distinct from the inexistence of a sentence. An inexistent sentence has not even

---

121. See "Votum de revisione sententiae," 122, no. 59.

122. See "De appellationibus," 316.

123. See *Adnotationes in m.p. "Causas matrimoniales,"* 10, no. 2d.

124. Cf. ibid., 12–13, no. 2.

125. See *Processus nullitatis matrimonii*, 88, o; *Novus processus nullitatis matrimonii*, 50, note 2.

126. See "Votum de revisione sententiae," 123, no. 69.

127. In one of his *vota*, he cited a doctoral thesis (by Emilio Ghidotti) that he directed, pertaining to the nullity of the definitive sentence as erudite and offering a contribution to the canonical doctrine. Cf. Ignacio Gordon, *votum* ("De quibusdam quaestionibus circa competentiam S. T. Signaturae Apostolicae"), *Nullitatis matrimonii*, prot. n. 35/70 CG, May 3, 1970: in SSAT Archives, 3, no. 5.

128. Cf. *Pars statica*, 43, nn. 68–69; *Pars dynamica*, 107, nn. 472–473. However, it was he who proposed the elimination of the canons on the *actio nullitatis* from the code (cf. 1917 *CIC* cc. 1679–1683), suggesting, however, the preservation on the canon that would become 1983 *CIC* c. 1405 §2 (the prior c. 1683 and draft c. 121). Cf. PCCICR Archives, *vol. 181. XI. De processibus. Sessio III⸗ Series II⸍diebus 23–28 octobris 1978 habita. Relatio*, 79; *Communicationes* 11 (1979) 77. He was the consultor in the minority in the discussion on the sanation of null acts, reported in ibid., 144 (see PCCICR Archives, *vol. 181. XI. De processibus. Sessio V⸗ Series II⸍diebus 11–16 decembris 1978 habita. Relatio*, 143–144).

the appearance of a sentence (*species sententiae*), "since it lacks an efficient cause (a judge) and a material or formal cause (the resolution of the cause expressed according to the norm of law)." A null sentence, though, has the appearance of a sentence but is defective in regard to some essential element or formality.[129]

56. – Even if certain grounds of nullity of the sentence should seem obvious, they need to be stated since they make the regime of nullity clear.[130] Simple prohibitions in law in this matter are insufficient, since it concerns a grave matter. For example, Father Gordon supported the explicit sanction of nullity (and indeed, that irremediable) for the illegitimate use of the oral process, "lest the intention of the legislator be frustrated."[131]

He was somewhat convinced by the pre-1983 opinion of another author about the illegitimate use of a single clerical judge as a cause of nullity of the sentence. However, he did sustain some doubt "since these nullities are established by analogy, rather than by the law."[132] Similarly, he was inclined to hold that the defect of motives in a decree of confirmation did not cause the nullity of the decree, since that defect was "expressly established for sentences."[133] On the other hand, he taught that judging in another instance a cause in which one already intervened is a matter of absolute incompetence, redounding to the irremediable nullity of the sentence.[134]

---

129. See *Pars dynamica*, 115, no. 517.

130. Cf. "'De processibus.' Relazione della sessione tenutasi dal 5 al 7 marzo 1981," in PCCICR Archives, *vol. 182, XI. De processibus, Parvus coetus (5–7 martii 1981). Relatio*, second folder, 19 at 2).

131. See *Novus processus nullitatis matrimonii*, 12, note a. See also *Processus nullitatis matrimonii*, 22, 1 and "'De processibus.' Relazione della sessione tenutasi dal 5 al 7 marzo 1981," in PCCICR Archives, *vol. 182, XI. De processibus, Parvus coetus (5–7 martii 1981). Relatio*, second folder, 27: "GORDON nota che la semplice proibizione è insufficiente nei casi in cui si tratti di materia grave. Seguendo poi questo criterio [i.e., that a simple prohibition would be sufficient] potrebbero essere soppresse tutte le sanzioni di nullità."

132. See *Adnotationes in m.p. "Causas matrimoniales*," 280.

133. Cf. ibid., 14–15, at IV.5.

134. Cf. *Processus nullitatis matrimonii*, 12, g; *Novus processus nullitatis matrimonii*, 7, note g.

CHAPTER VIII

The Supreme Tribunal of the Apostolic Signatura

A. History of the Apostolic Signatura

1. – Among modern canonical proceduralists, Father Gordon is notable for his historical research about the Apostolic Signatura, so much so that one author called him "the principal current historian on the Signatura of Justice."[1] Father Gordon alluded to some aspects of this history in his first major work in the area of canonical administrative law, the "De Tribunalibus administrativis." He attempted a more concentrated, chronological history in his introductory annotations to the *NS*, unofficially published in the journal *Periodica*. He would build upon these in subsequent years, culminating in several profound studies in the first part of the 1980s, the end of his formal scholarly profession. And these historical investigations yielded discoveries that he found useful even in his technical consultation.[2] He was credited by one author in 1984 with completing "the most

---

1. See Juan Ignacio Bañares, "Función judicial y supremacía de la Signatura de Justicia en el siglo XVII: en torno al testimonio del Cardenal De Luca," *Ius Canoncum* 28 (1988) 305–306, note 1.

2. See, e.g., Ignacio Gordon, *votum* ("Breves observationes ad *votum pro rei veritate* exaratum ab. Adv. [X]"), *Nullitatis matrimonii*, prot. n. 35/70 C.G.1., June 22, 1970: in SSAT Archives; idem, *votum* ("È possibile impugnare le decisioni de gli Em.mi e Ecc.mi Giudici con la querela di nullità e/o la *restitutio in integrum?*"), prot. n. 23136/91 VAR (cf. prot. n. 18190/86 CA), February 11, 1992: in ibid.

139

recent and rigorous investigations on the history and activity of the Signatura."[3] By means of this historical research, Father Gordon wanted to reveal, in part, that it was a "love of justice that had created the Signatura."[4]

2. – Father Gordon illustrates how the primitive form of what would become the Signatura was something expressed in its own way in earlier secular government. In the governance of the late Western Roman Empire, there was a particular official called the *referendarius*, who would make reports (*relationes/referre*) to the emperor about different requests and petitions directed to him. This same practice would enter the praxis of ecclesiastical curiae, including especially the papal chancery.[5] The history of the Signatura itself can be identified according to four periods: 1) its origin and primitive evolution, 2) its progress and especially its "golden age," 3) the codification of its laws, and 4) its transformation.[6] This is what the late Reverend Professor Carmelo de Diego-Lora called "the classic distinction of stages in its history, formulated by Gordon."[7]

1. The Origins of the Signatura

3. – The origin and primitive evolution of the Signatura emerges in the praxis of Pope Innocent III (13th cent.). When a report was given to him, he would reply by placing his signature (*signum*) on a document, granting the request. Those giving such a report were called referendaries (*Referendarii*, "reporters") under Innocent IV (1243–1254).[8] Under Eugenius IV (1431–1437), they had the faculty to sign for the Pope requests for non-judicial favors and judicial commissions, and so they came to be called *Referendarii Signaturae*. The body of them was called the *Signatura gratiae et commissionum*, signifying both kinds of requests they handled and a certain distinction within the Signatura itself. By the end of

---

3. See Vicente Cárcel Ortí, "Il Supremo Tribunale della Segnatura Apostolica. Cenni storici," in *Dilexit iustitiam. Studia in honorem Aurelii Card. Sabattani*, ed. Zenon Grocholewski and Vicente Cárcel Ortí (Vatican City: Libreria Editrice Vaticana, 1984) 173, note 29.

4. See idem, *votum*, February 11, 1992: 2, no. 8.

5. Cf. "Normae speciales," 76, no. 1.

6. Cf. "De Signaturae Iustitiae competentia," 351–352.

7. See Carmelo de Diego-Lora, "I tribunali della Sede Apostolica," in *Il processo matrimoniale canonico. Nuova edizione riveduta e ampliata*, Studi Giuridici 29 (Vatican City: Libreria Editrice Vaticana, 1994) 267, no. 32.

8. Cf. "Normae speciales," 76–77, nn. 2–3; "La renovación de la Signatura Apostólica," 573–574, note 1a. The findings of these two studies, together with those of the "De iustitia administrativa ecclesiastica," are presented in synthetic form in *Pars statica*, 283–314, nn. 413–459e, as Fr. Gordon himself points out on 283, in note ** [*sic*].

the fifteenth century, this would be a formally recognized distinction, such that the Signatura of Favor (*Signatura gratiae*) was headed by the Pope himself and had preeminence over the Signatura of Justice (*Signatura iustitiae*).[9]

2. The Golden Age of the Signatura

4. – The institution of the Signatura underwent progress beginning in the early sixteenth century, on account of this institutionalized bifurcation between the Signatura of Justice and the Signatura of Favor. Falling within this period was its golden age, spanning from Pope Alexander VII (1655–1667) to Pope Benedict XIV (1740–1758).

The referendaries and *votantes*, who comprised both Signaturas, were highly praised by the Roman Pontiffs, notably by Paul III in his constitution *Debita consideratione* of July 30, 1540. Later, in 1746, Pope Benedict XIV described them as "prelates of the Church laboring with us in this Roman Curia in order to treat the demanding and most difficult affairs of favor and of justice for the whole Catholic world."[10] For their work frequently involved the examination of a large volume of documented procedural history, including the various developments in a cause that had already resulted in a triple conforming sentence.[11]

5. – The Signatura of Justice (*Signatura iustitiae*) addressed *commissiones*, which Father Gordon defined as "a certain supplication whose *presupposition* was some judicial cause, at least somehow begun, but its *object* was the obtaining of some favor that had a connection with the aforementioned cause." The Signatura's favorable response always had to be issued within the limits of the law when issued in virtue of its ordinary power. It was called a *rescriptum*, and it mandated or "entrusted" a particular act or series of acts to some judge.[12] The object of these supplications varied. When it was not a request for the admission of some

---

9. Cf. "Normae speciales," 77, nn. 4–5; "La renovación de la Signatura Apostólica," 574, note 1b.

10. See "De referendariorum ac votantium dignitate," 200, no. 1. Citing this work, see, e.g., Niccolò del Re, *La Curia Romana. Lineamenti storico-giuridici*, 4th ed. (Vatican City: Libreria Editrice Vaticana, 1998) 215, note 13; Joaquín Llobell, "Il diritto al processo giudiziale contenzioso amministrativo," in *La giustizia nell'attività amministrativa della Chiesa. Il contenzioso amministrativo*, ed. Eduardo Baura and Javier Canosa, Monografie Giuridiche 31 (Milan: Giuffrè Editore, 2006) 244, note 45.

11. Cf. "De procedura sequenda," 600.

12. See "De Signaturae Iustitiae competentia," 356. Pius VII would later call the *commissio* a *domanda* (It., or L. *instantia*), or a request ("Codificationes legum," 89–90, no. 3.), but his successor restored the use of *commissio* (ibid., 94, no. 3).

appeal—the most common request, which at that time included complaints of nullity and requests for a *restitutio in integrum*—it might pertain to a question of the competent forum or some matter delegated to it by the Signatura of Favor. Rescripts issued with such a delegation could go beyond the limits of the law, since the Signatura of Favor was the Pope's organ for handling extraordinary requests and thus could exceed what was foreseen by law.[13] In any case, in handling the request, the Signatura would study the sentences or decrees of the inferior judges involved and decide whether the favor was to be granted or denied.[14]

6. – The Signatura of Justice was a tribunal by the mid-sixteenth century.[15] From the sixteenth to the eighteenth centuries—until its suppression by Napoleon in 1809—its officials were a Cardinal Prefect and a kind of college of several referendaries, among whom some were called *votantes*. Prior to June 13, 1659, the Prefect alone issued the decision in the congregation of the full Signatura. That day, however, Pope Alexander VII endowed the twelve *votantes* with the power to give a deliberative vote, such that they, together with the Prefect and the referendary proposing the cause to them, constituted a college of judges.[16] Its competence excluded the judgment of the merits of causes but included the following acts: to declare the nullity of judicial acts, to grant an appeal or *restitutio in integrum*, to remove suspect judges, to resolve conflicts of competence between tribunals, and to reply to judges about proper judicial conduct.[17]

Petitions submitted to it were decided either by the Prefect or the full Signatura (*Signatura plena* or *Congregatio Signaturae*). Which organ decided it was based on the criterion of clarity or certainty: if it was a petition that was clearly to be granted or denied, it was handled by the Prefect. If this was in doubt, the Prefect took care to defer the matter to the full Signatura. By the mid-eighteenth century, a lower-tier of jurisdiction was instituted in the person of the auditor. To his judgment were entrusted commissions of lesser importance, and recourse could be made against those to the Prefect. This was meant to avoid the deferral of numerous recourses to the full Signatura, which was being approached with increasing frequency and zeal by advocates. Recourse could only be made to it

---

13. On these, see "De Signaturae Iustitiae competentia," 366–369. On the frequency of the *commissio appellationis*, see also "De procedura sequenda," 586, no. 3.

14. Cf. "De Signaturae Iustitiae competentia," 360 and 386, no. 2.

15. Cf. "Normae speciales," 77, no. 6.

16. Cf. "De procedura sequenda," 602. See also "Normae speciales," 78, no. 7. On their collegial quality, see ibid., 92, no. 35.

17. Cf. "Normae speciales," 78, nn. 7–8; "La renovación de la Signatura Apostólica," 572, note 1d.

against decisions of the Prefect if the latter confirmed the decision of the auditor, if the object was the principal and not an incidental cause, and if the recurrent deposited a certain amount of money (four "scuta").[18]

7. – The Signatura of Favor (*Signatura gratiae*) was an organ over which, in 1588, Pope Sixtus V declared his intention to preside, as his predecessors did. This fact attributed it much prestige and authority but would also relate to its demise. For, on the one hand, it had superiority over the Signatura of Justice, whose decisions denying appeals could be overturned by this organ. On the other hand, since the Pope was otherwise burdened with care of the whole Church, it was only able to meet periodically. It would therefore regularly entrust its causes to the Signatura of Justice. It ceased *de facto* in 1839 and *de iure* in 1908.[19]

During the golden age of the Signatura, the Signatura of Favor had competence over merely favorable matters (i.e., when there was no opposing party) as well as over contentious matters. As was said, the Pope was the president of the Signatura of Favor, and so it was the organ that aided him in deciding extraordinary appeals and recourses, including cases in which there was neither an ordinary nor an extraordinary remedy of law available to the parties. Accordingly, it could entertain requests whose object was *contra legem* or reserved to the Roman Pontiff. It could grant the right of appeal when a cause had been entrusted to some judge with the clause "appellatione remota." When a provision had been made by the Apostolic See to which was attached immunity from litigation, this organ could receive a request for an *aperitio oris*, or a reconsideration of that clause by the Roman Pontiff. It could grant sanations of null sentences, such as when there was a defect of a citation. It could grant *restitutiones in integrum* beyond the competence or praxis of other tribunals. It handled questions of the competent forum beyond the competence of the Signatura of Justice. And it could grant further extensions of *fatalia legis* already extended.[20]

3. The Age of Codification

8. – The period of *codification* of the laws of the Signatura is seen especially from the pontificate of Pius VII to that of Gregory XVI (i.e., from about 1800 to

---

18. Cf. "De procedura sequenda," 577–580.

19. Cf. "Normae speciales," 83–84, nn. 13–15; "La renovación de la Signatura Apostólica," 572, note 1f. On the delegation of matters to the Signatura of Justice, see also "De Signaturae Iustitiae competentia," 368–369.

20. Cf. "De Signaturae Iustitiae competentia," 369–371.

1870). During most of the pontificate of Pius VI (1775–1799), the Signatura of Justice functioned normally. Its activity would be interrupted, though, for about nineteen months (February 1798–September 1799) during the first French occupation of Rome. Pius VI's successor, Pius VII, would introduce some laws in the first years of his pontificate affecting the Signatura, including the October 30, 1800 constitution *Post diuturnas*, by which he reordered the Roman Curia and civil tribunals, some of which material touched upon the competence and procedure of the Signatura of Justice. Once again, French invasion caused the Signatura's jurisdiction to cease, from 1809 to 1814.[21]

9. – After Napoleon's empire had been overthrown and the Papal States reconstituted, Pope Pius VII renewed and unified the governance of the Papal States. His first major legislative act in this regard was to promulgate general rules for such governance, which he accomplished by the motu proprio *Quando per ammirabile* of July 6, 1816. His plan to issue two codes was not completed, and he was able to issue only a code of civil procedure, on November 22, 1817, by the motu proprio *Nello stabilire*. Both of these bodies of norms impacted the competence and functioning of the Signatura of Justice since, without changing the norms of the Signatura, it gathered them for the first time into one *corpus*.[22]

The Signatura was treated in Book VI of *Nello stabilire*, as well as in some introductory constitutional norms.[23] That motu proprio established clearly that the Signatura was the only supreme tribunal, since to it were now clearly subject the tribunals of the Papal States and, by means of the Rota, all ecclesiastical tribunals of the Church herself. Its officials, in continuity with its tradition, were the Prefect, his auditor, twelve *votantes*, and several referendaries. The full Signatura comprised two *turni* of six *votantes* each, the oldest of them presiding; they each had a decisive vote in the cause before them. The auditor of the Signatura, and the Prefect if he wished, were present at each *turnus* gathering, which occurred once per week. Each *turnus* embodied the full Signatura, but all twelve *votantes* could treat a cause as the full Signatura.

Causes whose value was less than a certain amount (200 "scuta") were judged by the auditor of the Signatura, against whose decision a party could make recourse to the Prefect. If the Prefect's decision reformed the auditor's and the cause involved more than a certain amount (50 "scuta"), a further recourse

---

21. Cf. "Codificationes legum," 79–80, no. 1.
22. Cf. ibid., 80–83, no. 2.
23. Cf. ibid., 84–92.

could be made to the full Signatura; otherwise, the Prefect's decision was subject to no recourse.

Pius VII therein stated seven titles of competence enjoyed by the Signatura of Justice. (1) It could declare the nullity (*circumscribere*) of acts, decrees, and judicial sentences on one of the three classic grounds of nullity, viz., a defect of jurisdiction, of citation, or of mandate. Once it declared an act null, it could entrust the cause either to the tribunal *a quo* or to the tribunal of the Apostolic Camera or of the Rota. (2) It could decide questions of competence for all tribunals of Rome and of the Papal States, except for that of the Apostolic Camera. (3) It determined the effects of certain appeals, especially whether they were suspensive or only devolutive. It was competent to decide (4) allegations of suspicion against judges, (5) the unification of causes, and (6) the summoning (*avocatio*) of causes. And (7) the Signatura had the power to judge petitions for a *restitutio in integrum*, or requests for "second appeal" against a cause that had passed into the state of *res iudicata*, though it could not suspend the execution of a *res iudicata*.[24]

10. – These norms were reiterated by Leo XII (1823–1829)[25] in his October 5, 1824 motu proprio *Dopo le orribili calamità*. This legislation introduced a number of changes to the procedural law of the Papal States but largely confirmed the regulation of the Signatura of Justice.

Two years later, he also issued a motu proprio *Quum plurima* on the Signatura itself and on the payment, privileges, and character of the *Votantes*. In it, he also reduced the number of *votantes* to seven, which would always act as a single college with no *turni*. One of them was a Dean (the Dean of the *votantes*), who had a kind of intermediate place between the Prefect and the auditor, still the Prefect's principal assistant. These three constituted three levels of internal jurisdiction, such that recourses would result in a double conformity of decisions before ever needing to reach the full Signatura. Since the full Signatura was smaller and there would be no division of labor, the causes that reached it were those involving a higher minimum amount than under Pius VII (300 "scuta"). *Quum plurima* also recognized the right of parties to know the motivation, or supporting reasons, for a decision if they requested it. The writing up of such motivation was the duty of the *votantes* according to a predetermined order.

---

24. During its golden age, parties submitting a commission of appeal before the Signatura of Justice would often request *in limine* a "*supersessoria*," or the suspension of execution of the sentence against which the party wished to make an appeal (cf. "De procedura sequenda," 586–587).

25. Cf. "Codificationes legum," 83 (no. 3), 92–94.

11. – Pope Gregory XVI, by means of his motu proprio *Elevati appena* of November 10, 1834, confirmed the status of the Signatura of Justice as both a civil and ecclesiastical tribunal. He entrusted to it also the administrative faculty to judge controversies arising from decisions of the sacred congregations and to resolve conflicts of competence between them. This order would only last until 1870, when the Papal States were occupied and suppressed.[26]

4. Transformation of the Signatura

12. – The period of *transformation* of the Apostolic Signatura (1908–1967) is what would give birth to the modern Apostolic Signatura. It began at the time of the general reform of the Roman Curia just over one century ago.

13. – In his June 29, 1908 constitution *Sapienti consilio*, Pope St. Pius X would declare the formal bifurcation between the Signatura of Favor and the Signatura of Justice to be suppressed, establishing the Supreme Tribunal of the Apostolic Signatura as a merely ecclesiastical and seemingly a purely judicial tribunal. In addition to having competence to handle complaints of nullity and petitions for *restitutio in integrum* against Rotal decisions and exceptions of suspicion against Rotal judges, it could also judge criminal and contentious causes against Rotal auditors. These were the ordinary limits of its competence, until Pope Benedict XV enriched it with the competence to handle petitions for favors relating to the administration of justice. That the latter competence seemed to be added on to what was established by Pius X would seem to have placed the Signatura of 1908 at some distance from what it was at its origins, in 1908 being limited to what it was as the Signatura of Justice. For this reason, Father Gordon thought it might have been opportune for it to be given an alternate, descriptive name, such as "Supreme Tribunal of the Apostolic Signatura, or the Supreme Dicastery of Justice."[27]

In any case, the judicial and administrative functions were enshrined in the special pontifical legislation of *REU* under the designation of the first section (*prima sectio*) of the Signatura. This, together with the creation of the *sectio altera*, were "the two great innovations" introduced by Pope St. Paul VI into the Apos-

---

26. Cf. "Normae speciales," 79–82, 93–94 (note 8), nn. 9–10, 42 (where he traces the evolution of competence to resolve conflicts of competence between dicasteries); "La renovación de la Signatura Apostólica," 572, note 1e. On its suppression, see "Normae speciales," 83, no. 12.

27. Cf. "Normae speciales," 84–87, nn. 16–22; "La renovación de la Signatura Apostólica," 571–574, nn. 1–7. For a critical analysis of its name, see the same studies at 86–87, notes 44 and 46, and 577, nn. 17–19, respectively.

tolic Signatura by *REU*.[28] These sections remain in existence today, even if they are conceived of a little differently, as is explained below.[29]

14. – Dicasteries of the Roman Curia typically have consultors at their disposal in order to aid their deliberations about technical matters falling within their sphere of competence. Given the historical antecedents, Father Gordon observed that these consultors "in the Signatura take on the name and particular character of *Votantes* and Referendaries." However, more recently that distinction has been suppressed, such that all the ordinary consultors are called referendaries.[30]

B. Its Nature as a Supreme Tribunal

15. – "The Signatura is the Supreme Tribunal or Dicastery, since, on account of both Sections and competencies that it has, it is established in some way at the apex of the judicial and administrative hierarchy, such that no other is above it, except the Pope."[31] As is discussed in greater detail in Chapter IX *infra*, the Church's system is one of double jurisdiction. In other words, the judiciary has two distinct branches: there are judicial tribunals and there is an administrative tribunal. Thus the activity of the administrative authorities of the Church are subject not to the judicial tribunals but to the administrative tribunal. What is unique about the Apostolic Signatura, as supreme tribunal, is that it is itself an organ of double jurisdiction: it is both a judicial tribunal (with jurisdiction especially over certain acts of the Roman Rota) and an administrative tribunal.[32] The term "tribunal" here (i.e., in virtue of *REU*) takes on a broader sense: a jurisdictional organ that is both judicial and administrative.[33] The second section is administrative

---

28. See "La renovación de la Signatura Apostólica," 574, no. 8. At 574–575, nn. 9–11, esp. in note 19, he argues that the reference to a *lex propria* in no. 108 of *REU* is not implying the *Lex propria* issued by Pius X but is a generic expression that includes the *NS* and would not exclude additional norms issued by or for the Signatura.

29. *Vide infra* no. 19.

30. See "Normae speciales," 117, note 7. Cf. *NS* artt. 3, 12–13; *LP* art. 10. On this matter, see Raymond L. Burke, "La Segnatura Apostolica: gli organi individuali," in *La "Lex propria" del S.T. della Segnatura Apostolica*, ed. Piero Antonio Bonnet and Carlo Gullo, Studi Giuridici 89 (Vatican City: Libreria Editrice Vaticana, 2010) 84.

31. See "Normae speciales," 91, no. 28. Cf. "La renovación de la Signatura Apostólica," 576, nn. 15–16.

32. Cf. "Normae speciales," 106–107, no. 78.

33. Cf. "Normae speciales," 90–91, no. 27; "De iustitia administrativa ecclesiastica," 307, no. 84; "La renovación de la Signatura Apostólica," 567, no. 14.

"not only for its clear contrast with the first but especially because of the object of its competence."[34]

16. – As a supreme tribunal, its competence should not readily be challenged, since it would not admit a cause over which it were incompetent, lest it cause an injustice itself. It is an organ that itself resolves conflicts of competence; and so it surely can determine authoritatively whether it is competent over a particular cause. Nor is such authority lacking in precedent, recalling that the Supreme Congregation of the Holy Office has been able to resolve questions of its own competence.[35]

17. – A juridical consequence of its supremacy is the norm according to which the judicial sentences of the Apostolic Signatura are unappealable (1917 *CIC* c. 1880, 1º; 1983 *CIC* c. 1629, 1º). One may only make an extraordinary recourse against them to the Roman Pontiff.[36]

At the same time, some of its decisions are judicial decisions issued essentially at the first level of jurisdiction—namely, penal and contentious causes against judges of the Roman Rota. And these are said to be appealable even in law.[37] In the judgment of Father Gordon, given the nature of an appeal as a provocation to a judge extrinsic to the tribunal that issued the sentence, the appeal against such decisions of the Apostolic Signatura is an appeal *sui generis*, analogous to the *beneficium novae audientiae*, by which emendation of the sentence is sought but from the same judicial organ. Because of this analogy, it would be natural for the same judges to receive an appeal against their own sentence.[38]

---

34. See "La renovación de la Signatura Apostólica," 577, no. 22.

35. Cf. Ignacio Gordon, *votum, Nullitatis matrimonii; Incid.: competentiae Signaturae Ap.*, prot. n. 19032/87 CG, March 22, 1988: in SSAT Archives: "Videtur dedecere dignitatem Supremi Tribunalis, quod contendat solvere dubium circa propriam competentiam ex contentioso cum aliquo Advocato (si bene intellexi!)." On the cited praxis of the Holy Office, see "Normae speciales," 94–95; on the derogation of its competence in this regard, see "La renovación de la Signatura Apostólica," 584, no. 48.

36. Cf. "El recurso contencioso-administrativo canónico," 648, at b; "La responsibilità," 419, at d.

37. 1917 *CIC* c. 1604 §1 ("si forte locus sit iudicio appellationis"); *NS* art. 77 §1 ("datur facultas appellandi contra sententiam primae instantiae Signaturae Apostolicae"); *LP* art. 69 ("appellatione in casu haud exclusa"). Fr. Gordon notes this briefly also in *Pars dynamica*, 109, no. 482, "*Ad 1*."

38. Cf. Ignacio Gordon, *votum* ("È possibile impugnare le decisioni de gli Em.mi e Ecc.mi Giudici con la querela di nullità e/o la *restitutio in integrum?*"), prot. n. 23136/91 VAR (cf. prot. n. 18190/86 CA), February 11, 1992: in SSAT Archives, 4–5, 10, nn. 13–17, 37.

18. – While the other decisions of the Apostolic Signatura, in both judicial and contentious-administrative causes, are unappealable, they may nevertheless be challengeable or impugnable. "The basis for the principle of impugnability is human fallibility, which is common to the Supreme Tribunal and to its judges." In particular, they may be subject to a complaint of nullity or a petition for a *restitutio in integrum*. For the Apostolic Signatura, "like any other human tribunal, may be subject to committing errors in the administration of justice. Such errors would be graver, being committed by the Supreme Tribunal which, for the Church and in particular for inferior tribunals, must be the mirror of justice and honesty."[39] This indeed is provided in the current proper law of the Apostolic Signatura with regard to sentences that it issues in contentious-administrative causes, which the Apostolic Signatura alone is competent to issue.[40]

C. Competence

19. – Today one can appropriately speak of three sections in the Apostolic Signatura, even if they are not so designated in the general legislation. In virtue of its first section, it judges especially acts of the ordinary appellate tribunal of the Apostolic See, the Roman Rota. In virtue of its second section (*"sectio secunda"*: the second of three, no longer "second" meaning "other" [*altera*]), it stands as the supreme administrative tribunal of the Church, which above all judges the legitimacy of singular administrative acts placed or approved by the dicasteries of the Roman Curia. And in virtue of its third section, it provides for the correct administration of justice in all the non-apostolic tribunals of the Church, by exercising general vigilance, approving tribunals, extending judicial competence, and correcting ministers of justice.[41]

---

39. See ibid., 8–9, 12, nn. 30, 45. In the incidental cause raised before the Signatura against its sentence of December 17, 1988, the opinions of three experts were sought: Fr. Gordon and two others, whose *vota* were later published in the form of scientific articles. See Gianpaolo Montini, "De querela nullitatis deque restitutione in integrum adversus sententias Sectionis Alterius Supremi Signaturae Apostolicae Tribunalis," *Periodica* 82 (1993) 669–697, and Joaquín Llobell, "Note sull'impugnabilità delle decisioni della Segnatura Apostolica," *Ius Ecclesiae* 5 (1993) 675–698. They were all in agreement that these remedies of law can be used against the decisions of the Apostolic Signatura. Cf. Supreme Tribunal of the Apostolic Signatura, Decree of the College of Judges, prot. n. 18190/86 CA, June 30, 1990: in SSAT Archives ("Dilata et compleantur acta"); the incidental cause is filed under prot. n. 23136/91 VAR, which was opened on December 6, 1991 (ibid.).

40. *LP* art. 91 §1: "Adversus Collegii sententias, cauta tamen semper Supremi Tribunalis natura, tantum remedia querelae nullitatis ac petitionis restitutionis in integrum suppetunt."

41. Cf. c. 1445; *PB* artt. 122–124; *LP* artt. 33–35; Francis, apostolic constitution *Praedicate evangelium*, March 19, 2022: *L'Osservatore Romano* (March 31, 2022) I–XII, at artt. 196–198.

There was a proposal in favor of attributing to the Apostolic Signatura competence for judging the constitutionality of laws of the conference of bishops and of provincial councils. Together with Ciprotti and Pinto, Father Gordon opposed this proposal; in his mind, this was more suited to the competence of the Congregation for the Clergy.[42]

1. First Section: Judgment of Rotal Decisions

20. – In this sphere of competence, the Apostolic Signatura stands at the peak of the hierarchy of judicial tribunals, "since it is a true judicial tribunal and indeed the supreme one."[43] The law of the 1917 *CIC* included within the Signatura's competence the faculty to grant a new examination of a cause decided *by the Rota* that the Rota has also refused to admit to a new examination (c. 1603 §1, 5º). However, "the primary object of the recourse is the denial of a new examination made by the Rota, but not the fact that the sentence . . . was issued by the Rota or by another tribunal."[44] This anticipated the revision that would later occur in the 1983 *CIC*, wherein the Signatura is said to be competent to receive a recourse against the Rota's denial of a new examination of a cause (c. 1445 §1, 2º).

21. – In one cause of nullity of marriage decided in the negative with a double conformity of sentences, a request for a new examination of the cause was proposed to the Signatura. The secretary asked Father Gordon a question about the matter, and he justly declared his view that the Signatura was incompetent, in regard to both the concession of a new examination of the cause (since its competence was limited to treating such a request once it had been denied by the Rota) and to the grant of a pontifical commission (since the petitioner had a right by law already to approach the Rota with such a petition).[45]

2. Second Section: Contentious-Administrative Jurisdiction

22. – The major field of the Supreme Tribunal's competence instituted while Father Gordon was teaching procedural law and just before he assumed the office

---

42. Cf. "'De processibus.' Relazione della sessione tenutasi dal 5 al 7 marzo 1981," in PCCICR Archives, *vol. 182, XI. De processibus, Parvus coetus (5–7 martii 1981). Relatio*, second folder, 9.

43. See "Normae speciales," 96, no. 44.

44. See Ignacio Gordon, *votum* ("De quibusdam quaestionibus circa competentiam S. T. Signaturae Apostolicae"), *Nullitatis matrimonii*, prot. n. 35/70 CG, May 3, 1970: in SSAT Archives, 7, no. 14. Cf. *Processus nullitatis matrimonii*, 88, 18; *Novus processus nullitatis matrimonii*, 49, note 21.

45. Cf. Gordon, *votum*, May 3, 1970: in SSAT Archives.

of referendary of the Apostolic Signatura is that of its then-designated Second Section (*Sectio altera*). To that section was, and is, entrusted above all the judgment of contentious-administrative causes in which an aggrieved party requests its ministry of justice so that it may examine the alleged illegitimacy of a singular administrative act placed or approved by a dicastery of the Roman Curia and order the execution of its decision, as the case may be.

Contentious-administrative jurisdiction is a specialized area of procedural law still noted for "its [relative] novelty and importance."[46] Father Gordon dedicated significant effort to its study, and so it merits its own chapter in this book (*vide infra* Chapter IX). That context is naturally suited to treating also the Apostolic Signatura as supreme administrative tribunal. And so that area of its competence is largely reserved for the next chapter. Nevertheless, a couple of related aspects of its competence treated by Father Gordon—"the secondary object" of the *Sectio altera*'s competence[47]—are given brief treatment here.

23. – The 1967 apostolic constitution *REU* included among the titles of competence of the *Sectio altera* of the Apostolic Signatura the judgment of administrative affairs (*negotia administrativa*) deferred to it by the dicasteries of the Roman Curia (no. 107). Bearing in mind the private character of *negotia* according to the common doctrine, Father Gordon explained in a *votum*[48] that the expression refers to some "question, problem, litigation, or difficulty arising from an administrative act." More specifically, it would be a matter of a "contention arising within the realm of a Congregation, from an administrative act of the Congregation" when "the Congregation judges it not expedient for it to judge that contention itself hierarchically." In effect, a dicastery could decide to refrain from making a decision in a particular case, while instead entrusting the judgment of the matter to the Supreme Tribunal, which would judge the merits of the case, since this course of action would avoid any question of the alleged illegitimacy of a decision of a dicastery. It may do this, "for example, because it is a party in the cause, or because it concerns a particularly difficult affair, which it will be more satisfactory to defer to the expertise of the Signatura."[49] He would speak of the object of this title of competence in the cited *votum* as *negotia seu controversiae*

---

46. See "La renovación de la Signatura Apostólica," 575, no. 13.

47. See "De obiecto primario competentiae," 521.

48. See Ignacio Gordon, *votum* ("De indole 'negotiorum administrativorum' de quibus agitur in const. 'Regimini' [15.VIII.1967] n.107"), prot. n. 6278/75 VAR, [undated]: in SSAT Archives.

49. See "Normae speciales," 95, "*De 3º*." Cf. "La renovación de la Signatura Apostólica," 584, nn. 49–50.

administrativae. In fact, the expression would change in the universal legislation, which describes them simply as *controversiae administrativae.*[50]

24. – The Supreme Pontiff can defer administrative questions to the judgment of the Apostolic Signatura, thereby conferring delegated power upon it. As such, the Signatura "is established as a parallel and complementary organism to the Sacred Roman Rota." For the Supreme Pontiff as supreme judge can entrust judicial causes called to himself to the Rota, while as supreme administrator he can entrust administrative questions to the second section of the Signatura.[51]

25. – In virtue of no. 107 of *REU* (*NS* art. 96, 2°), the Signatura judges conflicts of competence between dicasteries of the Roman Curia. This had in the past been entrusted to various organs: the Sacred Congregation of the Consistory, some group of cardinals, and the Pontifical Commission of Interpreters of the Code of Canon Law. Its return to the Signatura is fitting and reveals something of its nature: "For it cannot be a party in a cause (as happened for the Sacred Congregation of the Consistory), and it is additionally a permanent organ (unlike that group of cardinals); and it is indeed supreme and therefore could be well endowed with the competent authority (which is less appropriate for the Commission of Interpreters)."[52]

3. Third Section: Vigilance over Ecclesiastical Tribunals[53]

26. – Its vigilance over the correct administration of justice includes protection of a correct jurisprudence. This does not mean, however, that the Apostolic Signatura is competent to intervene judicially in a cause in which a tribunal has employed an erroneous jurisprudence. It always acts in a way that respects "the authority of ecclesiastical tribunals and the *relative* firmness, which sentences issued in causes concerning the status of persons must have."[54] Nor therefore does it have the "prerogative of imposing the interpretations of law that it makes on the jurisprudence of inferior tribunals."[55]

---

50. See c. 1445 §2; *PB* art. 123 §3; *LP* art. 34 §3.

51. See "Normae speciales," 95, "*De 4°.*" Cf. "La renovación de la Signatura Apostólica," 584–585, no. 51.

52. See "Normae speciales," 94, no. 42. Cf. "La renovación de la Signatura Apostólica," 584, no. 47.

53. *Vide supra* Chapter V, no. 34.

54. See Gordon, *votum*, May 3, 1970: in SSAT Archives, 5, no. 13.

55. See "Normae speciales," 97, no. 45; "La renovación de la Signatura Apostólica," 578, no. 23.

It can be petitioned for the favor of a transfer of the cause to a different tribunal (cf. *CM* IV §3), even though this is no longer anticipated in the legislation. Such a request may be useful when, prior to or during the instruction of the cause, a significant number of the proofs have moved to a different territory.[56]

D. Manner of Proceeding

27. – Father Gordon appeared to have the aspiration to write a comprehensive study on the manner of proceeding before the second section of the Apostolic Signatura, but he was not able to do so.[57] Still, he did make several particular observations throughout his writings, which are too numerous and detailed to examine here.

But one unique question he raised that is noteworthy concerned the nature of a recourse to the Signatura. He taught that it is comparable to a recourse to the college of judges against a decree of a judge, and it is also similar to an appeal (while not being an appeal), since it is a matter of seeking the reformation of an act causing a grievance. And since a recourse to the Signatura has suspensive effect, a legitimate recourse within the Signatura, such as to the college of judges against a decree of the *Congresso*, is marked with a "continuation" of that suspensive effect.[58]

---

56. Cf. *Novus processus nullitatis matrimonii*, 19, note k.

57. *Vide infra* Chapter X, note 18.

58. Cf. Ignacio Gordon, *votum* ("De recursu contra Congressus decisionem latam in quaestione de iure appellandi"), prot. n. 2120/71 CG, April 3, 1973: in SSAT Archives, 29–30 and 31, nn. 124–125, 133. At the same time, he thought the matter of suspensive effect to be not altogether certain, even if it is more probable (ibid., 31, no. 135).

CHAPTER IX

Contentious-Administrative Jurisdiction

SUMMARY — A. The General Notion of Administrative Justice (nn. 1–4). ▪ B. Administrative Justice in the Church (nn. 5–11). ▪ C. Aspects of the Control of Legitimacy of Administrative Activity in the Church (nn. 12–16). ▪ D. The Object of Contentious-Administrative Recourse (nn. 17–26). ▪ E. The Parties (nn. 27–29).

A. The General Notion of Administrative Justice

1. – The sector of procedural law that concentrates on the judicial treatment of controversies arising from the exercise of the administrative power of governance is identified commonly as "administrative justice" (*iustitia administrativa*) or "administrative contention" (*contentiosus administrativus*). Father Gordon explains that these expressions, respectively, are from Italian and French juridical norms and doctrine—*giustizia amministrativa* and *contentieux administratif*, respectively. And he defines administrative justice as "the juridical institute whose purpose is to investigate and resolve, according to the prescripts of law, controversies or contentions arising between private persons and the public administration."[1]

---

1. See "De Tribunalibus administrativis," 612, no. 13. See also "De iustitia administrativa ecclesiastica," 252, 253, nn. 2, 4; "La renovación de la Signatura Apostólica," 586–587, nn. 53–55; "Origine e sviluppo," 1. This is quoted, e.g., by Eduardo Labandeira in his *Trattato di diritto amministrativo canonico*, trans. Lucia Graziano (Milan: Giuffrè Editore, 1994) 486. For Fr. Gordon's students, his instruction on administrative justice was something "completely new" to them (e.g., Paolo Bianchi, "Ricordo di padre Ignacio Gordon," private correspondence, May 6, 2019). It was a theme on which he also spoke often outside his strictly university work. For instance, on May 14, 1974, he gave a lecture for the Archsodality of the Roman Curia entitled "Civil Law Influences on contentious-administrative activity in the Church" ("Decisio Signaturae Iustitiae," 185, note 3). On the occasion of the celebration of the first centenary of the foundation of the Faculty of Canon Law of the Pontifical Gregorian University, he moderated a discussion on the morning of February 18, 1977 on organs of administrative justice in the Church, concluding the session that included presentations by Cardinal Dino Staffa, Prof. Ermanno Graziani, Msgr. Heinrich Straub, and Prof. Paolo Moneta (Pontifical Gregorian University Faculty of Canon Law, *Conventus internationalis iuris*

On several occasions, Father Gordon explained the three forms in which administrative justice has tended to be institutionalized. And these teachings have been much cited by canonical doctrine.[2] The three forms are (1) administrator-judge, (2) double jurisdiction, and (3) single jurisdiction.

2. – The system of "administrator-judge" originates in the thirteenth century French monarchy and was codified after the French revolution. While royal dispositions and decisions of the king's officials could not be appealed in any way, these same authorities could stand as judges over their own acts when subjects wished to challenge them. The authority in question, then, was the governor or administrator that placed the act, and he was also judge of the legitimacy of the act when it was challenged. This model flowed from the principle of the separation of powers, since the administration was seen to be in no way subject to the judiciary. This kind of judgment took place within the administration itself and was seen to be an expression of administration.[3] This system is clearly insufficient from the perspective of the subject, who is search of an impartial judgment, since the judge was also a party to the cause. It is thus seen to be a transitory model leading to the second.[4]

3. – The system of "double jurisdiction," which developed out of the system of administrator-judge, consists in a twofold judiciary. One branch is the series of ordinary tribunals before which civil and criminal causes are introduced (the judicial tribunals). The other is the series of tribunals before which claims against

---

canonici, 14–19 februarii 1977. Commemoratio primi centenarii Facultatis, brochure in the archives of the same Faculty, 16). And on April 6 and May 25, 1979 at an interdisciplinary seminar, he gave lectures on the historical origins of administrative justice in the Church and on the protection of subjective rights before the *Sectio altera* of the Apostolic Signatura (Pontificia Universitas Gregoriana, *Liber annualis, Roma 1980 Univ. 427°* [Rome: Universitas Gregoriana, 1980] 282).

2. In addition to the "De Tribunalibus administrativis" (*vide infra* notes 3 ff.), he describes these also in "De iustitia administrativa ecclesiastica," 253–254, 315–329, nn. 5–6, 94–116; in "La renovación de la Signatura Apostólica," 587–589, nn. 57–64; in "Origine e sviluppo," 8–9, no. 4; and, quite succinctly, in "Normae speciales," 106, no. 77 and "Interessi legittimi," 400, at 2). Citing this doctrine, see, e.g., Dino Staffa, "Dissertationes de administratione iustitiae in Ecclesia. II. De supremo Tribunali administrativo seu de secunda Sectione Supremi Tribunalis Signaturae Apostolicae," *Periodica* 61 (1972) 22, note 3; Ilaria Zuanazzi, "La possibilità di tribunali amministrativi a livello particolare," in *La giustizia nell'attività amministrativa della Chiesa. Il contenzioso amministrativo,* ed. Eduardo Baura and Javier Canosa, Monografie Giuridiche 31 (Milan: Giuffrè Editore, 2006) 134, 168, notes 2, 126–127; Gianpaolo Montini, "L'esecuzione delle pronunce giudiziali della Segnatura Apostolica nel contenzioso amministrativo," in ibid., 384, note 3.

3. Cf. "De Tribunalibus administrativis," 613–614, nn. 15–16.

4. Cf. ibid., 623, at b. See also "Normae speciales," 78–79, esp. notes 12–13.

public acts of administration are introduced (the administrative tribunals). A judicial tribunal is entirely independent from the public administration. An administrative tribunal is separate from and superior to the active administration, or ordinary governing organ. Just as in (but separate from) the hierarchy of judicial tribunals, there is a series of administrative tribunals, at the peak of which is the supreme administrative tribunal.[5]

The following convergent factors demonstrate how an administrative tribunal is distinct from both the active administrative organ and from a judicial tribunal. (1) It resolves controversies between private parties and the public administration or between two organs of public administration. (2) It applies to the case the law binding the parties, unlike the active administration, which predominantly exercises prudent discretion. (3) Its officials are part of neither of those two structures. And (4) it utilizes a judicial procedure, although a simpler one.[6]

Of the three models, this one is "highly commended." For it is the most commonly used in secular governments, some of which even transitioned to it from either of the other two models, which were seen to be inadequate. Its excellence is based not merely on historical circumstances or the influence of its originators "but rather on intrinsic circumstances, that is, in the very nature of the system. For this ordering of tribunals protects the rights of private parties, while at the same time providing for the dignity and protection of the administration."[7]

4. – The system of "single jurisdiction" concentrates judicial and contentious-administrative jurisdiction in the judicial tribunals. It is meant both to correct abuses in the active administration and to prevent conflicts of competence between judicial tribunals and the active administration.[8] Another expression of this includes special tribunals for administrative conflicts situated within the one judiciary, being clearly independent from the public administration.[9] This model has the benefit of simplicity, but it seems to endanger the public administration, which is subjected to the judicial authority without discrimination.[10]

---

5. Cf. "De Tribunalibus administrativis," 615–617, nn. 18–20.

6. Cf. ibid., 618, no. 23. He modestly quotes this text of his ("Liceat nobis afferre….") in "Normae speciales," 107, no. 79.

7. See "De Tribunalibus administrativis," 623–624, no. 27.

8. Cf. ibid., 619, nn. 25–26.

9. Cf. ibid., 622–623.

10. Cf. ibid., 623.

B. Administrative Justice in the Church

5. – Identifying these forms of administrative justice is useful for understanding the evolution of its regulation within the society of the Church. As Father Gordon illustrates in his lengthy treatise on the subject,[11] there is a long history of administrative justice in the Church. And up to the present, it has taken each of these three forms.

6. – For about eight centuries, one detects the existence in the Church of the system of single jurisdiction. Beginning in the twelfth century, the Roman Pontiffs permitted a *provocatio ad causam*, or an *"appellatio" extra iudicium* (or *extraiudicialis*),[12] and this would be a stable institute until 1908, when it was suppressed. The extrajudicial appeal is not a judicial appeal, which is a reaction to a judicial sentence, but the deferring of a grievance ("appeal" in a broad and now even improper sense) caused by a non-judicial act or a feared, future grievance—such as a decision or precept of a bishop, an election, or any personal injury—before a tribunal. The ordinary judiciary was competent, since this was a matter of introducing a cause before the competent tribunal claiming the illegitimacy of the act in question. Once that tribunal had issued a decision, subsequent appeals were judicial appeals. Thus, for example, the archdeacon might issue a decision (a singular administrative act in today's parlance), against which the aggrieved party would present an "extrajudicial appeal" before the diocesan bishop. His judicial sentence could then be appealed judicially to the metropolitan, whose sentence could be appealed to the Apostolic See.

---

11. "De iustitia administrativa ecclesiastica," at 257–280. He openly relies heavily on Heribert Schmitz' dissertation published in Munich in 1970. At 269–273, he relates some Rotal jurisprudence from causes originating as extrajudicial appeals, which is drawn from the dissertation of Jaime Traserra, directed by himself and published in 1972. See also "Origine e sviluppo," 1–18; "De obiecto primario competentiae," 505–521; "La renovación de la Signatura Apostólica," 589–591, nn. 68–75; "Interessi legittimi," 398, no. 2; "Decisio Signaturae Iustitiae," 185, no. 1; "De Signaturae Iustitiae competentia," 362–363. Fr. Gordon's scholarship on this matter remains a useful point of reference for authors of canonical administrative law; see, e.g., Julián Herranz, "La giustizia amministrativa nella Chiesa dal Concilio Vaticano II al Codice del 1983," in *La giustizia amministrativa nella Chiesa*, Studi Giuridici 24 (Vatican City: Libreria Editrice Vaticana, 1991) 18, note 16; Joaquín Llobell, "Il *'petitum'* e la *'causa petendi'* nel contenzioso-amministrativo canonico. Profili sostanziali ricostruttivi alla luce della cost. ap. *'Pastor bonus*,'" in ibid., 98, note 3; Francesco Salerno, "Il giudizio presso la *'Sectio altera'* del S.T. della Segnatura Apostolica," in ibid., 128, note 6 *et passim*; Eduardo Baura, "Discrimine tra la via amministrativa e la via giurisdizionale nella tutela dei diritti nei confronti dell'amministrazione ecclesiastica," in *Studi in onore di Carlo Gullo*, Annales IV (Vatican City: Libreria Editrice Vaticana, 2017) 1:5–6, notes 4 and 7.

12. Fr. Gordon cites especially X 2.28.5 and 7 and Clem. 2.12.13.

The extrajudicial appeal was not itself precisely equivalent to single jurisdiction, since it could also be used against acts of private persons or private matters. The system of single jurisdiction is observed in the aspect of challenging the act of administrative authority. Furthermore, it was limited to the challenge of acts below the level of the Apostolic See. Acts of Sacred Congregations could not ordinarily be challenged before any tribunal, including the Signatura of Justice and other apostolic tribunals, since they acted in the name of the Supreme Pontiff. The Sacred Congregations, for their part, were in a position to receive the complaints of subjects against their bishops, especially in place of the extrajudicial appeal, which were a possible cause of scandal. Pope Gregory XVI (1831–1846), under the influence of French law, established the principle according to which ordinary tribunals were not competent to judge acts of administrative governance, and he created a certain contentious-administrative order excluding any tribunals.[13] This is a rule he had already instituted in the form of legislation for the Papal States in which, prior to June 19, 1834, one could challenge administrative acts before the Roman Rota and the Signatura of Justice, but not so on or around that date. For by way of the *oraculum Pontificium* given to the Prefect of the Signatura of Justice in the context of a particular cause, Gregory XVI had at that time declared that ordinary judges have no jurisdiction to investigate and define matters first decided by "administrative, political, and directive power." And this would become the rule according to which the Signatura of Justice would determine its own competence in the matter.[14]

7. – In 1908, Pope St. Pius X instituted in the Church the system of administrator-judge, inasmuch as he situated the Sacred Congregations in the position of "judge" over governmental acts of lower administrative authorities.[15] The norm of canon 16 of the 1908 *Lex propria* of the Sacred Roman Rota and the Apostolic Signatura indeed excluded administrative "dispositions of Ordinaries that are not sentences issued in judicial form" from the competence of the Rota and reserved them to the Sacred Congregations. This was then received into canon 1601 of the code that would come into effect about ten years later: "There is no appeal or recourse to the Sacred Rota against the decrees of ordinaries; but the Sacred Con-

---

13. On the last-mentioned order, see "Normae speciales," 82–83, no. 11, esp. note 28.

14. See "Decisio Signaturae Iustitiae," esp. 185, 186–191, nn. 2, 5–19. By means of original documentation and his own detailed annotations and scholarship, Fr. Gordon shows that the Roman Pontiff was introducing into the Church a rule from French law that probably would have been known in the Roman Rota due to the establishment of the Napoleonic court of appeal in Rome and of the Parisian court of cassation (cf. 191–210, nn. 20–210).

15. Cf. "De iustitia administrativa ecclesiastica," 280–303; "De Tribunalibus administrativis," 624–629, nn. 28–33; "Normae speciales," 97, no. 46.

gregations exclusively judge such recourses."[16] In other words, decrees of ordinaries, like those of Sacred Congregations since the sixteenth century reform of the Roman Curia, became immune from judicial authority (no single jurisdiction); they could be judged only by the superior authority of the competent congregation of the Roman Curia, to which final judgment was entrusted (no double jurisdiction). The regime of the extrajudicial appeal was not merely refashioned as hierarchical recourse; rather, the latter replaced the former, being no longer a "provocatio *ad causam*" (i.e., for a true judicial trial) but a hierarchical and extrajudicial examination of the challenged act.

There is no constitutional reason why administrative authority in the Church should necessarily be subject to judicial authority. That is, there is no basis for insisting that an act of administrative power should be subject to litigation before a tribunal. It is notable that in the history of the Signatura, there was to be no subjection of a Congregation to it, except by commission of the Supreme Pontiff. For the Congregations are vicars of the pope, such that he alone would seem to be their superior, and there would be no other judicial authority to which they are subject. At the same time, the same Congregations may be presumed to have had an institutional bias in favor of the superiors whose decisions were being challenged, since they have "an (active) administrative nature . . . in virtue of which they belong to the same hierarchy of governance as the bishops against whom recourse is made." Additionally, any process they would have used lacked the safeguards of the judicial process and was less effective at uncovering the truth. Thus, some change came to be necessary.[17]

8. – Indeed, the ecclesiastical system of administrator-judge was transformed into a system of double jurisdiction with the institution of the *Sectio altera* in the Supreme Tribunal of the Apostolic Signatura on August 15, 1967 (*REU* nn. 106–107). This was, in Father Gordon's judgement, *REU*'s "greatest innovation 'after the mentality of contemporary people' in procedural matters,"[18] and "the boldest innovation and the one of greater importance for the life of the Church that Paul VI introduced with th[at] constitution."[19] For, even if it may be subject to some

---

16. 1917 *CIC* c. 1601: "Contra Ordinariorum decreta non datur appellatio seu recursus ad Sacram Rotam; sed de eiusmodi recursibus exclusive cognoscunt Sacrae Congregationes."

17. See "De obiecto primario competentiae," 510.

18. See "De Curia Romana renovata," 95–96.

19. See Ignacio Gordon, "Prólogo" [September 30, 1972], in Jaime Traserra, *La tutela de los derechos subjetivos frente a la administración eclesiástica*, Colectánea San Paciano 18 (Barcelona: Editorial Herder, 1972) preamble.

further perfections, this change introduced a new kind of jurisdiction in the Church: contentious-administrative jurisdiction. And this was "the ultimate and definitive step in the path of solicitude by which the Church strove ever better to provide for the just protection of the rights of both the faithful and of the ecclesiastical administration."[20]

This situated within the Apostolic Signatura both a tribunal that is not a judicial tribunal and an organ that is outside the active public administration for the controversies deferred to it. It is an organ of administrative justice, which is to say one endowed with contentious-administrative competence.[21] It is "at the apex of the administrative hierarchy," since it can resolve conflicts between dicasteries that enjoy vicarious papal power and can decide recourses against their decisions "with supreme authority."[22] This transformation is not dubious simply because there is only one administrative tribunal. For while "a hierarchical ordering of administrative tribunals pertains to the perfection of the system" of double jurisdiction, it remains true that there is a judicial control over the public administration by an administrative tribunal that is independent both from that administration and from the hierarchy of judicial tribunals.[23]

9. – Father Gordon's assessment is that in the long period of the system of single jurisdiction, the judiciary "evidently favored subjective rights a little too much, at the expense of the public administration of the Church, whose governance often remained blocked." This was reversed by the institution of the system of administrator-judge, which favored the public administration and left subjective rights with little protection. And so this transition to the system of double jurisdiction may leave the Church with "the hope of arriving at an equilibrium."[24] As will be seen below, however, Father Gordon would insist that the new system of double jurisdiction did not accomplish its full potential in giving protection to subjective rights before the public administration.

10. – One hallmark of the current system of double jurisdiction is its protection of the stability of public order and of the dignity of ecclesiastical authority.

---

20. See "De iustitia administrativa ecclesiastica," 312, no. 90.

21. Cf. "De Tribunalibus administrativis," 630–633, nn. 34–35; "Normae speciales," 105–106, 108 nn. 75–76, 82.

22. See "Normae speciales," 98, no. 47.

23. See ibid., 108, no. 83; "De iustitia administrativa ecclesiastica," 311, no. 89. Cf. "De Curia Romana renovata," 96, note 18.

24. See "Origine e sviluppo," 17–18.

He explains the rationale for this in a *votum* from a cause in which the aggrieved parties introduced causes against eight bishops before their own diocesan tribunals. He teaches:

> It belongs to the character of canon law that the authority of the superiors of the Church, namely, of the Roman Pontiff and of Bishops, is held in great reverence—not only as this is necessary in any society, but also because in the Church the primacy and the episcopate are instituted by the divine law. Therefore, while it is true that the Church was always concerned about greatly restraining delicts even of prelates and about withstanding the ecclesiastical administration from harming the rights of the faithful, nevertheless she has also been diligently careful, because of the abovementioned duty of reverence, that ecclesiastical administrators, or bishops, not be subjected to common tribunals.[25]

11. – He taught a similar lesson in the context of a cause in which a priest challenged his bishop's decree establishing that the priest could not use money for his personal ministry since it was bequeathed to him for his ministry in a particular parish from which he had been transferred. In that case, the Congregation for the Clergy had confirmed the bishop's decree, in response to which the priest attempted an alternate remedy: to introduce a cause of rights before the Roman Rota. The priest made recourse to the Apostolic Signatura against the decree of rejection *in limine* issued by the Dean of the Roman Rota, who declared the Rota's absolute incompetence. Father Gordon taught in his *votum* that the decisions of the dicasteries of the Roman Curia are not subject to the judgment of tribunals, since they are immediately subject to the Roman Pontiff, who alone can entrust judicial authority over them to another. "On account of the dignity of Congregations, which are vicars of the Pope, . . . no one can judge their decisions unless it is the Pope himself or from his commission or concession"—a concession that has been made in a legislative manner by the institution of the Second Section of the Apostolic Signatura. Father Gordon's *votum* thus advised the rejection of the priest's recourse, which was indeed rejected by the Supreme Tribunal.[26]

---

25. See Ignacio Gordon, *votum alterum circa causas [X] et [Y] et aliarum*, prot. n. 270/70 CG, October 24, 1970: in SSAT Archives, 31–32, nn. 121–122. For the December 1, 1970 decree of the *Congresso* issued in the cause, see *Periodica* 61 (1972) 169–180; see also the February 23, 1974 definitive sentence of the college c. Staffa in *Periodica* 64 (1975) 222–233.

26. See Ignacio Gordon, *votum* ("De restitutione in integrum contra Decretum Rotale"), prot. n. 1025/69 CG, April 29, 1971: in SSAT Archives, 10. The *Congresso*'s decree of rejection was issued on May 11, 1971 (see SSAT Archives, document no. 31).

C. Aspects of the Control of Legitimacy of Administrative Activity in the Church

12. – The institute of the Synod of Bishops can be understood as "a representative assembly of those who exercise administrative power in the Church." For most are or participate in organs of the active public administration. The Synod therefore legitimately addressed the question of the control of administrative activity in the Church at its assembly in October 1967. That assembly approved, among other things, the erection of administrative tribunals in the Church. Bearing in mind that this meant that even their own acts could be subject to judicial complaint, this vote of approval constituted proof that administrators in the Church love justice and truth (*documentum amoris erga iustitiam et veritatem*).[27]

13. – A system of administrative justice in the Church itself reduces the risk of arbitrariness in the public administration. For

> the arbitrary administrator fears nothing more than that he be investigated, refuted, and punished; and tribunals are practically the only effective means for uncovering arbitrary administrators: for tribunals are like light. And since "everyone who does evil hates the light and does not come to the light, lest his works be exposed" (John 3:20), the administrator therefore takes care appropriately to refrain from malice and whim, lest he be dragged to the tribunals. And thus every suspicion of arbitrariness completely disappears in the ecclesiastical administration.[28]

It is fitting, though, that a member of the faithful aggrieved by an administrative act have a right to approach the administrative tribunal only after the administrative pathway has been exhausted. For there is a certain unity to the active public administration, or the governance of the Church at the local and higher levels. These are to try to address the matter satisfactorily before formal litigation begins (cf. 1917 *CIC* c. 1925; 1983 *CIC* c. 1446). "This successive order is also demanded by Christian mildness and charity, which first attempt the sweeter and easier remedies and only then rise to the graver ones."[29]

---

27. "De Tribunalibus administrativis," 603, no. 3.

28. See ibid., 634–635, no. 37. However, this should not lead to paralysis in the governance of the Church: the law should limit the accessibility of the administrative tribunal, and the tribunal should have the ability and obligation to reject recourses devoid of foundation (ibid., 636, no. 38).

29. See ibid., 643, no. 53.

14. – Part of this administrative pathway is some institute, where it exists, that fosters the reconciliation of the administration and the party aggrieved by it. Use of such an institute, however, has to be carefully implemented in order to be authentic and impartial. Thus, if there is an organ of conciliation or mediation before which a diocesan bishop and a member of the faithful aggrieved by a decision of his may seek a peaceful resolution, the members of the conciliation organ should not be appointed by the bishop "on account of suspicion of partiality."[30] This was an observation made by Father Gordon in the context of a particular case before the Apostolic Signatura; and the Signatura confirmed this argument of Father Gordon, making it its own.[31]

15. – During the period between the issuance of *REU* in 1967 and the promulgation of the 1983 *CIC*, authors were accustomed to speak about the power of the hierarchical superior of an administrative authority as contentious administrative power. This distinguished it from the ordinary circumstances of governance in which administrative power was exercised—namely, by the organs of *active* public administration (active administrative power). However, Father Gordon perceived a difficulty with the use of the word "contentious" here, since it has a primarily judicial meaning.[32] Causes introduced before and handled by the Church's judiciary are either contentious (formerly, civil) causes or penal/criminal causes. Such contentious causes may concern either judicial questions, such as those handled before most tribunals of the Church, or administrative questions, such as those handled by the sole administrative tribunal of the Church, the Apostolic Signatura. Such causes are, respectively, contentious-judicial and contentious-administrative.[33]

16. – One difficulty that seems to have existed within the membership of the supreme administrative tribunal of the Apostolic Signatura—that is, among its judges—is an accumulation of functions that are "not mutually 'compatible'"—

---

30. See Ignacio Gordon, *votum* ("De decreto generali Conferentiae Episcoporum N. circa instrumenta iuridica conciliationis"), prot. n. 15781/83 VT, May 20, 1989: in SSAT Archives, 4, no. 3a.

31. Supreme Tribunal of the Apostolic Signatura, *Animadversiones Congressus*, prot. n. 15781-28/83 VT, November 30, 1989: in SSAT Archives, 2, II.2: "Haec Signatura Apostolica tamen reiterandam censet observationem Rev.mi Votantis ad suspicionem partialitatis amovendam. . . ."

32. *Vide supra* Chapter V, no. 21.

33. *Pars statica*, 52–53, no. 79d. In the usage of the Apostolic Signatura, causes involving Rotal decisions or judges are given the letters CG (*contenzioso giudiziale*), while those that challenge the legitimacy of an act placed or approved by a dicastery of the Roman Curia are given the letters CA (*contenzioso amministrativo*, or *contentiosus administrativus*).

namely, that some prefects of dicasteries have been judges. Thus, one official would be a functionary in the active administration and a judge in the administrative tribunal (i.e., the second section of the Signatura), as well as a judge in the supreme judicial tribunal (i.e., the first section of the Signatura). Father Gordon proposed two solutions.[34] (1) It would be optimal for this rule of art. 4 §2 of the *NS* to be applied also to members: "There are twelve *Votantes* and Referendaries, among whom major or minor officials of Dicasteries of the Roman Curia cannot be admitted." (2) The members of the Signatura, all of whom would be convoked as the full Signatura, should exclusively judge causes either in the judicial section or in the administrative section, "not only for the greater distinction of both pathways, but also because the diverse character of the tribunal demands diverse special preparation, and also so that they may attain greater expertise and facility in the activity of judging in either section alone."[35]

D. The Object of Contentious-Administrative Recourse

17. – The basic elements of contentious-administrative recourse to the *Sectio altera* are these.[36] The *recurrent* is the party aggrieved by the decision of the dicastery. The *respondent* (*conventus* or *pars resistens*) is immediately the dicastery, mediately or perhaps equally immediately the ordinary that placed the original act, or the dicastery alone if the ordinary is the one aggrieved.[37] The *object* of the recourse is the overturning of the dicastery's decision and, as the case may be, the act of the ordinary. The *reason for petitioning* (*ratio petendi*) is the violation of the law.

In general, the object of the recourse is what is now designated a singular administrative act. Father Gordon defines an administrative act as "any act proceeding from the power of jurisdiction and which, on the one hand, is neither a legislative nor a judicial act and, on the other, in any way promotes the public good within the limits of the law." Such an act "cannot be judged by a judicial tribunal but only by the competent administrative dicastery."[38] It includes an authoritative

---

34. Evidently, if a challenged act were placed by one such Prefect, he would not be assigned as a member of the college.

35. See "Normae speciales," 107–108, nn. 80–81. See also ibid., 117, note 10.

36. Cf. ibid., 100, 101, nn. 58, 60.

37. While this is not evident in the law of *REU*, not only the aggrieved private party but also the aggrieved administrative authority can make recourse to the Apostolic Signatura (cf. "El recurso contencioso-administrativo canónico," 645). He notes his "satisfaction" at seeing the Prefect of the Signatura, Dino Card. Staffa, confirm his view on this point (see ibid., note 21).

38. See Ignacio Gordon, *votum* ("De recursu ad S.Tribunal Signaturae Apostolicae contra decretum Decani S.R.Rotae dierum 21–25 octobris in una [X]"), prot. n. 715/68 CG, July 7, 1969:

act of warning that is a declaration both of judgment and of the will, such as a notification of the faithful about the harmful content of theological writings.[39]

More particularly, though, the object of recourse concerns the legitimacy or effects of such an act. There have been some contested questions about all of the above-identified elements of recourse, but the one that gained significant attention from Father Gordon was this particular object of recourse. It was a question of whether the administrative tribunal could judge only the conformity of the act with the law or also the alleged injury of subjective rights and even of juridical interests.

18. – The question of the object of contentious-administrative recourse at the time of Father Gordon's research and writing was regulated by three norms: no. 106 of the apostolic constitution *REU* issued in 1967, art. 96, 1° of *NS* issued in 1968, and two authentic interpretations issued in 1971.[40] Here are the centrally relevant texts with an unofficial English translation:

REU 106 — Per alteram sectionem Signatura Apostolica contentiones dirimit ortas ex actu potestatis administrativae ecclesiasticae, et ad eam, ob interpositam appellationem seu recursum adversus decisionem competentis Dicasterii, delatas, quoties contendatur actum ipsum legem aliquam violasse. In his casibus videt sive de admissione recursus sive de illegitimitate actus impugnati.

REU 106 — By means of the second section, the Apostolic Signatura resolves controversies arising from an act of ecclesiastical administrative power and deferred to it on account of the introduction of an appeal or recourse against the decision of the competent Dicastery, whenever it is alleged that the same act had violated some law. In these cases, it makes a judgment about the admission of the recourse and the illegitimacy of the challenged act.

NS art. 96, n. 1 — Per sectionem alteram Signatura Apostolica cognoscit…contentiones ortas ex actu potestatis administrativae ecclesiasticae, ad eam delatas ob

NS art. 96, 1° — By means of the second section, the Apostolic Signatura judges controversies arising from an act of ecclesiastical administrative power deferred to

---

in SSAT Archives, 6–7, nn. 21–22. The Apostolic Signatura decreed in accord with what Fr. Gordon argued—namely, that the act that was being challenged before the Roman Rota was in fact an administrative act that could only be challenged "via hierarchica" (no. 3, 3°), i.e., by way of administrative recourse and, as the case may be, contentious-administrative recourse (cf. decree of the *Congresso*, prot. n. 715/68 CG, December 1, 1970: *Periodica* 61 (1972) 180–183; see *Periodica* 64 (1975) 208–221 for the February 23, 1974 definitive sentence of the College *coram* Staffa issued in the cause).

39. See Gordon, *votum*, October 24, 1970: in SSAT Archives, 13–14, nn. 48–53.

40. *DR* 1:399; *AAS* 63 (1971) 329–330, *sub* II.

interpositam appellationem seu recursum adversus decisionem competentis Dicasterii, quoties allegetur legis violatio.

it on account of the introduction of an appeal or recourse against the decision of the competent Dicastery, whenever a violation of the law is alleged.

Responsa diei 11 ianuarii 1971 — 3) D. – Quid intelligendum sit per comma *quoties contendatur actum ipsum aliquam violasse,* de quo in n. 106 Constitutionis Apostolicae *Regimini Ecclesiae universae.* R. – Pro violatione legis intellegi errorem iuris sive in procedendo sive in decernendo.

Responses of January 11, 1971 — 3) Q. – What is to be understood by the phrase "whenever it is alleged that the same act had violated some law" used in no. 106 of the apostolic constitution *Regimini Ecclesiae universae.* R. – By "violation of the law" is to be understood an error of law in the procedure used or in the substance of the decision.

---

4) D. – Utrum in casu de quo in dubio tertio, Supremum Signaturae Apostolicae Tribunal - Sectio Altera - videat tantummodo de illegitimitate actus impugnati an etiam de merito causae. R. – Affirmative ad Ium; negative ad IIum; seu Supremum Signaturae Apostolicae Tribunal - Sectionem Alteram - videre tantummodo de illegitimitate actus impugnati.

4) Q. – Whether, in the case mentioned in the third question, the Second Section of the Supreme Tribunal of the Apostolic Signatura is to make a judgment only about the illegitimacy of the challenged act or also about the merits of the cause. R. – Affirmatively to the first; negatively to the second; that is, the Second Section of the Supreme Tribunal of the Apostolic Signatura is to make a judgment only about the illegitimacy of the challenged act.

The object as specified further in art. 96, 1º of the *NS* (see also 106, 2º) is solely the alleged violation of the law. Other grounds stated in secular (especially Italian) law—namely, incompetence of the public administration and abuse of power—are not at issue in an ecclesiastical contentious-administrative trial.[41]

19. – In its foundational norm (*REU* 106), it was unclear whether the object of the Signatura's competence was unitary or double. In saying that it "resolves controversies (*contentiones dirimit*) arising from an act of ecclesiastical administrative power," the legislator did not exclude violation of a subjective right as an object of the contention. However, in saying that it "makes a judgment . . . about the illegitimacy of the challenged act," he appeared to be stressing the act's con-

---

41. Cf. "Normae speciales," 103–105, nn. 70–73. On this Italian law, see "De iustitia administrativa ecclesiastica," 326, no. 114.

formity with the norm of law. The object of the trial can be understood in terms of the injury of subjective rights, at least inasmuch as the allegedly injured right is one that enjoys protection in a law that was allegedly violated. The question is whether the *Sectio altera* was and is competent to judge only the legitimacy of the challenged act or also, and instead, its alleged violation of a subjective right.

Father Gordon did not consider this question to be resolved by the above-quoted authentic interpretation. This was because of "the objective weight of the reasons" favoring the inclusion of subjective rights, the authority of several canonists arguing for it, and "the period of *ius condendum* in which we abide," that is, in the period of final drafting of the *CIC* to be promulgated eventually in 1983.[42]

20. – It would appear that the *Sectio altera* was destined to be a tribunal competent to judge not only the legitimacy of a singular administrative act but also its alleged violation of subjective rights. This is what was being prepared especially by the code commission with the approval of the Synod of Bishops in the seventh guiding principle. The inclusion of both elements with the seeming prevalence of the judgment about legitimacy seems to be a compromise with or even an intrusive influence of the Italian system of administrative justice.[43]

Father Gordon argued in favor of the double competence of the *Sectio altera* (two "branches") for these reasons:[44] resolving a controversy often is not accomplished merely by a declaration of illegitimacy; the violation of subjective rights and the violation of the law are indeed distinct questions; and the definitive sentence of the Signatura is seen in its jurisprudence to be constitutive, not merely declarative. The question of the alleged illegitimacy is the *condicio sine qua non* for its deferral to the Signatura; however, it does not seem fitting that passage to the contentious-administrative tribunal should depend upon a violation of the law, when in any case one can allege the violation of a subjective right.[45] It is true that the Supreme Tribunal may not make a judgment about the merits (*de merito*) or fittingness (*opportunitas*) of the challenged administrative act. But the judgment about the alleged injury of subjective rights is something distinct from the merits of the case, which principally concerns the discretionary judgment proper to administrative activity.

---

42. See "De obiecto primario competentiae," 521–522.

43. Cf. ibid., 519–521.

44. See "De iustitia administrativa ecclesiastica," 331, 332–339, nn. 120, 123–124, 126–131; "La responsibilità," 419; "Interessi legittimi," 398–399; "Origine e sviluppo," 17–18; "De obiecto primario competentiae," 520–521. On this discussion, see also "La renovación de la Signatura Apostólica," 593–604, nn. 82–129.

45. Cf. "Interessi legittimi," 401.

21. – It seems clear that the Apostolic Signatura has not been one to precisely handle contentious causes of subjective rights in the way they had once been handled in the French government. Rather, the object is a "mix of contention about a subjective right and of [French and Italian] contention about annulment or legitimacy, with an evident prevalence of the latter." This Father Gordon found to be an "internal and grave inadequacy," in view of the kinds of controversies that the Signatura was seemingly erected to address and its character as a contentious tribunal.[46]

22. – In his reading, the norm of *REU* 106 suggests that the *Sectio altera* directly and immediately resolves controversies about subjective rights. However, if in practice the *Sectio altera* only makes a judgment about the legitimacy of an administrative act, it is only indirectly and mediately resolving the controversy—namely, "by means of resolving the question of legitimacy and, if the case warrants it, by means of a new act of the administrative authority." This he deemed unacceptable, since it "openly contradicts the immediate and direct sense which the first part of no. 106 undoubtedly has."[47] Limitation to judgments of illegitimacy without addressing subjective rights "does not correspond to a certain necessity of the Church but is something artificial" based on the historical influence of Italian law.[48] It was Father Gordon's hope that "the full efficiency of this institution" would be realized, such that it would be able to make judgments not only about alleged violations of the law but also about the alleged violation of subjective rights.[49]

23. – For, as he taught in his intervention at an international gathering of canonists in 1973,[50] 1) this is the purpose of administrative tribunals as envisioned in the guiding principles for the revision of the *CIC*—which, he notes elsewhere, say "not one word" about judgments of legitimacy;[51] 2) in canonical tradition, administrative contention has always concerned the alleged violation of subjective rights, especially in the early-identified phenomenon of the extrajudicial *gravamen*;[52] and 3) the early jurisprudence of the *Sectio altera* (1968–1971) reveals

---

46. See "De iustitia administrativa ecclesiastica," 331, no. 118.
47. See "De obiecto primario competentiae," 528–529.
48. See "De iustitia administrativa ecclesiastica," 336, no. 125.
49. See "La renovación de la Signatura Apostólica," 610, no. 157. See also "El recurso contencioso-administrativo canónico," 645, note 19.
50. Cf. "Interessi legittimi," 399–400.
51. See "De obiecto primario competentiae," 518, 4a.
52. Cf. ibid., 507–509.

the intent and ability to resolve controversies about subjective rights.[53] Also, as he demonstrated six years later, in addition to being expressed at the beginning of *REU* 106, it was the vision of the commission that drafted *REU* that the *Sectio altera* was to be fashioned in light of the administrative tribunal of the Second Vatican Council, which judged controversies of rights arising between the fathers (or members) of the council and its moderators, who had the quality of superiors within the council.[54]

24. – He therefore proposed that to the *Sectio altera* of the Apostolic Signatura be attributed the primary and single competence of making judgments about the alleged violation of subjective rights on the part of administrative authorities, and that the *Sectio altera*'s competence of judging the alleged illegitimacy of singular administrative acts be suppressed so as to remove all confusion. The reformed text of *REU* 106 that he supported, proposed largely by Professor Paolo Moneta, is this: "Per alteram Sectionem Signatura, instructa omnibus facultatibus iurisdictionis contentiosae, definit controversias ortas ex actu potestatis administrativae ecclesiasticae, qui ius subiectivum violaverit."[55]

Within the code commission, he proposed in particular that the competence of the *Sectio altera* be restated among the canons on the administrative procedure and administrative tribunals. And he envisioned an expansion of its competence, such that "it may judge not only the illegitimacy of the challenged act but also the merits of the cause."[56] This would be *"perfectly coherent"* with the model of the tribunal of the council and with the kind of tribunals proposed and called for by the commission and the Synod of Bishops.[57]

---

53. He would recognize that this jurisprudence changed in mid-1971 as a result of the authentic interpretation, but he argues that "that change is not at all based on the response given by the commission on January 11, 1971 (whose authentic sense we have already noted) but in the free interpretation of it, which in fact, it seems to us, is not faithful to either the prescript or the finality of no. 106 of the Constitution *Regimini*" (see "De obiecto primario competentiae," 536).

54. Cf. "De obiecto primario competentiae," 533; on that tribunal, see ibid., 512–516 and *infra* Chapter X, no. 18 (§§4–5). On this teaching, see Ilaria Zuanazzi, *"Praesis ut prosis." La funzione amministrativa nella diakonia della Chiesa* (Naples: Casa Editrice Jovene, 2005) 376, note 75.

55. "De obiecto primario competentiae," 542. English translation: "By means of the Second Section, the Signatura, having been endowed with all the faculties of contentious jurisdiction, defines controversies arising from an act of ecclesiastical administrative power that has violated a subjective right."

56. See PCCICR Archives, *vol. 181. XI. De processibus. Sessio VII · Series Altera diebus 14–19 maii et die 11 iunii 1979 habita. Relatio*, 231; *Communicationes* 43 (2011) 441. This was rejected, as is well known.

57. Cf. "De obiecto primario competentiae," 537–542, quotations, respectively, 542 and 541, no. 3.

25. – His proposals in this regard, however, have not been accepted. For, since the period in which he was writing, the legislator has four times declared his choice to limit the competence of the Supreme Tribunal in this matter to the question of a violation of the law. That is, it may not immediately examine whether the singular administrative act placed or approved by a dicastery of the Roman Curia violated some subjective right, but only whether it committed a violation of the legislation (*violatio legis*) in regard to the substance of the decision (*in decernendo*) or the procedure used (*in procedendo*). Nevertheless, Father Gordon's active and eloquent insistence undoubtedly advanced the question to the point of a legislative clarification implicit in the *CIC* and explicit in subsequent norms.[58]

26. – Father Gordon taught that there is no basis for concluding that the distinction between subjective rights and legitimate interests—the so-called "fundamental criterion" in the Italian system of contentious-administrative jurisdiction—exists in or has been received by the canonical system.[59] An especially important implication of this is the conviction that the public administration of the Church is not sued before the ordinary tribunals of the Church on account of its acts of governance when a complainant can claim only a juridical interest in the matter. This was established in canon 1601 of the 1917 *CIC* and reinforced six years later in an authentic interpretation.[60] The public ecclesiastical administration could only be summoned before the ordinary tribunal for causing damages as a private person apart from the exercise of public power.[61]

---

58. Cf. c. 1445 §2 but esp. *PB* art. 123 §1 and *LP* art. 34 §1, and most recently *Praedicate evangelium* art. 197 §1.

59. Cf. Gordon, *votum*, October 24, 1970: in SSAT Archives, 15–31, nn. 58–119; idem, *votum*, April 29, 1971: in SSAT Archives, 6–7. On the fundamental criterion, see especially "De iustitia administrativa ecclesiastica," 342–349, no. 138–148; on the debate in doctrine, see ibid., 351–378, nn. 155–199. See also "La renovación de la Signatura Apostólica," 605–609, nn. 130–155; "Interessi legittimi," 391–398. For a summary of his position, see, e.g., Zuanazzi, *"Praesis ut prosis,"* 399, note 150.

60. *AAS* 16 (1924) 251. On the problematic early applications of this distinction theoretically resolved by this authentic interpretation, see "De iustitia administrativa ecclesiastica," 284–286, nn. 49–52.

61. Cf. "La responsabilità," 418, at b: "Se il responsabile del danno è un ufficiale della P.A. della Chiesa, ma in veste in privato, può essere deferito o per via gerarchica al suo Superiore (…), o per via contenziosa al tribunale giudiziale ecclesiastico competente, avuto conto dello stato ecclesiastico del convenuto."

E. The Parties

27. – Special care is to be taken in contentious-administrative trials that the dignity of the ecclesiastical administration—which is a common good—not be harmed. On the one hand, one can speak of the "equality of procedural rights which is due the contending parties" before the Signatura. On the other, there is a particular "minimum reverence that is to be shown to the public authority."[62] One implication of this concerns the publicity of such a trial. "Having safeguarded the essential publicity," in causes of contentious-administrative recourse "a little greater secrecy is demanded" than in other contentious trials.[63]

28. – The text of no. 106 of *REU* seemed not to grant the faithful the right to introduce recourse before the Signatura against an act of a dicastery placed singularly, without any inferior authority having first placed an act. In other words, the dicastery would not be an original party but only a party by association with a lower level of the administration. For the legislator envisioned a prior act of an inferior authority and a decision of the dicastery. And so, under that law, this should be presumed to be the precise scenario that qualified for contentious-administrative recourse. For "the legislator willed to proceed slowly and cautiously in establishing 'administrative contention,' and so he did not grant everything that he could have granted but only some aspect of it and, as it were, experimentally."[64] This seemed too restrictive to Father Gordon, who was therefore pleased that an authentic interpretation extended this competence to include an administrative act of a dicastery, whether or not it resolved a hierarchical recourse.[65]

29. – Finally, it is interesting to note that Father Gordon was present at the March 3, 1987 gathering of consultors of the Pontifical Commission for the Authentic Interpretation of the *CIC*, which led to the well-known authentic interpretation on the active legitimation of a group of the faithful. This authentic interpretation responded to a *dubium* proposed by the Apostolic Signatura itself

---

62. See "Normae speciales," 102, no. 64.

63. See ibid., 149, note 1.

64. See ibid., 103, no. 69; see also ibid., 156, note 3.

65. Cf. "El recurso contencioso-administrativo canónico," 644, at b. For the authentic interpretation, see *AAS* 63 (1971) 329, *dubium I*.

within the context of a particular contentious-administrative cause.[66] At that gathering, Father Gordon declared his conviction that the mere fact of being a grouping of the faithful does not attribute it even private juridical personality, which is what would be necessary for it to act as a group. Moreover, even a group with active legitimation would be bound to demonstrate the existence of a *gravamen*, that is, an injustice, or a violation of a subjective right and not a mere "juridical interest," the latter of which concepts is not found in canon law and has introduced confusion.[67]

---

66. See Supreme Tribunal of the Apostolic Signatura, decree of the *Congresso, Demolitionis ecclesiae*, prot. n. 17447/85 CA, August 22, 1987: in *Ministerium Iustitiae. Jurisprudence of the Supreme Tribunal of the Apostolic Signatura. Official Latin with English Translation*, Gratianus Series, trans. William L. Daniel (Montréal: Wilson & Lafleur Ltée, 2011) 441–446.

67. "Consulta (3 marzo 1987). Relazione," in PCCICAI Archives, *Consulta VII (3 marzo 1987)*, 5, 6.

CHAPTER X

Summaries of Major Studies Written by Father Ignacio Gordon, SJ

For the benefit of the reader, who may not have convenient access to all of Father Gordon's works, this final chapter offers summaries of each of his major publications in the area of canonical procedural law in chronological order of publication. It also gives further recognition to the fact that Father Gordon's reflections on procedural law are not fully represented in the foregoing pages, for reasons described in the Introduction. This book aims to consolidate his contribution to general and particular questions; but this approach admittedly does not allow the reader to appreciate the full methodological integrity of his argumentation. The summaries below are an attempt to remedy this.

This chapter includes our author's *dispense* that have the quality and length of a book or article, since—as he describes in one place—he "deem[s them] to pertain to scientific work of an especially didactic character."[1] And they have indeed frequently been cited in canonical doctrine. On the other hand, this chapter omits minor publications of a more journalistic or reporting character, and those of only peripheral relevance to procedural law. It also naturally does not include his unpublished *vota* which, while often having the length, technicality, and complexity of a scholarly article, contain many facts particular to causes under examination before the Apostolic Signatura, which it is not this author's place to reveal.

1. "De Tribunalibus Regionalibus cum respectu ad iudicum delectum et ad processus breviationem." *Periodica* 56 (1967) 579–596.

The first article written by Father Gordon (hereafter G.) in the area of judicial procedural law is from a paper given on June 7, 1967 at a canon law conference in Lugano, Switzerland. It takes as its point of reference a 1964 conciliar *votum* that proposed, among other things, measures for simplifying the marriage nullity process and for protecting the suitable selection of judges. This prompted G. to examine the institute of the regional tribunal (i.e., the interdiocesan tribunal).

---

1. See *Pars statica*, 46, no. 75.

For—as G. might have known—related conciliar documentation briefly addressed regional tribunals.[2]

After a detailed first section identifying the various regional tribunals in the Church, he asked whether this institute contributes to the proper selection of judges. He replied in the affirmative since: 1) it encompasses a larger territory in which there are more people, among whom there would exist more clerics suitable for the office of judge ("regionality"); 2) it facilitates supervision by the competent dicastery of the Apostolic See; and 3) it can promote the greater distribution of causes, especially where the exclusive competence of a regional tribunal would be that of second instance, thus allowing it to be focused on appellate work.

Moreover, the institute of the regional tribunal is meant to address the causes of delays that occur in the completion of the process. In principle, its ministers of justice are to be free to dedicate themselves without distraction to the administration of justice. And the goal is that there will be a more or less equal distribution of causes between the various regional tribunals, leaving no one of them disproportionately burdened with causes. Moreover, the handling of causes is also expedited when the appellate tribunal is exclusively competent in second instance, since it builds up an expertise and can thus advance causes more rapidly.

2. "De Tribunalibus administrativis propositis a Commissione Codici I. C. recognoscendo et suffragatis ab Episcoporum Synodo." *Periodica* 57 (1968) 602–652.

The Second Vatican Council declared in *Dignitatis humanae* and especially *Gaudium et spes* the right of all to be treated with justice, including the availability of means for protecting their rights before organs enjoying true independence. This was applied to the Church's juridical order by the Pontifical Commission

---

2. The source cited by Fr. Gordon was a report published in *L'Osservatore Romano* 104/270 (Venerdì, 20 Novembre 1964) 2. He offers an excerpt of the Latin text in his "De nimia processuum matrimonialium duratione," 562–564, Appendix I. For the full text, which was distributed to the council fathers on November 10, 1964, see "Votum de matrimonii sacramento," in *Acta synodalia Sacrosancti Concilii Oecumenici Vaticani II. Pars VIII: Congregationes generales CXXIII–CXXVII. Sessio publica V* (Vatican City: Typis Polyglottis Vaticanis, 1976) III/8:467–473. It was the April 27, 1964 *Schema voti de matrimonii sacramento* that observed that the praxis of establishing regional or interdiocesan tribunals has been useful in many places, while it may not be suitable everywhere (see ibid., 1157, no. 4a). This statement related to no. 15 of the July 19, 1963 *Schema Decreti de matrimonii sacramento*, which called for the preparation and selection of suitable ministers of justice to work in "regional or interdiocesan tribunals" (cf. ibid., 1078).

for the Revision of the Code of Canon Law, which proposed among its guiding principles the protection of the rights of the faithful, freedom from arbitrariness in the exercise of administrative power, and the institution of administrative tribunals. These proposals were approved by the Synod of Bishops.

The Council taught that the Church enjoys the *munus regendi*, which includes legislative power, judicial power, and the power to direct all things (*omnia moderandi*), or administrative power—by no means to the exclusion of coercive power. These powers are distinct but also united in the Supreme Pontiff and the bishops, who may exercise them alone or, in many respects, through others. Administrative power is "that part of the power of jurisdiction that promotes the public good within the limits of law" by a variety of operations (no. 10). One aspect of it is "its function of resolving controversies," which resembles judicial power (no. 12).

Administrative justice is the treatment of a controversy arising between the public administration and private persons. It has taken different forms: administrative-judge, double jurisdiction, or single jurisdiction. Each of these forms arose from particular historical circumstances and are expressed in the many governments of the world. In the 1917 *CIC*, the first model was in effect, inasmuch as the administrative superior, which would make or receive recourses against administrative decisions, was also the one to which judgment was reserved, to the exclusion of the Sacred Roman Rota (c. 1601). The 1917 *CIC*'s drafters would have had no experience of double jurisdiction, and single jurisdiction had long become something foreign to the Church and the praxis of the Apostolic See. With the issuance of *REU*, however, the system of double jurisdiction was established, and this was highly supported by the Synod of Bishops, which also voiced some fears. These fears, which concerned hindering governance and undermining obedience, can be overcome by suitable legislation and appropriate formation.

Administrative tribunals in the Church ought to be arranged according to different levels, especially three levels. For: 1) the fallibility of human judgments demands the opportunity of appeal and the possibility of a double conformity of sentences; 2) levels of administrative justice were foreseen in the seventh guiding principle for the revision of the *CIC* and thus in the drafts of the future law; and 3) some ordering according to levels is verified in the secular organization of administrative contention, of whatever model. This arrangement by levels is tempered by two principles: 1) the right to approach an administrative tribunal presupposes that the administrative pathway has been exhausted; and 2) it is impossible for acts of the Roman Curia ordinarily to be submitted to a non-apostolic authority. These principles would seem to be mutually exclusive, since one cannot introduce a contention before the local administrative tribunal after the matter has already been decided by the Apostolic See.

Some authors have proposed other structures, e.g., a national administrative tribunal for matters of lesser importance, or a procedure for the ordinary to act as administrator-judge with the metropolitan as an intermediate higher authority. Another approach envisions a priest-delegate or diocesan commission for contentious matters. However, the metropolitan ought not be situated as an intermediate administrative authority, since this prolongs the administrative pathway, delaying the ability to approach an administrative tribunal, and it would create tensions between the bishop and the metropolitan. Apostolic administrative tribunals, competent to judge acts of the Roman congregations, could have three levels: first instance before the apostolic nunciature or delegation, and second and third instances in commissions (resembling Rotal *turni*) before the Apostolic Signatura; or all three levels before the Signatura.

3.　"De nimia processuum matrimonialium duratione. Factum – Causae – Remedia." *Periodica* 58 (1969) 491–594 and 641–735.[3]

Both the Fathers of the 1967 Synod of Bishops and numerous authors were harboring grave concerns about the excessive duration of marriage nullity trials, such that it seemed an undeniable fact and one that clearly had a negative impact on the good of souls. In a carefully progressing and comprehensive study, G. set out to identify and examine this problem, and its causes and remedies, in relation to the practical work of the persons involved (especially ministers of justice and advocates) and to the procedural norms themselves.

I. He analyzes the fact of excessive length by examining the ideal length of a trial in law and human reality, the unfortunate excesses that are verified in practice, and the harm that the latter cause. He then examines the causes and remedies to those causes—five of which depend on persons, and a complex of which depend upon procedural law itself and suggest areas for its reform.

II. 1. The first cause is that ministers of justice are either unavailable, or that their numbers are disproportionate to the number of causes to be treated by the tribunal. This problem exists because the number of priests is shrinking, the bishop moderator has other pastoral priorities, ministers of justice have to take on other functions for their livelihood, and the number of causes is ever increas-

---

3. He had given a lecture on this theme, with the same principal title, in June 1969 in Brescia (Pontificia Universitas Gregoriana, *Liber annualis 1970* [Rome: Universitas Gregoriana, 1970] 431).

ing. The primary remedy for this is the erection of regional tribunals, though some also argue for the collaboration of lay people in the work of judging.

2. The second cause is insufficient or even nonexistent remuneration for ministers of justice in some tribunals, leading them to assume additional functions apart from the administration of justice. The remedy is obviously to make sufficient funds available, which may be obtained from judicial fees, the establishment of a fund by the bishop, or the concentration of resources in a regional tribunal.

3. The third cause is the lack of preparation, or lack of academic formation, of those appointed to be judges, which exists in some places in the Church. This has a detrimental impact on the manner of proceeding and is a grave matter affecting the individual judges and the whole Church. The remedy is a thorough formation in canon law, and particular formation in judicial doctrine and praxis.

4. The fourth cause is the delay that is sometimes caused by the parties and witnesses, the defender of the bond, experts, and other tribunals. Some remedies for this part of the problem are the following: to send documents to parties and witnesses prompting them to appear, to have the judge instead of the defender prepare the questions to be posed to the parties and witnesses, to ensure that the defender works in the tribunal full time, to be able to consider a single expert report sufficient (while the law envisioned two), not to exclude *a priori* an expert who had already cared for a party, to impart general instruction to the clergy about inter-tribunal assistance, to encourage willingness on the part of the judge (with a notary and defender of the bond) to travel in order to collect proofs.

5. The fifth cause is the delay attributed to advocates. This occurs in part because the number of advocates is unequal to the number of causes needing their patronage—whether because lay people often cannot earn sufficient income as advocates or they lack knowledge of law and jurisprudence, or because there are not enough priests to satisfy the demand for this work. Also, there are problems with the timely submission of their *restrictus iuris et facti* and lax attitudes toward less lucrative or important causes. The roots of these problems are often lack of juridical expertise and offenses against the truth. Remedies to this include the promotion of canon law studies among laypeople so that they may be able to become advocates, the practical reservation of advocates for more difficult cases, ongoing instruction in judicial praxis and judicial deontology, and the creation of a college of advocates in tribunals.

A remedy for the principal causes of delays is the institution of regional tribunals. For they require fewer priests to dedicate themselves to judicial activity, and they foster the pooling of clergy and financial resources. They can also free former diocesan judges to serve as advocates.

III. Several authors propose modifications to procedural law. 1. The proposal for the suppression of matrimonial tribunals is based on false premises and erroneous notions about marriage, and thus cannot be admitted. Tribunals may need to be reformed, but they do not need to be suppressed; yielding the judgment about the nullity of marriage to the spouses is contrary to good sense and settled principles of justice. A diocesan commission for examining the spouses' already-made decision to consider their marriage null is useless and arbitrary. (See publication no. 6 below.)

2. Limited legislative decentralization is legitimate in regard to what is accidental (not substantial) to the process, or to the local application of what is substantial.

3. Some reforms in the introductory stage of the process would promote the celerity of the process, such as inclusion of a forum of the petitioner's domicile or place of residence if this would also facilitate the instruction of the cause, the competence of the *officialis* or presiding judge to admit or reject the *libellus*, and the *contestatio litis* without requiring the parties to appear at the tribunal.

4. When there are no contrary arguments and the one confessing to the nullity of his marriage is judged credible, a single confession can have the force of full proof.

5. The proposal that the judicial standard of moral certitude be replaced with that of "the preponderance of the evidence" would harm the stability of marriage. However, there has been an absolutization of the former in procedural law and in regard to nullity of marriage, and that could be profitably adjusted in accord with canonical tradition.

6. The obligation of the defender of the bond to appeal should not be eliminated or converted into a mere prudent judgment. However, it would foster the just abbreviation of a matrimonial trial to institute an abbreviated appellate process. Proposals to decentralize third instance from the Roman Rota, despite some advantages, are not suitable and would practically suppress a unity of jurisprudence in the Church.

4.   "Normae speciales Supremi Tribunalis Signaturae Apostolicae. Editio aucta introductione, fontibus et notis." *Periodica* 59 (1970) 75–165.

In a work including many bibliographical notations, G. traces the history of both Signaturas (i.e., of Justice and of Favor). This begins with information about the Apostolic Signatura's origins (13th–15th cent.), continues with its more formal institution in the sixteenth century, and extends to its restoration by Pope St. Pius

X in 1908 and the innovations introduced by Pope Benedict XV and Pope St. Paul VI. He then offers a treatise on the Apostolic Signatura in the (then-)*ius vigens*, identifying the norms that govern it and explaining its structure, especially its *Sectio altera*. The heart of this work is the very text of the *Normae speciales* of 1968, for which he offers some annotations, outstanding among which are the *fontes* for individual norms in the form of footnotes. It concludes with an index identifying the various officials of the Signatura and in which norms they are mentioned.

5.   "De iustitia administrativa ecclesiastica tum transacto tempore tum hodierno." *Periodica* 61 (1972) 251–378.

Intended to be a continuation of the work listed in no. 2 above, this lengthy treatise opens with some review of what he had addressed in that one. Administrative justice is the treatment of a controversy arising between the public administration and private persons, though, as other authors have pointed out, it may also arise between organs of public administration and even be initiated by one. It takes the three forms discussed above, and it is not uncommon to observe in juridical orders a passage from one system to another. This occurred not only in France, Belgium, and Italy, but also in the canonical system. History indeed shows that the Church transitioned from a long period of single jurisdiction (12th cent.–1908), to the system of administrator-judge (1908–1967), to the system of double jurisdiction (1967–present).

The system of single jurisdiction existed, in effect, thanks to the institute of the extrajudicial appeal, in virtue of which one could sue a bishop or superior for a non-judicial act, including an act of what is now called executive or administrative power. This was first authorized explicitly by Pope Alexander III (as the *provocatio*), and it was confirmed by Popes Gregory IX and Clement V. It would be examined by canonists from the classical period of canon law to the end of the nineteenth century. It was the basis for some decisions of the Roman Rota, but it did not include acts of the sacred congregations, which were therefore immune from judicial control. Gradually, they, and not tribunals, became the hierarchical (administrative) superiors, instead of any tribunals.

The system of administrator-judge was instituted by Pope St. Pius X in canon 16 of the *Lex propria* of the Rota and the Signatura and confirmed in canon 1601 of the 1917 *CIC* and in a 1924 authentic interpretation. Despite some efforts to prolong the existence of the extrajudicial appeal in doctrine and jurisprudence, the law itself envisioned the institute of hierarchical recourse to the congregations of the Apostolic See, which did not admit of any ordinary challenge. Following

1924, the majority of authors taught that administrative decrees of ordinaries could in no way be challenged before tribunals, while Rotal jurisprudence would not accept this seemingly until the mid-1940s.

Finally, the Church was transformed into a system of double jurisdiction with the institution of the *Sectio altera* of the Supreme Tribunal of the Apostolic Signatura. For this tribunal is a true administrative tribunal with jurisdiction over the whole administration of the Church: immediately over the central administration (the Roman Curia), and mediately, through it, over all subordinate administrations. Influenced by the French juridical order (which had contentious jurisdictions of subjective rights and then of annulment or [il]legality) and the Italian juridical order (which had and has a contentious jurisdiction of [il]legitimacy), the Signatura examines rights with the prevailing object of a violation of the law but not the merits of the challenged act.

Understanding of the competence of the *Sectio altera* as an administrative tribunal is further deepened by comparing it to the competence of an ordinary judicial tribunal. This distinction is detected in the juridical orders of France, Germany, and Italy, and likewise in that of the Church. A distinction in the Italian juridical order has been proposed by some authors as if it exists or should exist in canon law: the distinction between subjective rights (which are vindicated before ordinary tribunals even when undermined by the public administration) and legitimate interests (which are vindicated before administrative tribunals when violated by the public administration). Pio Ciprotti and Ermanno Graziani argue that this distinction exists in canon law, but G. demonstrates that in fact it is absent from the 1917 *CIC*, the word *interesse* consistently has other meanings not the same as "legitimate interest," and it is absent from the doctrine of most major commentators. This distinction is not necessary, it is not completely accepted even by Italian jurists, and it is superfluous for canon law. And so it should not be introduced into canon law since it would interrupt strong and organic developments in contentious-administrative jurisdiction, ordinary tribunals are not well-equipped to judge the public administration, the italianization of canon law should be avoided, and it does not clearly promote the good of the Church.

6.   "La soppressione dei tribunali ecclesiastici negli scritti di Mons. St. J. Kelleher (1966–1969)." In *Atti del Congresso internazionale di diritto canonico: La Chiesa dopo il Concilio. Roma, 14–19 gennaio 1970*, 2.1:737–751. Milan: Giuffrè Editore, 1972.[4]

An American canonist, Msgr. Stephen J. Kelleher, *Officialis* of the Archdiocese of New York, began proposing radical reforms in the area of matrimonial law in the middle to late 1960s. Among these proposals was the suppression of tribunals. He arrived at this proposal because of his distress at seeing the experience of the faithful before the tribunals of the Church and his conviction that, even if tribunals were functioning optimally, they do not offer a satisfactory solution in instances of so-called "intolerable marriages." Msgr. Kelleher presumes that there must be some solution to the problem of such marriages and that this is meant to be the aim of matrimonial procedural law.

Msgr. Kelleher has three main proposals in regard to the transformation of the tribunal. The first is that tribunals are to be suppressed, since they are a source of injustice and inhumane treatment, they harm human dignity, are not Christian, and do not and cannot solve the problem of "intolerable marriages." The second is that spouses must be accorded the right to make a personal decision about whether they are free before God from their matrimonial bond. The third is that a "matrimonial commission" should be set up in each diocese, which can examine such marriages and make non-binding recommendations to the spouses.

G. demonstrates, with the support in fact of other canonists of the New York Tribunal, that the concept of the "intolerable marriage" from which one should be able to be released is inherently flawed, since some such marriages may in fact be valid. The goal of releasing spouses from any marriage is contrary to the Church's teaching on marriage and is not the object of a matrimonial trial. If tribunals are imperfect, they need to be reformed, not suppressed. Spouses are obviously unable to objectively determine the binding character or invalidity of their marriage. And such a matrimonial commission seems to be a useless institute that only fosters a modern form of clandestine marriage.

[This article is, as G. says (at 751), a "condensed re-elaboration" of what he wrote in "De nimia processuum matrimonialium duratione," 644–668, nn. 119–159.]

---

4. In September 1969 in Pozzuoli, Naples, he had given a lecture on this theme, entitled "Theoria Stephani J. Kelleher circa Tribunalium matrimonialium suppressione ac substitutione" (Pontificia Universitas Gregoriana, *Liber annualis 1970* [Rome: Universitas Gregoriana, 1970] 431).

7. *De iudiciis in genere. II. Pars dynamica.* Rome: Pontificia Universitas Gregoriana, 1972.

This *dispensa* is much more abbreviated than that treating the *Pars statica* of
the process (*vide infra* no. 14), spanning just 130 pages. Standing as a second part
of the aforementioned volume—since both constitute his course notes *De iudiciis
in genere*—it lacks any introduction of its own. Rather, it simply begins with the
introductory stage of the judicial process. Following the sequence of this section
of the *CIC*, he presents the basic teaching on the following themes: the introduction of the cause, the *litis contestatio*, the instance of litigation (the notion of
instance and its cessation), interrogations, the various forms of proof (this section
is quite lengthy, spanning about 50 pages), incidental causes, the publication of
the acts together with the conclusion in and discussion of the cause, the sentence,
ordinary remedies against the sentence, the *res iudicata* and *restitutio in integrum*,
concluding with only some doctrinal citations on judicial expenses and the
execution of the sentence. Throughout the *dispensa*, G. offers insets on causes of
nullity of marriage, citing especially the pertinent norms from *PME*.

8. "La renovación de la Signatura Apostólica." *Revista Española de Derecho
   Canónico* 28 (1972) 571–610.

The Apostolic Signatura has a long history dating back in its primitive form
to the thirteenth century and undergoing developments as a result of the praxis
of the papal chancery, the reform of the Roman Curia, and the Napoleonic invasion and eventual withdrawal. It was reestablished as supreme tribunal by Pope
St. Pius X, and its traditional administrative competence over judicial activity was
restored by Pope Benedict XV. Pope St. Paul VI established its *Sectio altera* and
approved its *NS*.

The Signatura is a true tribunal, or judicial organ, and a supreme tribunal,
having jurisdiction over aspects of the activity of both the Roman Rota and the
administrative dicasteries of the Roman Curia. Its two sections are rightly considered judicial and administrative. In its first section, it keeps vigilance over the
correct administration of justice and exercises either ordinary or delegated power
depending upon the nature of the matter, especially in regard to its traditional
judicial competences but also in certain novel titles of competences, especially
the disciplining of advocates. Among the administrative questions included
within its competences are the following: the examination of decisions in view
of their obtaining civil effects, addressing requests for pontifical commissions,

extending the competence of tribunals, resolving conflicts of competence, and approving the erection of regional tribunals. In addition to the judgment of contentious-administrative causes, its *Sectio altera* is competent to resolve conflicts of competence between dicasteries of the Apostolic See and to judge administrative questions entrusted to it by them as well as by the Roman Pontiff.

The second half of this article treats the competence of the *Sectio altera* as an administrative tribunal having competence over controversies arising from a singular administrative act. It essentially consists of a Spanish translation and synthesis of the themes described in the last two paragraphs in no. 5 above.

9. "El recurso contencioso-administrativo canónico." *Sal Terrae* 61 (1973) 641–648.

The object of contentious-administrative recourse is a contention between any member of the faithful and an administrative superior in the Church, who has issued an act of administrative power. The superior may be a bishop, religious superior, or the conference of bishops, and its act is clearly a non-normative and non-judicial act of power or the administrative silence of such a superior. The conditions for introducing recourse before the Signatura are these: 1) that a dicastery of the Roman Curia issued a decision that resolves the controversy and 2) that the decision is deemed by one of the parties to violate the law.

Such recourse can be proposed, through a qualified advocate, by the subject aggrieved by the original act or by the author of the original act if he is aggrieved by the decision of the dicastery. The *libellus* introducing the recourse must be submitted within thirty days of the notification of the decision. A factor that was in effect in the earliest era of the *Sectio altera* was the date of the issuance of acts in relation to the coming-into-effect of *REU*: those issued thirty days prior to it were not subject to contentious-administrative recourse. The execution of the challenged decision can be suspended, and indeed some were considered suspended by the very fact of the recourse, such as those against the removal of a pastor and the dismissal of a religious.

The first step of the recourse is the preliminary judgment about the admission or rejection of the recourse. If it is admitted, the judgment about the alleged illegitimacy is made. A decision judged illegitimate is null or rescinded. This decision is not appealable, except by means of a recourse to the Roman Pontiff. The decision must be accepted by those affected.

10. "De appellationibus iuxta m.p. '*Causas matrimoniales.*'" *Periodica* 63 (1974) 285–316.[5]

Immediately following the issuance of *CM*, much literature was produced about it, including several addressing particular questions. In this article, G. takes up three particular questions.

1. *CM* refers to the defender of the bond's obligation to appeal to "the superior tribunal." It is the common doctrine that this was inclusive of both the local appellate tribunal and the Sacred Roman Rota, which had concurrent jurisdiction. A minority opinion rejected that notion, but G. defended the majority position, since *CM* remitted itself to the procedural law of the 1917 *CIC*. Speed is a goal of *CM*, but it is subject to the main judicial goals of truth and justice, and the Rota is an appellate tribunal already for the second level of jurisdiction.

2. Some authors maintained that the affirmative sentence that would be examined by means of the *processus brevior* of *CM* was that issued at any level of jurisdiction. G. shows that the majority opinion is certain and even supported by Rotal jurisprudence. According to that view, the affirmative sentence after which the *processus brevior* could be used (see *CM* VIII §1) was only that issued in first instance or "as if in first instance" after a ground has legitimately been added at the level of appeal. This is clear especially from elements in VIII §§2–3 of *CM*[6]— which G. calls the "intrinsic argument" (299).

3. The norm of *CM* VIII §1 mentions the defender of the bond's obligation to appeal but mentions no other party. This led some authors to hold these extreme views: i) *CM* derogates from the right of a spouse defending his marriage to appeal an affirmative sentence, such that only the defender of the bond may

---

5. See the introductory note at no. 11 below.

6. See *CM* VIII: "§1. From the first sentence (*A prima sententia*) declaring nullity of marriage, the defender of the bond is bound to appeal to the superior Tribunal (*ad superius Tribunal*) within the legitimate time period: should he neglect to do this, he is to be compelled by the authority of the presiding judge or sole judge. §2. Before the Tribunal of second instance (*Apud Tribunal secundae instantiae*), the defender of the bond is to present his observations stating whether or not he has some opposition to make against the decision issued at the first level (*in primo gradu*). Against these observations, the college, if it judges it opportune, may seek the observations of the parties or their procurator-advocates. §3. Having seen the sentence and weighed the observations of the defender of the bond and, if they have been sought and submitted, of the parties or their procurator-advocates, the college by its decree either ratifies the decision of the first level (*decisionem primi gradus*) or admits the cause to an ordinary examination at the second level (*ad ordinarium examen secundi gradus*). In the first case, if no one makes recourse, the spouses who are otherwise not impeded have the right to contract a new marriage after ten days have elapsed from the publication of the decree" (at 444).

appeal; ii) the *processus brevior* may not be used if one of the spouses also appeals the affirmative sentence at the same time as the defender of the bond; in such a case, the cause is treated according to the ordinary process immediately. There were also some more moderate views. These include the following: the respondent does not appeal but can express some opposition to the affirmative sentence; the respondent's right of appeal is suspended until the cause is admitted to an ordinary examination; the respondent can indeed appeal and his observations must be sought by the appellate college when he does so; the respondent's right of appeal gives rise to the ordinary process in place of the *processus brevior* only if the appellate college decrees it.

G.'s position is that, under the regime of *CM* VIII §1, the defender of the bond alone could appeal against an affirmative sentence issued in first instance or as if in first instance. For that law makes no mention of the respondent's particular rights as an appellant, and it overrides the respondent's supposed right to an ordinary appellate process by virtue of the fact that all trials pending in second instance due to an appeal of an affirmative sentence (even including by the respondent) were to be treated in the *processus brevior*. It is thus for the defender to protect the rights of the respondent in this procedural context. Whatever is argued during the *processus brevior*, it is for the appellate college of judges to decide whether or not to confirm the sentence immediately.

11. "De diverso regimine appellationum inducto in m.p. '*Causas matrimoniales.*'" In *Studi di diritto canonico in onore di Marcello Magliocchetti*, 2:713–724. Rome: Catholic Book Agency, 1975.

[While this study was published in 1975 in a collective work, it was clearly a precursor to another published in 1974 (*vide supra* no. 10). For, in the first paragraph of this article (at 713), G. indicated that he would leave "for another time" an examination of particular questions pertaining to appeals in *CM*. And in the 1974 article (at 285 and 292 [*Ad secundum*]), he stated that he had already "recently treated" fundamental questions about the appeal.]

CM introduced a new regime for handling appeals in causes of nullity of marriage. When an affirmative sentence was issued in first instance and the defender of the bond appealed it, a preliminary decision was to be made about whether or not to confirm it within an abbreviated procedure (*ritus brevior* or *processus brevior*). After the appeal of all other sentences, it was to be treated according to the norms of the ordinary appellate process. This article is G.'s defense of that legislative choice.

The fundamental defense concerns the definitive sentence's relationship to the objective truth. An affirmative sentence is a declaration of the truth about the nullity of marriage, while a negative sentence declares only that that truth is unknown. Accordingly, an affirmative sentence (a kind of presumed finding of the truth) requires only a superior judgment confirming whether or not that is the truth; a negative sentence is an admission that the truth may demand a deeper investigation. This is not so, however, when an affirmative sentence is first issued at a level higher than the first level, since there is already a disparity of judgments.

The statistics taken from a ten-year period at the Tribunal of the Vicariate of Rome would seem to illustrate this. In that sample, the vast majority of affirmative sentences were confirmed. Among the negative sentences, almost half were not appealed and almost a third were confirmed; about 17% of them were overturned. All of this suggests that single affirmative sentences are largely deemed to be just in practice, while causes resulting in a negative sentence have a more varied future. Thus, *CM*'s diverse governance of appeals is just.

In response to those that argue *CM* to create an inequality among the parties, G. offers three arguments. (1) *CM* does not absolutely favor the petitioner since it still demands an ordinary appellate process beyond second instance. (2) A uniform appellate process would either injure the discovery of truth (which can only be accomplished via an ordinary process after an appeal of a negative sentence), or it would prolong a trial that had already justly resulted in a confirmable affirmative sentence. And (3) the rights of the parties to be heard prior to any decree of confirmation are intact and may persuade the appellate judges to admit the cause to an ordinary appellate process. In response to those that argue the inconsistency of *CM*, since it expedites only certain causes, G. declares that the principle of speed is always subordinate to the search for the truth.

The article concludes with a demonstration of how the *processus brevior* of *CM* was already being proposed by some authors and enjoys some normative precedents, especially in canon 1992 of the 1917 *CIC*.

12. "Interessi legittimi, diritti soggettivi e giustizia amministrativa ecclesiastica."[7] In *Persona e ordinamento nella Chiesa. Atti del II Congresso Internazionale di Diritto Canonico, Milano 10–16 settembre 1973*, 391–401, 455. Milan: Vita e Pensiero, 1975.

Two questions related to the recognition and defense of subjective rights are whether the legitimate interests of the faithful are recognized in the Church's legislation and whether they are accorded jurisdictional protection. Among Italian jurists, there are two opposing views: 1) such interests exist in the 1917 *CIC* and *REU*, and 2) such interests do not exist but should be introduced into the Church's legislation. G.'s view is contrary to both of these for several reasons. (1) The concept of "legitimate interest" (i.e., diverse claims on the legitimate exercise of administrative authority) is absent from the 1917 *CIC*. The word *interesse* is used 78 times: usually in the sense of "to take part" or "to be present," other times as an expression of utility in relation to a subjective right. Most authors do not speak of this concept, and those few that do are unconvincing. (2) The concept has not been introduced by *REU*. For "legitimacy" does not necessarily include "legitimate interest." (3) It should not be introduced, because it is a historically conditioned Italian construct. Italian jurists themselves are divided about its meaning and importance. The canonical doctrine on subjective rights is adequate to address questions of judicial protection.

The defense of subjective rights ought to be clearly accepted as a component of administrative justice in the Church. For this is the stated purpose of administrative tribunals, it is the consistent essence of administrative contention in the Church, and it is verified in jurisprudence.

13. "Dichiarazione di nullità e dispensa del matrimonio." In *Amore e stabilità nel matrimonio*, 133–150. Rome: Università Gregoriana Editrice, 1976.

It is necessary ever to distinguish the declaration of nullity of marriage and dissolution of the matrimonial bond on the one hand from secular legal divorce on the other, which is contrary to the indissolubility of marriage. This can be seen by means of a careful consideration of the two aforementioned ecclesiastical processes.

---

7. In this book, the individual interventions are not entitled as a heading at the beginning of them. Rather, the designated moderator of the individual roundtable discussions declares the title by way of introduction (in the same book, see Stephan Kuttner, 390).

The declaration of matrimonial nullity relates to the incipient nullity of a marriage due to defects based simply on the natural law or on positive ecclesiastical laws, the latter of which concretely express the natural law, pertain to the protection of the faith, or pertain more generally to the protection of the public nature of marriage. Canon law identifies who may accuse a marriage of nullity and who is competent to declare that nullity. This is done sometimes by means of a summary or documentary process, but more typically by the ordinary or "normal" process, which has several defined phases and the potential of appeal. Among the problems introduced on the occasion of the process are its duration, its costs and fees, and the general difficulty of caring for those in unhappy marriages, whether they are null or not.

The dissolution of a non-consummated marriage is reserved to the pope, who grants a dissolution under certain conditions. Proofs are gathered under the supervision of the bishop. It may be granted when there is a grave cause, such as the irreconcilability of the spouses, the desire of the petitioner to enter a new marriage, or a danger of incontinence, and when there is no danger of scandal. The petition is transmitted to the Apostolic See, which either denies the favor, requests additional information, or advises the pope to grant it.

14. *De iudiciis in genere. I. Introductio Generalis, Pars statica.* Rome: Pontificia Universitas Gregoriana, 1976 (second printing, 1979).

A first, relatively brief section (41 pages) presents the general introduction to procedural law. This includes the following themes: the notion, origin, and evolution of canonical procedural law in general; difficulties and advantages of studying it; the elements of Book IV of the 1917 *CIC* together with rules of interpretation and a bibliography; and basic notions for studying trials.

The remainder of the book (341 pages) presents the whole *pars statica* of procedural law. This is divided into a preliminary chapter, followed by five chapters. The preliminary chapter explains the concept of an ecclesiastical trial, kinds of trials, the object of judicial power, and the force of procedural legislation. Chapter 1 is on the competent forum; chapter 2, the hierarchy of tribunals; chapter 3, the discipline to be observed in tribunals; chapter 4, the parties; and chapter 5, actions and exceptions.

15. Gordon, Ignacio, and Zenon Grocholewski, eds. *Documenta recentiora circa rem matrimonialem et processualem cum notis bibliographicis et indicibus*, vol. 1. Rome: Pontificia Universitas Gregoriana, 1977.

This is the *de facto* third edition of two previous, much thinner collections of documents compiled by G.[8] It is not formally identified as the third, perhaps because it is so much larger than the previous two; but in the preface G. does recognize it as a third version, stating that copies of the second edition have run out (cf. *DR* 1:5). It is co-edited by then-Monsignor Zenon Grocholewski, Whose Eminence informed me that, "since this volume was completed by me as something practically new in relation to the preceding editions circulated, Father Gordon did not wish to appear as an author with me. But to me it seemed honest, because it was his inspiration."[9] And later G. would identify it as published "by the Most Illustrious and Very Reverend Monsignor Z. Grocholewski and by myself,"[10] though he credited Grocholewski with accomplishing the work of expansion from the previous versions: he "carried the weight" of the project "largely alone" (5).

The book contains 74 documents pertaining to marriage and procedural law, including administrative procedures and contentious-administrative causes. Part 1, on marriage, includes documentation on the nature of marriage, mixed marriages, delegation of a deacon to assist at marriage, and the then-evolving revision of universal legislation on marriage. Part 2 gives documentation for various aspects of matrimonial procedure: the universal marriage nullity process, particular laws (e.g., APN) and responses, cases of the presumed death of a spouse, petitions for dissolution *super rato*, and causes of separation. Part 3, on "other processes," contains documents on the administrative procedure and on the procedures for dispensation from obligations of the clerical state and dismissal of religious in particular. Part 4 is on the Supreme Tribunal of the Apostolic Signatura. There are also two Appendices with documents pertaining to Eastern marriage nullity trials and special faculties for mission territories. There are extensive bibliographies throughout the work, as well as four useful indices.

---

8. The much less dispersed edition is the first one: *Documenta recentiora circa rem matrimonialem et processualem collegit I. GORDON S. I., Ad usum privatum* (Rome: Pontificia Universitas Gregoriana Facultas Iuris Canonici, 1971). The brief preface authored by Fr. Gordon is dated September 15, 1971. It is located in *Archivio del primo corso per giudici (1971–1972)*, FICPUG Archives, II.13. A second edition was published in 1972 (preface dated July 16, 1972). As he states in the latter, these books were printed precisely for the upcoming *Cursus* events.

9. See Zenon Grocholewski, private letter, October 7, 2018.

10. See *DR* 2:5.

16. "Decisio Signaturae Iustitiae diei 19 iunii 1834 qua nova forma contentiosi-administrativi in Statu Pontificio introducta est." In *Investigationes theologico-canonicae*, 185–210. Rome: Università Gregoriana Editrice, 1978.

From the twelfth century until 1908, the system of single jurisdiction was in effect, such that acts of administrative power could be challenged before ordinary tribunals by means of the extrajudicial appeal. However, already in 1834, Pope Gregory XVI introduced into the jurisprudence of the Signatura of Justice the contrary rule in relation to civil administrative acts issued within the Papal States. Until this time, such acts were indeed subject to judicial litigation, but the Prefect of the Signatura questioned its own competence in a particular cause leading to this declaration of the Roman Pontiff (*oraculum Pontificium*), which in turn guided the subsequent judgments of the Signatura. The source material, which comprises over half of the pages of this article (which is also richly endowed with historical annotations), reveals that the source of Gregory's rule was in the jurisprudence of the Napoleonic courts in Rome and in Paris. These influenced a particular Rotal decision *coram* De Cursiis from June 6, 1825, which contains principles resembling Gregory's pronouncement. The decision of the Signatura of Justice, signed by the Prefect Giovanni Francesco Cardinal Falzacappa and issued on June 19, 1834, solemnly declares and defends this principle of the Roman Pontiff.

In reproducing the documents, G. first gives the text of the decision of the Signatura of Justice (*Lauretana, Circumscriptionis,* June 19, 1834), and then offers the key texts in an appendix, with annotations. They are the 1811 decision of the appellate court of Rome, the November 11, 1811 decision of the Parisian Court of Cassation, and the Rotal decision *coram* De Cursiis (*Romana, Refectionis damnorum,* June 6, 1825).

17. "Discorso generale sui libri IV e V del *Codex*." Apollinaris 52 (1979) 62–79.

This article represents a half-hour presentation given by G. on February 18, 1978 at a conference on Roman law and canon law. There were three presentations on particular questions of procedural law and penal law, and his was meant to offer an overview of these two disciplines so as to offer a context for the other three. The vast majority of it (about 15 pages) is spent on the ordinary contentious trial, while the remaining fews pages are on penal law.

In the section on the judicial process, he reflects by way of introduction on the notion of *actio* from Roman law and its reception into canon law. He then explains the five fundamental parts of the ordinary contentious process: the introduction, the instruction, the discussion, the definitive sentence, and the challenge of the sentence. Given the context, he maximizes his references to historical sources, most of which are found also in his *dispensa* on the *pars dynamica* (no. 7 *supra*). In the section on penal law, he limits himself to three concepts: the delict, the purpose of penalties in general, and *latae sententiae* excommunication.

18. "De obiecto primario competentiae 'Sectionis Alterius' Supremi Tribunalis Signaturae Apostolicae." *Periodica* 68 (1979) 505–542.

This article appears to be G.'s grand appeal for clarity on the object of competence of the *Sectio altera* of the Apostolic Signatura. It is his only article presented in all three of his major languages: Latin, Spanish (no. 21 *infra*), and Italian (no. 29 *infra*).

There are certain historical presuppositions to the institute of ecclesiastical administrative justice. In the first period, controversies between superiors and subjects could be introduced before ordinary tribunals in the form of the extrajudicial appeal. In the second period, such controversies remained before administrative organs thanks to the institute of hierarchical recourse. In the third period, after hierarchical recourse, the controversy could be introduced before an administrative tribunal—namely, the *Sectio altera* of the Apostolic Signatura. Throughout these developments, it has been a question of the vindication of subjective rights allegedly violated by the public administration. This was implicit in the medieval concept of the *gravamen*.

The passage from the second to the third period was influenced by different factors. Above all, in the second period, the protection of rights had been quite weakened due to the lack of procedural safeguards (e.g., publication of acts, the assistance of advocates.) and the institutional bias of the sacred congregations, which belong to the same hierarchy of governance as the bishops. Some improvement of the institute of hierarchical recourse was seen to be necessary, and various proposals were made, among which, however, seems not to have been included a "jurisdiction of legitimacy for the defense of subjective rights" (511).

At its inception, the *Sectio altera* was likened by the secretary of the commission that drafted *REU* to a kind of administrative tribunal erected within the Second Vatican Council. That tribunal was an expansion of a similar institute at the First Vatican Council—namely, the judges of excuses and the judges of complaints. These judges received and, before the plenary session of the council, reported on individual bishops' requests to be absent from the council or to leave early (*excusationes*), and came to agreements about controversies (*querelae*) regarding the order of seating and the right of precedence or, if they could not agree, referred the case to the general assembly. The administrative tribunal of the Second Vatican Council included some questions of excuse and complaint but also questions about the discipline of the council; a member of the council could thus complain before it that some moderator violated his right to do or omit something. This was an administrative tribunal constituted to judge administrative acts of the authorities within the council; by its nature, it was separate from the hierarchy of judicial tribunals. Judgments were made by a *turnus* of three members, and recourse could be made to the whole tribunal (*videntibus omnibus*).

In this same era, the first Synod of Bishops approved a principle (no. 7) for promoting the protection of subjective rights against the public administration of the Church. This was to be done by true tribunals that were administrative in nature, ordered according to levels and kinds, for the purpose of the defense of rights according to a proper canonical procedure. These tribunals and those of the Second Vatican Council have these marks in common: they are true tribunals, they are endowed with contentious-administrative jurisdiction, they directly and exclusively judge controversies arising between superiors and subjects, they have the same faculties as ordinary judges, and their judges must be endowed with knowledge and dignity.

Debate continues about the primary object of the Signatura's competence in causes of contentious-administrative recourse. There are two dominant views. The first view, limiting it to the question of legitimacy of the challenged decision, finds support in three arguments. (1) A restrictive reading of *REU* 106 does not mention any contention between parties. G. argues, though, that the identity of the parties is clearly implicit: the public administration and the one aggrieved by the administration's act. (2) The 1971 authentic interpretation limits competence to the illegitimacy of the act, to the exclusion of a judgment about its merits. G. shows, though, that the violation of subjective rights is not clearly a question of the merits, as would be the fittingness of the act or the proper use of discretion. (3) The judgment of the *Sectio altera* is tantamount to the *restitutio in integrum* within the competence of the *Sectio prima*; for just as the latter does not judge the merits of a cause but, as the case may be, removes the *res iudicata* and returns the cause to the Rota, so does the former refrain from judging any question of merit but returns the matter to the dicastery. For G., though, this analogy fails for several reasons. All of these arguments neglect to address the fact that *REU* 106 prescribes that the *Sectio altera* immediately and directly (not mediately and indirectly) is to resolve contentions that cannot be resolved if the violation of subjective rights cannot be addressed.

The second view, which G. espouses, argues that in the law in force, both elements are included in the primary object of competence of the *Sectio altera*. This is indicated in the first part of *REU* 106 itself; the secretary of the commission drafting it compared it to the administrative tribunal of the Second Vatican Council, which treated complaints about the rights of the members; this competence is repeated in *NS*; and the jurisprudence of the Signatura addresses questions of subjective rights. At the same time, this view holds not only that the competence concerning subjective rights should be preserved but also that the competence over legitimacy should be suppressed. For it creates confusion about the dependence of the question of subjective rights upon the question of legitimacy; an administrative tribunal by its nature (*pace* Italy) judges the injury of subjective rights by the public administration (not merely the violation of laws like a tribunal of cassation); and it appears to attribute the effects of nullity or rescindability to the violation of the law by an administrative authority.

19. *Adnotationes in m.p. "Causas matrimoniales" (Excerptum ex "Adnotationibus Professorum", 3ᵃ edit., pp. 241–287 addito brevi commentario 20 paginarum circa appellationem).* Cursus renovationis canonicae pro iudicibus. Rome: Pontificia Universitas Gregoriana, 1979.

This is the *dispensa* of G. that was distributed at the 1979 *Cursus*, in which he examines Paul VI's reform of the marriage nullity process by way of the motu proprio *CM*. He explains what occasioned the reform and the various solutions that were being proposed. The reform enacted was partial, universal, and temporary, since it modified only some aspects of the process, applied to all tribunals, and remained in effect only until the eventual promulgation of the revised code. Among the sources of the reform were the norms granted by the Apostolic See for the tribunals of the U.S.A. (the APN). These retained their effect with the promulgation of *CM*, but they introduced an improper sense of moral certitude, which needs to be understood in accord with canonical tradition and especially the teaching of Pope Pius XII.

The forum of the "non-precarious residence" of the respondent was that in which the party had a stable residence that was not necessarily supported by the passage of time or the intention of remaining there. This has some basis in other canonical norms, and it respects the principle *actor sequitur forum rei*. The new forum of proofs fosters the more rapid instruction of a cause when the four conditions stipulated in *CM* are fulfilled. The transfer of the instance to another competent tribunal under the conditions stated in no. IV §3 is a welcome innovation, since it promotes the better and faster instruction of the cause.

The principles of priestly character and collegiality informed the exercise of the office of judge in the 1917 *CIC*, even if exceptions to collegiality were made in mission lands. In *CM* both of these principles were made relative in causes of nullity of marriage; collegiality was also prioritized in relation to priestly character. Now, once various conditions are fulfilled, a cause may be entrusted to a college of judges composed even of two clerics and one layman or, failing that, to a single clerical judge. Lay people may also exercise other functions in the tribunal.

CM also elaborates upon the norms of the 1917 *CIC* on the special cases in which the documentary process is used. However, it unfortunately ignores several important responses given by the Apostolic See about that process. That process primarily concerns non-dispensed diriment impediments, and here "impediments" is to be understood in a technical sense, not improperly speaking such as when it is applied to *amentia* or fear. Its secondary object includes the defects of legitimate form and of a procuratorial mandate.

This *dispensa* concludes with a lengthy section sharing the same title as no. 10 above and which answers seven questions pertaining to appeals under the regime of *CM*—some of which G. had treated before. (1) See no. 11 above. (2) See point 2 in no. 10 above. (3) See point 1 in no. 10 above. (4) See point 3 in no. 10 above. (5) The decree of confirmation or admission to an ordinary examination is one issued according to the standard of moral certitude, and it must be motivated. (6) The decree of ratification, or confirmation, is judicial and decisional in character. It may be issued even on only one of several grounds decided in the affirmative in the definitive sentence or for different reasons used in it. It may be challenged with a recourse within ten days or anytime by a new proposition of the cause; but G. was inclined to say that it could not be accused of nullity simply for a lack of motives. The decree, not the affirmative sentence, is what was to be executed. (7) The decree admitting the cause to an ordinary examination is not a decisional but an ordinatory decree, since it decides no controversy. It is unappealable.

The *dispensa* concludes with excerpts from responses from the Apostolic See, a supplementary bibliography, and sample decrees.

20. "De Signaturae Iustitiae competentia inde a saec. XVI ad saec. XVII." *Periodica* 69 (1980) 351–386.

In the sixteenth century, during the "golden age" of the Apostolic Signatura's history, the judiciaries of both the Church and the secular sphere were highly active. Many recourses and appeals arrived at the Apostolic See, being integral to this judicial activity, and not least because of its jurisdiction over the Papal States, in which even causes of a worldly nature would appear at the threshold of St. Peter. In this context, it was not uncommon to discover abuses of the right of appeal as a means of delaying and obstructing the execution of a sentence. This came to be noticed by the Roman Pontiffs, who corrected it and, in cases when such delay was effected by beating, mutilation, or death, even established the penalty of *latae sententiae* excommunication. In order to prevent abuses of the right of appeal or recourse, the pope centralized requests for appeals (*commissiones*) to the Signatura of Justice.

In general, the competence of the Signatura of Justice included the broad category of "commissions," which were requests for some favor pertaining to a trial or judicial activity. The act of the Signatura was also called a commission but was in fact a mandate given to some judicial authority. There were many synonyms for the word *commissio*, especially *supplicatio* and *causa*. They pertained to all kinds of causes to be treated in any kind of tribunal under the authority of the pope, whether it was an ecclesiastical/spiritual matter or a "profane" cause in relation to the Papal States. The object of such commissions was various. The majority of them had to do with appeals, while others dealt with requests for a *restitutio in integrum* or a question of the competent forum.

During this period, there was a hierarchy of tribunals both within and outside the Roman Curia. The appellate tribunal was typically the Sacred Roman Rota or a special commission of judges. When a cause was appealable, appellants had a right to choose among competent appellate tribunals. Appealable causes resulted in a *res iudicata* when an appeal was not made or pursued within the time limits or after three conforming decisions had been issued or, in some cases, two. The remedies in question were the judicial appeal, the complaint of nullity (due to defects of jurisdiction, the citation, or a mandate, or for a notorious injustice), and a *restitutio in integrum*.

When considering a request for an appeal, the Signatura would weigh questions of competence and the suspension of execution of the sentence as well as whether the sentence was appealable and, if not, for what reason. The question of appeal at times also raised the possibility of a transfer to another remedy—

namely, to a complaint of nullity or a *restitutio in integrum* if there were a question of nullity or of grave injustice flowing from a *res iudicata*. In any event, these matters were included within commissions of appeal (*commissiones appellationis*), due to the historically broad sense of the word "appeal," which had been the name given to any challenge of a judicial sentence. Thus among the commissions of appeal were included questions of appeal in the strict sense, of nullity (including *attentata*), of *restitutio in integrum*, of requests for the reform of a commission previously granted to the opposing party (*commissiones reformatoriae*), and of the correction of acts illegitimately placed by a judge.

Commissiones circa forum included conflicts of competence, the kind of trial (contentious or criminal), challenges relating to the recusal of a judge, and the calling of a cause due to injustices committed in a tribunal. Commissions delegated by the Signatura of Favor were also handled by the Signatura of Justice; this was common, since it was difficult for the Signatura of Favor to meet with its head, the Roman Pontiff himself. When it acted with the delegation of the Signatura of Favor, the Signatura of Justice could act beyond the limits of law that usually restricted it.

The chief limits to the competence of the Signatura of Justice were three. (1) It could not treat commissions reserved to the Signatura of Favor, unless the latter delegated competence to the former. (2) It could not treat prohibited commissions, unless certain stated conditions were fulfilled. And (3) it could not entertain commissions involving judges or tribunals not subject to it. Among these tribunals, G. lists and describes the following: those of the congregations of cardinals (i.e., of the Roman Curia—"tribunals" in an improper sense), other congregations, the Apostolic Camera and its subordinates, the Capitoline Curia, the patriarchal basilicas, the cities and dioceses of Ostia and Velletri, legates, and certain pious places. Also, certain tribunals could be granted exemption from the Signatura of Justice. In this work, G. relies heavily on the seventeenth century *auditor Sanctissimi* Giovanni Battista De Luca.

21. "El contencioso-administrativo eclesiástico. Génesis, historia y competencia actual." In *Curso de derecho matrimonial y procesal canónico para profesionales del foro (IV)*. Bibliotheca Salamanticensis, Estudios 31, 145–171. Salamanca: Universidad Pontificia, 1980.

Despite the varied title, this is essentially a Spanish version of the study summarized at no. 18 above.

22. "El M. P. '*Causas matrimoniales*' y las normas americanas." In *Curso de derecho matrimonial y procesal canónico para profesionales del foro (IV)*. Bibliotheca Salamanticensis, Estudios 31, 191–216. Salamanca: Universidad Pontificia, 1980.

During the decade of 1970–1980, there had developed a conviction among many canonists that the APN was more effective than the reform of Pope Paul VI in *CM* and that the provisions of the former should be adopted in the reform of the marriage nullity process in the revised *CIC*. This article is a comparative assessment of the principal provisions of the two legislative bodies.

It first explains the genesis, content, and characteristics of the two documents. The APN originated from the Canon Law Society of America and was advanced by the U.S. conference of bishops in order to receive the approval of the Apostolic See. It was a temporary body of particular law that introduced certain simplifications to the marriage nullity process. Some of these created tensions with bishops of other countries and led to corrections from the Apostolic See, which are summarized individually. The influence of the APN and the proposal of particular legislation by other conferences led to the issuance of *CM*, which was an attempt to avoid the risks that accompany the multiplication of particular procedural legislation in the area of holy matrimony. *CM* was based on the revisions proposed but not yet "carefully touched up" by the code commission. The documents treat three foundational questions in diverse ways:

1. *Competent forum* (CM IV; APN 7, 12). (a) Both documents effectively abolished the forum of domicile or quasi-domicile of the respondent, replacing it with the non-precarious dwelling of the respondent (*CM*)[11] and residency of either spouse (APN).[12] The latter made the respondent's defense difficult, until the Apostolic See required the prior consent of the respondent's tribunal, which, "with [all] due respect," itself could still leave the respondent unaware of the introduction of the *libellus*. (b) The documents also establish a forum in relation to the proofs. *CM* established four conditions to be fulfilled for use of the forum of "the majority of the depositions or proofs," while the APN established the competence of the approached tribunal when it decided that it was in a better con-

---

11. About this he stated: "It is greatly hoped that this discipline, which has been happily implemented for causes of nullity of marriage, may be extended to all judicial causes" (see *Pars statica*, 131, no. 191a).

12. He identifies this as the source, "tempered by three conditions," for what would become c. 1673, 3º of the 1983 *CIC*, which conditions have now been derogated by *MI* c. 1672, 2º. See *Processus nullitatis matrimonii*, 4, c; *Novus processus nullitatis matrimonii*, 2, note c.

dition to treat the cause than the other competent tribunals and it had fulfilled the same conditions, though without the prior hearing of the respondent. *CM* is a bit excessive in its conditions, while the APN is a bit subjective and leaves the respondent undefended personally at this moment. (c) The transfer of the instance is also established by both documents but with much greater precision in *CM*. Abuses of the APN in regard to these fora were corrected by the April 12, 1978 declaration of the Apostolic Signatura, especially in regard to violations of the respondent's right of defense.

2. *Single judges* (*CM* V §§2–3; APN 3, 23.I.). *CM* permitted this under certain conditions, among which was that it was granted for individual cases, which meant for individual tribunals. The APN contained ambiguous elements, such as the requirement of a grave reason (which in *CM* was a matter of an impossibility of constituting a college). The APN required the intervention of the Apostolic See. It was also unwise for the APN even to allow a single judge in second instance.

3. *The appeal* (*CM* VIII–IX; APN 23). (See no. 11 above, the major conclusions of which are rehearsed by way of premise.) In *CM*, upon appeal of an affirmative sentence by the defender of the bond, the cause is automatically set on the pathway of the *processus brevior*, which is meant to be truly brief while also respecting the right of the respondent to appeal a decree of confirmation. The APN states the rule according to which an ordinary process is always followed after an appeal, and the exception according to which the defender of the bond can be dispensed from the obligation to appeal if it would be superfluous. According to G., the criterion given in the APN in this matter is vague; dispensation from appeal should not have involved the defender of the bond; and the respondent's right of appeal in this context or to be heard prior to a dispensation seems neglected. Moreover, in practice the exception became the rule, and the rule became the exception. This is why regulations for the examination of dispensation requests were issued by the conference of bishops and approved by the Apostolic Signatura.

In sum, while there may be some imperfections in *CM*, its clear aspiration was to achieve a simpler and quicker process. And it is marked with a clear and precise juridical style. APN has this same aspiration, but it also seems to favor the petitioner. It has many points of juridical imprecision, which can give and have given rise to abuses in tribunals. This has necessitated several interventions by the Apostolic See, resulting (if observed diligently) in a procedural law similar to *CM*.

23. "Votum de revisione sententiae primo affirmantis nullitatem matrimonii." August 10, 1981. In *Congregatio plenaria diebus 20–29 octobris 1981 habita.* Acta et documenta Pontificiae Commissionis Codicis Iuris Canonici recognoscendo. Edited by the Pontifical Council for the Interpretation of Legislative Texts, 111–127. Vatican City: Typis Polyglottis Vaticanis, 1991.[13]

Once the 1980 schema of the revised *CIC* had been produced by the Pontifical Commission, a plenary assembly of an enlarged body of members of that commission was held in Rome. Six special questions were posed for discussion at that event, among which was the question of whether a superior examination and confirmation of a single affirmative sentence declaring the nullity of a marriage was necessary before it could be executed. This question included consideration of whether the decision to appeal could be left to the conscience of the defender of the bond or whether a superior judgment should be required only when the affirmative sentence was issued by a single judge.[14] In order to prepare the Fathers of the commission for the discussion, they were given copies of observations written by some of their fellow commission members and the *vota* of then-Archbishop Aurelio Sabattani, Secretary of the Supreme Tribunal of the Apostolic Signatura, and of G.

1. In the first part of his *votum*, G. treats the question of whether the obligatory examination of all affirmative sentences should be removed or retained. He introduces the theme by tracing the history of opinions—from the 1967 Synod of Bishops, to the opinions of authors, to the suggestions proposed within the code commission. The first opinion was that the obligation of examination of an affirmative sentence be totally removed, since the corresponsibility of the parties, the defender of the bond, and the judge better ensured moral certitude and justice, and since a hierarchical revision is not essential to the process. To

---

13. On Fr. Gordon's contribution on this occasion, see Bassiano Uggé, *La fase preliminare/ abbreviata del processo di nullità del matrimonio in secondo grado di giudizio a norma del can. 1682 §2,* Tesi Gregoriana – Serie Diritto Canonico 60 (Rome: Editrice Pontificia Università Gregoriana, 2003) 79–90.

14. See Pontifical Commission for the Revision of the Code of Canon Law, letter, "Elenchus 'Quaestiones Speciales in Congregatione Plenaria Disceptandae' seu dubiorum," prot. n. 4747/81, August 22, 1981: in *Congregatio plenaria,* 29, no. 2: "*a)* Whether in causes of nullity of marriage it should be necessary always to demand an examination of the sentence first declaring nullity, to be carried out by the tribunal of appeal, as is stated in canon 1634? *b)* Whether it better suffices to leave it to the conscience of the defender of the bond? *c)* or at least to demand it only if the sentence has been issued by a single judge?" The cited canon 1634 is the verbatim text of canon 1682 of the *CIC* as promulgated in 1983, now derogated by *MI* (cf. new c. 1679).

these G. replied (1) that the choices of parties, who know little of canon law, of the defender of the bond, who may be under social pressures, and of the judges, who may err, do not guarantee the objective veracity and justice of the sentence. And (2) while such is indeed not essential to the process, the facility with which marriages are declared null in the current age urges the legislator to retain it for the same reasons that Benedict XIV instituted it. The opinion also held that abuses could be corrected by other means, but G. observed that no such means were proposed, and the hierarchical examination actually works when carried out correctly.

The second opinion favored a tempering or restricting of the obligation, such that the appeal would be left to the conscience of the defender of the bond if the sentence was issued by a collegial tribunal, but it would be obligatory if the sentence was issued by a single judge. However, the appellate defender could withdraw the appeal. Thus, even if this approach theoretically emphasizes the excellence of the collegial tribunal, it at the same time renders "the benefit of that obligation to appeal . . . entirely illusory" (120, no. 52).

The third opinion supports the preservation of the necessary or obligatory examination of the sentence, which is meant to be done swiftly according to the institute of the *processus brevior* established by *CM* to be received into the *CIC*. Contrary to certain objections made to this, it is necessary that this examination include an evaluation of all the acts of the cause, since this alone allows the superior tribunal to weigh the objectivity of the conclusions in the affirmative sentence. This seems to be the common understanding of canonical doctrine. If some bishops deem this work too burdensome for their tribunal officials, they should consider erecting regional tribunals.

2. The second part of the *votum* examines the mechanism for implementing the necessary examination of an affirmative sentence before the appellate tribunal. The original mechanism (still in force at the time the *votum* was written) was the imposition of the obligation to appeal upon a distinct officer, the defender of the bond. There was also a "security clause" introduced according to which the judge could compel the defender to fulfill this obligation (1917 *CIC* c. 1986). The security clause evolved in the first schema of the revised *CIC*, whereby the presiding judge ordered the transmission of the acts to the appellate tribunal if the defender was negligent. A further evolution was proposed by the French conference of bishops and the University of Louvain which, in part and in a somewhat strained manner (seeing the defender more as a private person than an officer), proposed that an obligatory "appeal" be established "*ipso iure.*" This would be executed by the judge, such that there would be not an appeal but a transmission of the acts.

24. *Processus nullitatis matrimonii sub luce Schematis Codicis I.C. recogniti cum notis et appendicibus.* Cursus renovationis canonicae pro iudicibus. Rome: Pontificia Universitas Gregoriana, 1981.

This is a *dispensa*, dated November 1, 1981, distributed to the participants in the final *Cursus* event, which was held that year. In a time when the universal law on trials was revised but not yet promulgated, it was advantageous already to begin studying what would likely become the universal law. This manual thus had that end. After an introduction, 116 pages present (on the odd numbered pages) the text of the revised canon as it stood in its present state in the autumn of 1981 and (on the even numbered pages) G.'s annotations. These annotations explain the meaning of the law in the manner of a commentary, identify the change from the law of the 1917 *CIC*, and underscore still useful norms from *PME* or even the 1917 *CIC*.

As the title suggests, it is not all the canons of procedural law that are presented but only those truly applicable to marriage nullity trials. At times, in an entirely transparent way, the text of the canon is altered slightly when a special canon on the marriage nullity process impacts its application. There are eleven chapters followed by two additional sections on the documentary process and incidental causes. The eleven chapters treat these themes: 1) the competent forum or tribunal, 2) the tribunal to be constituted, 3) the parties and the right to challenge a marriage, 4) the introduction of a cause, 5) the *litis contestatio*, 6) proofs, 7) the publication of the acts, the conclusion in the cause, and the discussion of the cause, 8) pronouncements of the judge, 9) the challenge of the sentence, 10) the execution of the sentence, and 11) judicial expenses and gratuitous legal assistance.

The work concludes with three appendices. Appendix I (9 pages) conveys the draft text of canons from throughout the soon-to-be promulgated code that are cited throughout the *dispensa*. Appendix II (7 pages) is an index of draft canons cited in the *dispensa*, their location in the *dispensa*, and the corresponding canons of the 1917 *CIC*. The similar Appendix III (7 pages) is an index of the canons of the 1917 *CIC*, the corresponding draft canons, and their citation in the *dispensa*.

25. *Novus processus nullitatis matrimonii. Iter cum adnotationibus.* Rome: Pontificia Universitas Gregoriana, 1983.[15]

In 1982, professors of the Pontifical Gregorian University delivered lectures in Brescia on the texts of the code about to be promulgated, and they distributed relative *dispense.* G.'s, which likely bore a close resemblance to the work reported in no. 24 above, was updated after the code was promulgated. And on September 8, 1983, he published this work, hoping that it would be useful especially to those who had participated in the *Cursus* events of the past as well as ecclesiastical judges at large.

It follows almost the same sequence and contains almost the very same text as the work reported in no. 24. The main structural change is that chapter ten is not on the execution of the sentence but on "those things which must be done after a double conforming sentence in favor of nullity." It does not contain the three Appendices of no. 24 but a simpler index of canons cited from the 1983 *CIC.*

26. "De referendariorum ac votantium dignitate, privilegiis, labore, in aetate aurea Signaturae iustitiae." In *Dilexit iustitiam. Studia in honorem Aurelii Card. Sabattani.* Edited by Zenon Grocholewski and Vicente Cárcel Ortí, 197–210. Vatican City: Libreria Editrice Vaticana, 1984.[16]

Among those who gave counsel to the Successors of St. Peter in the medieval governance of the Church were those called referendaries. These referendaries held a function endowed with great dignity, since they were given the trust of the Supreme Pontiff to lighten his labor in governing the Church and in carefully aiding him in making just dispositions through their immediate, daily counsel.

---

15. A Polish translation of this work was published at Czestochowa in 1985 (Beyer, 24, no. 64; Zenon Grocholewski, "L'appello nelle cause di nullità matrimoniale," *Forum* 4 (1993/2) 22, note 6).

16. For the proofs of this article with Fr. Gordon's handwritten corrections to the body and the footnotes (which are endnotes in the manuscript), see SSAT Archives, files on *Dilexit iustitiam.* It appears that this was meant to be but a chapter of a much more complete historical study of the Signatura, which was never published. We read this testimony: "... prof. I. GORDON, S.J....ha in fase molto avanzata di preparazione una vasta monografia storico-giuridica sulla Segnatura Apostolica, sin dalle sue origini fino ai nostri giorni, dove vengono trattate con ampio respiro le attività dei votanti e referendari, i loro diritti e privilegi. P. Gordon ha voluto anticipare un capitolo di questa esauriente monografia nell'articolo riportato nelle pagine 197–210 del presente volume" (Vicente Carcél Ortí, "Il Supremo Tribunale della Segnatura Apostolica. Cenni storici," in *Dilexit iustitiam,* 173, note 29).

Highly were the referendaries of the golden age of the Signatura of Justice (16th–18th cent.) praised for their labors, especially by the popes. They were stellar churchmen, several of whom themselves became popes. Their work of technical consultation was of a great volume and complexity and was completed in brief periods of time.

The referendaries offered also a generous service, since they carried out their work without particular compensation. They had to have benefice-provided support so that they could freely serve the Roman Pontiff in concrete acts out of devotion. At the same time, the popes spontaneously bestowed them with benefits that were material (e.g., exemption from taxes, annual gifts of wine), spiritual (e.g., the choice of a confessor with special faculties, use of a portable altar, certain indulgences), and liturgical (e.g., service at their Masses as acolytes, having a private oratory at which Mass may be celebrated).

At various times they also enjoyed jurisdictional privileges, including exemption of their persons, benefices, familiars, servants, and goods from the jurisdiction of ordinaries, as well as the faculties to appoint notaries and ordinary judges, to dispense from illegitimacy, and to confer academic degrees. They also were bestowed with honors, such as the right to remain a referendary in perpetuity (e.g., even after promotion to the episcopate and assumption of diocesan governance), the general title of ecclesiastical dignity, and the use of violet-colored attire, a rocchetto (in public), and a cappa magna (in the papal chapel and in sessions of the full Signatura).

Additionally, they enjoyed a certain precedence, or the prevailing right to sit and enter. Referendaries, who were prelates, had precedence over non-prelate officials of the Roman Curia and over prelates who could not wear a rocchetto. They followed auditors of the Sacred Rota and *votantes*, but they had precedence over superiors general of religious orders and over canons. *Votantes* had precedence over secretaries of sacred congregations, the subdatary, and the auditor of the pope but not over auditors of the Sacred Rota or clerics of the Camera.

While so many of these matters differ from the style and culture of modern times, they have an impact on the structure of the Signatura. For they accentuate the activity and dignity of the work of the Signatura from its golden age until the present day.

27. "Codificationes legum Signaturae Iustitiae a Pio VII et Leone XII elaboratae."
In *Miscellanea in onore del Professore P. Esteban Gomez O.P.* Edited by Pontificia
Università S. Tommaso d'Aquino – Roma, 79–100. Milan: Massimo, 1984.[17]

The codification of the laws governing the Signatura of Justice needs to be
placed in the context of the pontificates when this was done. During the pontificate of Pius VI, the stability of office of the Signatura's notary was confirmed in
the face of certain social difficulties raised by the College of Scribes of the Roman
Curia's Archives. The Signatura of Justice was inactive for nineteen months of this
pontificate when the French invaded Rome. Pius VII issued some laws affecting
the operations of the Signatura of Justice prior to its temporary, five-year cessation
during the next French invasion. In 1814, though, once liberated, he appointed a
new Prefect and would proceed to issue two bodies of norms reforming the governance of the Papal States, including its tribunals in general and the Signatura
of Justice in particular. These prescriptions on the Signatura were confirmed by
Leo XII.

The codification of Pius VII, by the November 22, 1817 motu proprio *Nello
stabilire*, devoted Book VI to the Signatura of Justice: Title I, general norms; Titles
II–III, the manner of proceeding before the auditor and Prefect or before the full
Signatura; Title IV, the auditor of the pope, who was also the secretary of the Signatura of Favor and the link between the two Signaturas. It established clearly
that the Signatura of Justice was situated in Rome and was the only supreme tribunal in both the Papal States and the Church herself. The motu proprio contained one hundred articles covering the Signatura's composition, competence,
manner of proceeding, time limits, and the issuance of decisions.

The codification of Leo XII in the motu proprio *Dopo le orribili calamità* of
October 5, 1824 aimed to reform that of his predecessor. It did alter certain procedural rules but it largely kept the regulation of the Signatura of Justice intact. His
April 11, 1826 motu proprio *Quum plurima* called itself a new ordering of the
Tribunal of the Signatura of Justice. In reality, it largely confirmed what had
already been established in regard to its structure and procedure (except for certain adjustments, such as the reduction of the number of *votantes* to seven, and
the constitution of the office of Dean of the *votantes*). Its main innovation was
the introduction of certain rules pertaining to secrecy, payment, and privileges.

---

17. He manifests his aspiration eventually to complete a concentrated study of Gregory XVI's
codification ("Complementum adicietur praesertim a Gregorio XVI, ut speramus adiquando [*sic*]
scribere" [89, no. 2, *in fine*]), though such would never be published.

28. "Origine e sviluppo della giustizia amministrativa nella Chiesa." In *De iustitia administrativa in Ecclesia—La giustizia amministrativa nella Chiesa*. Edited by Pio Fedele, 1–18. Rome: Officium Libri Catholici, 1984.

This work, delivered as a lecture on April 6, 1979, is a condensed, Italian version of the major work listed as no. 5 above. See the second, third, and fourth paragraphs in that summary.

29. "L'oggetto primario della competenza della 'Sectio altera.'" In *De iustitia administrativa in Ecclesia—La giustizia amministrativa nella Chiesa*. Edited by Pio Fedele, 167–195. Rome: Officium Libri Catholici, 1984.

This work was delivered as a lecture on May 25, 1979 and "is strictly connected with that" just mentioned in no. 28. It is essentially an Italian version of the study summarized at no. 18 above.

30. "De procedura sequenda coram Signatura Iustitiae inde a saeculo XVI ad saeculum XVIII." *Periodica* 74 (1985) 575–604.[18]

The manner of proceeding during the golden age of the Signatura of Justice was more or less elaborate, depending on the gravity and clarity of the case. The process before the Cardinal Prefect was more abbreviated, while that before the full Signatura was more complex.

A case whose resolution was clear—a clear grant or rejection of a request— was decided by the Prefect. The interested party's procurator would prepare the petition and submit it to a referendary, who would study the matter, formulate his opinion, and defer it to the Prefect. The Prefect would have another official (the *Revisor*) examine the case and then issue the decision. This was accomplished relatively quickly. To this could be added the live hearing of the interested parties, when there was some doubt. The Prefect would convoke them and inform them of his decision; if they could not accept it, the matter would be submitted to the full Signatura, by way of a kind of recourse. Since this became abused by advocates, additional rules were developed: commissions of lesser importance were to be decided by the auditor, against whose decision recourse could be made

---

18. He seemed to have plans back in 1972 to carry out a complete study on the contentious-administrative process itself in the then-*ius vigens*, NS ("La renovación de la Signatura Apostólica," 575, no. 13: "Dejamos para otra oportunidad todo lo referente a la procedura"), but he never did so.

to the Prefect; only principal causes could be submitted to the full Signatura; recourse could be made to the full Signatura if the Prefect confirmed the auditor's decree, but only if the recurrent submitted a deposit of a certain amount.

Before the full Signatura, there were normative efforts to limit the number of commissions being considered at any one time. By the late sixteenth century, each referendary could propose two (or, if a recent gathering of the Signatura had been omitted, three) commissions at one gathering. Some exceptions were made with the permission of the Prefect, but these were multiplying and thus were declared to be truly exceptional in the late seventeenth century until they were suppressed the next century. In 1742, it was decided that the number of commissions to be decided in one session could not exceed forty.

The handling of each commission to be decided by the full Signatura typically spanned eight or ten days, depending upon the exact time period. During these days, the commission was submitted, transmitted to the other party, arguments were submitted in writing and orally, responses were given and, on Thursdays, the Signatura convened and made its decision.

Preliminary to commissions of appeal, the party wishing to appeal the unappealable sentence would often request a *supersessoria*, or temporary suspension (i.e., until the decision of the full Signatura) of execution of the sentence that had given rise to a *res iudicata*. He would submit this request to the auditor of the Signatura and, with assistance of a cursor, would cite the party favored by the sentence. The auditor would then either issue a decision on the commission immediately, or grant the *supersessoria* and simultaneously cite the other party to the gathering of the full Signatura, or deny the request.

After the petition for a *supersessoria* had been resolved or when no such petition was made, the commission process evolved beginning with the "transmission of the commission." This was the submission of the petition by the party's procurator, in duplicate, to a cursor, to which was attached the citation of the opposing party—that is, the invitation to that party to state his cause in preparation for the decision. All of this was communicated to the opposing party by the cursor. Around this time or even before the procurator submitted the commission, the recurrent would select the referendary whom he wanted to eventually propose the commission before the full Signatura. In response, the opposing party could object to the proposal of the commission before the full Signatura, or remain silent. His objections would be addressed by the auditor, who may demand that the recurrent supplement or amend his commission. In any case, the opposing party would be informed of the name of the referendary and the date of the Signatura's gathering. The referendary would propose the commission before the Signatura in an act or document called a "*Proponam*," with an indication of which commission of his it was—the first, second, third, or fourth.

Prior to the gathering of the Signatura, procurators and advocates would prepare three kinds of documents. These were the *summarium* (or the collection of key documents, including the commission and the challenged decision), the *informatio in scriptis* (or the factual and technical arguments of defense), and *responsiones* (or the previously distributed arguments given in response to those of the other party). Prior to the two parties offering responses to the other's arguments, there was an opportunity for the two sides to offer *informationes in voce*, or oral arguments before the referendary who would propose the cause in the Signatura. Once all arguments had been completed, it was for the referendary to formulate his recommendation. This was a most demanding task, since it required a thorough study of each cause he would present before the full Signatura, and usually such causes had an extensive procedural history. It also required him to weigh the arguments of advocates, which frequently were unhelpful due to lack of diligence, learning, and experience.

The decision was finally issued in the full Signatura. Prior to June 13, 1659, the Prefect alone was the judge, having a decisive vote, while the *votantes* had only a consultative vote. Alexander VII's disposition of that day, however, endowed the *votantes* and the referendary proposing the cause before the Signatura with deliberative votes, such that they constituted a college of judges. The form of the decision included the dispositive part together with the "*signatura*" or conclusive signature and declaration of the Prefect. It was then communicated to the parties. If it granted the appeal, the rescript of the Signatura was sent to the apostolic chancery, which arranged for the distribution of admitted causes to Rotal auditors.

31. "Nota. Responsio nonnullis quaestionibus de interpretatione quorundam canonum Libri VII C.I.C." *Periodica* 75 (1986) 639–645.

This appears to be G.'s final publication in the area of procedural law. It consists of a series of questions and answers pertaining to three topics: I. interdiocesan tribunals (3 questions), II. the minority dissent of a judge in a collegial tribunal (6 questions), and III. the procedure *super rato* (1 question).

I. He teaches that the March 25, 1971 norms of the Apostolic Signatura on interdiocesan tribunals remain in force after the coming-into-effect of the 1983 *CIC*. When those norms mention the "senior bishop," they mean senior in age, not ordination. The norms of an individual tribunal would cease only insofar as they are contrary to the universal law, such as in the manner of designating the bishop moderator.

II. The judge who decides to dissent from the majority of the college is to do that in the discussion itself. The notary does not sign the act, since he is not involved in the discussion of the college. Rather, the matter is taken care of, in turn, by the judicial vicar and the presiding judge: the former has a small register that notes dissents, so that when there is an appeal he may remind the latter to defer the sealed dissent together with the acts. The dissent is viewed only by the superior judges of the next instance—not the defender of the bond, advocates, or procurators, nor the judges of further instances. When a cause is decided by a sole judge employing an assessor instead of by a college of judges, the judge does not reveal to the assessor his "dissent" from his advice, since the judge's *votum* constitutes the decision.

III. If a cause of nullity of marriage should be suspended in order to instruct a non-consummation petition within an interdiocesan tribunal, it is the bishop of the petitioner that writes the *votum*, not the bishop moderator of the tribunal.

Conclusion

1. – An examination of Father Ignacio Gordon, SJ's published and unpublished scholarly work and his service to the Pontifical Gregorian University and the Apostolic See reveals a rich body of scholarship in the discipline of canonical procedural law by a man who was serious about the edification of the Church through his work and priestly ministry. As a scholar and jurist, he labored during a time of great transition, especially in regard to the general legislation of the Church, which was undergoing revision during most of his academic career and implementation in its revised form as that career was ending. His academic work wisely balanced continuity with the canonical tradition and the just revision of law in order to promote the good of the ecclesial society, attentive to the real circumstances of Christian life at the present time. This allowed him both to offer a critical reading of the norm in force while always respecting firm principles inherited from the ages.

2. – The reform of legislation is not an end in itself for the jurist in the Church. Father Gordon's teaching and scholarship in the area of procedural law direct one's attention to those goals that transcend the norm of positive law. In particular, the judicial process is to be carried out in a just manner, attributing to the parties the practical right to intervene appropriately and effectively. And the just process is only truly just when it leads to the discovery and pronouncement of the truth. Trials are to progress without needless delay, with as much celerity as is possible, though ever in a position of subordination to truth and justice (*quam primum, salva iustitia*). This principle is to be observed with the greatest care when the object of the trial concerns the alleged nullity of marriage, so that marriage may be duly protected and the spouses not be left waiting for a decision for an inordinate amount of time in a matter that concerns the *ratio peccati*. In his immense efforts to provide and promote the due preparation of judges and other ministers of justice, Father Gordon sought to impart knowledge of the concrete norms of procedural law and above all these higher norms and deontological principles.

3. – Also transcending any period of reform is the history of juridical institutes, which reveals the perennial mind of the legislator in certain stable organisms of the Church. The Apostolic Signatura's history bears witness to the Church's constant commitment to the just social relations of her children. The evolution of

norms governing the Signatura of Justice in particular manifests the Church's consistent efforts at the highest levels of her judiciary and central government to provide for the administration of justice in a way that respects the rights of parties while also eliminating obstructionism and undue delay as far as possible. Father Gordon also seems to have been personally inspired by the *Votantes* and Referendaries preceding him by centuries. For he, like them, appears to have spent himself in generous service of the Supreme Pontiff, for his part, by his work of study and of drawing up detailed *vota* for the Apostolic Signatura, and by promoting devotion to the Successor of St. Peter among those who attended the *Cursus renovationis canonicae pro Iudicibus et Tribunalium administris*.

4. – One can imagine that he was left dissatisfied, though probably personally resigned, in regard to the restrictive scope of competence of the Second Section of the Supreme Tribunal of the Apostolic Signatura. He so aspired that it would in practice be competent to resolve controversies about subjective rights allegedly violated by the public ecclesiastical administration. His teaching in this matter remains valuable nevertheless, since it was accompanied by eloquent lessons about the reverence due the authority of the Church and the right of the faithful to just treatment by the public administration. And perhaps his proposal may be useful in a future regulation of ecclesiastical administrative justice.

5. – Father Gordon's teaching epitomizes one particular aspect of the position in which the canonical proceduralist finds himself. On the one hand, the careful study of procedural law and the correct administration of justice are to be encouraged and promoted. On the other hand, litigation within the household of faith is to be avoided after the model and teaching of Christ the Lord. And so judicial activity is ever to be placed at the service of charity:

It is for the Church to tend to the honor of God and the salvation of souls. Consequently, in general, it belongs to her to provide for the observance of the law of God and of the principles of the natural law. In particular, it is for her to protect fraternal charity as well as peace and harmony, which is the bond of charity, and, where fraternal correction may not be sufficient, even by means of a judicial sentence.[1]

---

1. See *Pars statica*, 91–92, no. 133.

Indices

These indices direct the reader to themes treated (A.), persons whose work is cited (B.), and norms referenced (C.). The reference numbers are not page numbers; rather, they signify a major part of the book and the section number within that part. Each chapter is indicated according to the appropriate Roman numerals (I, II, III, etc.), while the Introduction is indicated with the abbreviation "Intr" and the Conclusion "C." The abbreviation "FM" means front matter. The Arabic number indicates the section number in the body of the work, but if it is preceded by the letter "n" it indicates a footnote. Multiple footnotes are preceded by "nn."

A. Subject Index

Absence, Declaration of, VII.16

Accumulation, VI.24

Acta Apostolicae Sedis, I.4

Action (*actio*), IV.25; V.9,16–17

    De spolio, IV.33

    Reconventionalis, VI.24,n59

Active Legitimation, I.12; IX.29

Administrative Authority: *See* Public Administration

Administrative Justice: *See* Contentious-Administrative Jurisdiction

Administrative Power, V.21,22; VII.41; IX.6,12,15; X.2

Administrative Tribunals, IV.6; V.32; VIII.15,19; IX.3,8,12,n28; X.2,12,18

Advocate, I.22; III.3; IV.32; V.30,31; VI.39,42,48–49; VII.5–7,30,33; VIII.6; X.3(II.5),30

Avocatio causae, V.n36; VII.45(*b*); VIII.9

American Procedural Norms, I.8,n95; II.9; IV.11,n20; V.7; VI.20,n89; VII.48–50,n106; X.15,19,22; *see also* C. Index of Norms Cited *infra*

Aperitio oris, VIII.7

Apostolic Signatura, Supreme Tribunal of the, Intr.2,3,4,7,n3; I.6–7,8,13,n29; II.6,9; IV.12; V.34,nn14,36,65–66; VI.3,9,10,22,nn14,25,121; VII.44,45,48,nn91–92,97,106; VIII; IX.7,8,11,14,16,29,nn31,38,66; X.*incipit*,4–5,8,15,22; C.3–4

Congresso, I.7; IX.nn25,26

Normae speciales, IV.13; VIII.1; X.4,8,18,n18; *see also* C. Index of Norms Cited *infra*

Sectio altera, II.9; IV.n74; VIII.22–25; IX.8,11,16,17–25,nn1,37; X.4–5,8–9,18,29; C.4

Signatura of Favor, VIII.3,4,5,6,7; X.4,20

Signatura of Justice, VII.30,n86; VIII.1,3,4,5–6,7,8–11,nn1,19; IX.6; X.4,16,20,26,27; C.3

    Auditor in, VIII.6,9,10; X.27,30

    See also Contentious-Administrative Jurisdiction, Referendary, Vigilance, and *Votans*

Appeal, VI.2; VII.15,39,40,42–45,52; VIII.5,6,7,9,17,27,n13; IX.6; X.2,10,20

    Appellatione remota, V.23; VIII.7

    Extrajudicial, IX.6,7,23; X.5,18

    Processus brevior of CM, IV.12,32; V.30; VI.n108; VII.48,51–54; X.3(III.6),10–11,22(3),23

    See also Defender of the Bond: Appeal by

Assessor, V.n44; VI.40,41; X.31

Auditor, VI.41; VII.17,18,nn6,46

Beneficium novae audientiae, VIII.17

Bishop Moderator, V.10,22,34; VI.3,9,14,27–28; VII.n106; X.3(II.1),31

Canonist, Intr.1

Canon Law Society of America, X.22

B. Index of Persons

C. Index of Norms Cited